Advance Praise

Stephen Cook's new commentary on Deuteronomy captures the reforming spirit of this biblical book. With his own fresh and dynamic voice, Cook unleashes the forceful, commanding voice of Deuteronomy. Read in light of Cook's long and deep scholarship, Deuteronomy emerges as a powerful source for theological reflection for the church today. Most highly recommended for courses in seminaries, divinity schools, and programs in theology.

—Mark S. Smith
Skirball Professor of Bible and Ancient Near Eastern Studies
New York University

Stephen Cook's new theological commentary puts Deuteronomy's compelling reinterpretation of an earlier minority tradition in ancient Israel in lively dialogue with other like-minded representatives of this "outsider" stream of tradition within the Old Testament (Hosea, Micah, Jeremiah, Malachi, the Elohist, Psalms of Asaph, Joshua–2 Kings). All this is done in service to Cook's overall aim to bring out the "vibrant liveliness and pressing relevance" of Deuteronomy as a resource for constructive theological formation for contemporary people of faith today. An insightful and accessible study of the theology and ethics of Deuteronomy.

—Dennis Olson
Charles T. Haley Professor of Old Testament Theology
Chair, Biblical Studies Department
Princeton Theological Seminary

Stephen L. Cook provides an accessible yet profound theological commentary on the theologically rich book of Deuteronomy. Often thought-provoking and always insightful, Cook's contribution illumines the ancient biblical text so modern readers, particularly lay and clergy, can come to a deeper understanding not only of the book itself but also of the God who reveals himself through it.

—*Tremper Longman III*
Robert H. Gundry Professor of Biblical Studies
Westmont College

READING DEUTERONOMY

SMYTH&
HELWYS

Smyth & Helwys Publishing, Inc.
6316 Peake Road
Macon, Georgia 31210-3960
1-800-747-3016
© 2015 by Stephen L. Cook
All rights reserved.

Library of Congress Cataloging-in-Publication Data

Cook, Stephen L., 1962- author.
Reading Deuteronomy : a literary and theological commentary / by Stephen L. Cook.
    pages cm
ISBN 978-1-57312-757-8 (pbk. : alk. paper)
1. Bible. Deuteronomy—Commentaries. I. Title.
BS1275.53.C66 2014
222'.1507—dc23
                        2014042231

1-23, 27-36
59-71

Reading Deuteronomy

A Literary and Theological Commentary

Stephen L. Cook

SMYTH&HELWYS
PUBLISHING, INCORPORATED MACON, GEORGIA

Also by Stephen Cook

Conversations with Scripture: 2 Isaiah

The Social Roots of Biblical Yahwism

The Apocalyptic Literature (Interpreting Biblical Texts)

Prophecy and Apocalypticism: The Postexilic Social Setting

To my wonderful young daughter,
Rebecca Ketziah Cook (You Fu Xuan),
with gratitude for filling my life with spirit,
strength, daring, beauty, and fun.

Contents

Editor's Foreword xiii
Author's Preface xv

Reading Deuteronomy: Issues and Approach 1
    Appreciating the Book...1
    A Respectful, Theological Approach 2
    The Significance of Deuteronomy...3
    Literary and Theological Form 4
    Historical Circumstances of Composition 6
    Village Israel versus the Royal Court 9
    A Flowing Stream of Theology and Tradition 11
    Literary History..13
    Structure of the Book 15
    Deuteronomy's Theology and Message 19
    Using this Commentary 21

The First Discourse of Moses, 1:1–4:43 25
    Israel's Past at Mount Horeb and at Kadesh-barnea, 1:1-46 27
        Introductory Note, 1:1-5 27
        The Tradition of Mosaic Judges, 1:6-18 29
        Israel at Kadesh-barnea, 1:19-46..32
    Israel's Journey from Kadesh to Moab, 2:1–3:11 37
    The Allotment of Transjordan, 3:12-29 45
        Distributing the Land, 3:12-22...45
        Moses' "Gethsemane" Prayer, 3:23-29...47
    Israel on the Plains of Moab, 4:1-43 49
        A Call to Obey Moses' Teaching, 4:1-40 49
        Appendix: Cities of Refuge in Transjordan, 4:41-43 55
    The Second Discourse of Moses, 4:44–29:1 57

Introducing the Torah, 4:44–5:5 59
   Introduction to Moses' Second Discourse, 4:44-49 59
   Actualizing the Covenant, 5:1-5 60
God's Revelation of the Decalogue, 5:6-33 63
   The Ten Commandments, 5:6-21 63
   The Mediator of the Covenant, 5:22-33 69
The Command to Love an Integral Lord, 6:1-25 73
The Command to Show No Mercy, 7:1-26 81
The Rejection of Dependence on Self, 8:1-20 87
The Rejection of Self-righteousness, 9:1–10:11 93
A Summative Call to Commitment, 10:12–11:32 99
A Central Sanctuary, 12:1-32 105
A Command to Resist Sedition and Insurrection, 13:1-18..........117
A People Called by God's Name, 14:1-29 123
   Choose Holiness, Choose Life, 14:1-2 123
   Ritual Requirements for Table Fellowship, 14:3-21 125
   Tithes and Firstlings, 14:22-29 127
A People of Sacred Interruptions, 15:1–16:17 129
   The Relief of Debts, 15:1-11 130
   The Release of Debt Servants, 15:12-18 132
   Sacrificing Firstlings, 15:19-23 134
   Concerning Festivals, 16:1-17 134
Leadership and Polity for God's People, 16:18–18:22 137
   Judges, 16:18–17:13 138
   Kings, 17:14-20 139
   Altar Ministers, 18:1-8 141
   Prophets, 18:9-22 142
Protecting Innocent Life: The Public Order, 19:1-21 147
   Cities of Refuge, 19:1-13 147
   The Boundary Mark, 19:14 148
   Witnesses, 19:15-21 148
Protecting Innocent Life: Warfare, 20:1-20 151
The Confrontation of Life and Death, 21:1-23 155
The Obligation to Protect Life, 22:1-8 161
Exposition of the Commandment against Adultery, 22:9–23:18 165
Exposition of the Commandment against Theft, 23:19–24:7 173
Exposition of the Commandment against False Witness, 24:8–25:4 ..177
Do Not Covet Your Neighbor's Wife, 25:5-12..........................181
Do Not Long for Anything that Belongs to
   Your Neighbor, 25:13–26:15 187

Conclusion to the Legal Corpus: A Mutual Covenant, 26:16-19 193
Ceremonies at Shechem, 27:1-26 195
Covenant Blessings and Curses, 28:1–29:1 201
The Third Discourse of Moses, 29:2–30:20 207
Ratification, Part 1: Review of Israel's History, 29:2-9 209
Ratification, Part 2: A Reciprocal, Immutable
    Commitment, 29:10-29 211
Ratification, Part 3: Assurance of the Future, 30:1-10 215
Ratification, Part 4: A Word Very Near, 30:11-14 219
Ratification, Part 5: A Necessary Choice, 30:15-20 221
Epilogue: The Death of Moses and the Torah's Formation, 31:1–34:12 223
Transferring Leadership and Depositing Witnesses, 31:1-29 225
The Song of Moses, 31:30–32:47 231
Moses Commanded to Die, 32:48-52 239
The Blessing of Moses, 33:1-29...241
The Death of Moses, 34:1-12 249

Works Cited..255

Editor's Foreword

The *Reading the Old Testament series* shares many of the aims and objectives of its counterpart, *Reading the New Testament*. Contributors to the current series, like those to its predecessor, write with the intention of presenting "cutting-edge research in [a form] accessible" to a wide audience ranging from specialists in the field to educated laypeople. The approach taken here, as there, focuses not on the minutiae of word-by-word, verse-by-verse exegesis but on larger literary and thought units, especially as they function in the overall conception of the book under analysis. From the standpoint of method, volumes in this series will employ an eclectic variety of reading strategies and critical approaches as contributors deem appropriate for expli-cating the force of the text before them. Nonetheless, as in RNT, "the focus [will be] on a close reading of the final form of the text." The overarching goal is to provide readers of the commentary series with an aid to help them become more competent, more engaged, and more enthusiastic readers of the Bible as authoritative Scripture.

The title of the series prompts several comments. For the editor, at least, the term "Old Testament" is a convenient convention, since any alternative seems either awkward or provocative. The Hebrew Bible is the shared heritage of Judaism and Christianity, the body of believers whom Paul once described as branches from a wild olive tree who have been "grafted contrary to nature into a cultivated olive tree" (Rom 11:24). Since the beginnings of Christianity, questions concerning how and in what sense the Hebrew Bible/Old Testament functions as Christian Scripture have perpetually confronted the church. Nonetheless, throughout its history, in the spirit of Paul, the church has insisted that the God of Abraham, Isaac, and Jacob is the God of the New Testament. Rather than impose a detailed doctrine of the unity of the two Testaments or specify a particular hermeneutical approach, the editor and the publisher have chosen to invite contributions to the series from scholars selected because of their learning and insight, again in the spirit of Paul, we hope, without regard to faith tradition or denominational identity.

The books of the Hebrew Bible were the fountainhead for the faith of both Paul and Aqiba. May it be that, through the scholarship presented in the pages of this series, the books of the "Old Testament" water the faith of another generation.

—Mark E. Biddle, General Editor
Richmond, Virginia

Author's Preface

Deuteronomy has made a big splash in Jewish and Christian history, wielding profound influence from the earliest infancy of the two religions. Contemporary biblical scholars have been so persuaded of this influence that some have been overzealous in seeing the hand of Deuteronomy's proponents almost everywhere they have looked within Scripture. The book's language and thought echo even in theologically unrelated biblical works, such as Ezekiel and Zechariah. This is some effective theology. Wherein lay Deuteronomy's power for the ancestors of the faith, power repeatedly to nourish and renew? I have kept this question before me as I wrote this Reading the Old Testament volume.

In search of answers, I have scoured Deuteronomy for authentic truth-telling about the anguish in our world, about the uniqueness of the covenant of God within the marketplace of religions, and about what kind of lifestyle can renew God's people. I have found that Deuteronomy astonishes the reader with its profound insights into God's intended journey of human ennoblement on earth. I have become ever more convinced that the book's vision of a deepening devotion to God and a broadening commitment to human mutuality commends itself now more than ever.

Many individuals and groups have assisted and encouraged me as I wrote this commentary on Deuteronomy. For their many penetrating insights and for their willingness to be guinea pigs as I tested my interpretations, I thank the members of my spring 2010 Deuteronomy seminar (OTS 607): Pierre-Henry Buisson, Rebecca Nelson Edwards, Elizabeth H. Farquhar, Stephen Drew Foisie, Catherine E. Guy, and Josiah D. Rengers. For granting me a sabbatical devoted to this project in spring 2011, I thank my institution, Virginia Theological Seminary; our dean and president, the Very Reverend Ian S. Markham; and our trustees. The staff at our seminary library met all my bibliographic needs with their legendary grace and efficiency, and I thank them, including head librarian and friend, Dr. Mitzi Jarrett Budde.

I am especially grateful to then Vice President of Academic Affairs Timothy F. Sedgwick for convening a Meade Seminar around my Deuteronomy research, hosting us in his home on multiple evenings. These dinner and discussion meetings allowed me to vet key drafts of my work and offered invaluable critique and insight. Tim pushed me especially to work out the connection between divine absence and Israel's freedom for relationship. Seminar members included Judy Fentress-Williams (Hebrew Bible), John Y.-H. Yieh (New Testament), and Elisabeth (Lisa) M. Kimball (Christian Formation). I am greatly indebted to two colleagues in Hebrew Bible who joined us from nearby universities: Nyasha Junior from Howard University and Robert Miller II from the Catholic University of America.

My understanding of Deuteronomy's theology benefited greatly from participation in the *Göttliche Anwesenheit und Abwesenheit Tagung* (Divine Presence and Absence Colloquium), Georg-August-Universität, Göttingen, Germany, May 12–15, 2011. Nathan MacDonald, who organized the colloquium, has strongly influenced my reading of Deuteronomy, as has Ben Sommer, another participant at the meeting.

I was able to share more of my work on two significant occasions in 2011–2012. "Difficult Deuteronomy" was my focus in presenting the MAR-SBL Presidential Address at The Mid-Atlantic Region of the Society of Biblical Literature. "Moses' First Discourse in Deuteronomy" was my sample chapter at the Lemadim Olam Colloquium of Hebrew Bible Scholars at the SBL Meetings in San Francisco. I warmly thank colloquium members for their vigorous responses to my draft, including John T. Strong, Jerome F. D. Creach, Steven Shawn Tuell, Corrine L. Carvalho, Bill Bellinger, James Nogalski, Nancy L. de Claissé-Walford, James W. Watts, Pamela Scalise, and Mark E. Biddle. Mark Biddle, of course, is the general editor of the series in which this commentary appears. I am especially grateful to him for inviting me to contribute and for skillfully nurturing the volume through all phases of production.

In all my research and publishing, my deepest appreciation goes to my wife of twenty-five years, Catherine Elizabeth Cook, LPC, for her unfailing inspiration and encouragement. I dedicate this work to our eight-year-old daughter, Rebecca Ketziah Cook, with deep gratitude to God for the unspeakable joy that she brings me.

—*Stephen L. Cook*
Alexandria, Virginia

Reading Deuteronomy: Issues and Approach

Appreciating the Book

For large segments of the modern world, the book of Deuteronomy is a lost treasure, a forgotten gem. The average person on the street in America or Europe cannot say why the book might be of interest. Those better informed about biblical matters may have more to say, but they often lack enthusiasm. Skimming the surface, Deuteronomy appears a boring read: lots of talk and rule-making but little action. To move beyond surface impressions, however, is to be immediately and powerfully surprised. In the pages of this commentary I aim to bring out the vibrant liveliness and pressing relevance of this book.

At least among Christians, misconceptions about the nature of Deuteronomy abound. Among them are the following: The book consists of tired laws, of "works-righteousness." It champions a stern and wrathful God who orders violence—the execution of Canaanites, idolaters, and rebellious children. It proffers a naïve view of divine justice, understanding all suffering as divine punishment and prosperity as divine favor. This commentary aims to expose these commonplace conceptions as far off base indeed.

I penned these comments with enthusiasm about Deuteronomy and with determination to dispel the prejudices against it. Far from a static, deadly book, this is Scripture pulsing with immediacy. This is divine word unleashed. Here Moses' voice speaks in the present tense, declaring *today* the day of commitment, the day of new journeying to God. The journey at issue is open to the future. Deuteronomy's texts reinterpret the past; they hear older teachings in a new way, speaking to the present.

In Deuteronomy Moses addresses a new generation poised to enter the promised land. The trials in Egypt and in the wilderness are over. He points the way forward on the trek with God, the journey toward God's reign. Modeling the sacrificial nature of faith's journey, Moses explains how the people must go on without him. He must die, bearing God's anger at the larger group (1:37; 3:26; 4:21).

Moses does indeed speak of violence along the journey of faith, but only because conflict and anguish are real parts of life. Deuteronomy's first readers, faced with the violence of the Assyrian empire, experienced it first-hand. In this book, their God takes a stand against Assyria's horrific boasts, but *co-opts* the language of violence as a "weapon" of devotion. Tired images of violence become new metaphors of resolve. This is a careful, critical appropriation of the contemporary culture's symbols of violence.

Deuteronomy's trek to God's reign is no naïve promise of reward for obedience and disaster for sin. This is no gospel of material gratification as the right of God's people. "One does not live by bread alone," the book insists (Deut 8:3; unless otherwise marked, all biblical quotations are from the NRSV). Those on the book's journey find a quieter, subtler flow of blessing. They find alignment with God's ways so that their lifestyle naturally, inevitably gravitates toward God's saving health.

Deuteronomy's gripping discourses yank readers out of the doldrums and back to Mount Horeb to an encounter with God's fearsome presence and voice. There at Horeb, the divine word issues forth from blazing fire. Divine presence and word stir deep longing for God, compel readers to bow, and provoke realization of the profundity of human inadequacy, vulnerability, and lack.

Moses' addresses move imperfect, frail readers to a place where they can stand before God's blazing presence, finding intimacy with a God of otherness and morality. Moses' covenantal teaching in Deuteronomy, his explaining of *torah* (God's "instruction," "teaching"), sets readers on a path to full communion with God, with other human beings, and with the natural world. Not content merely to compel a decision of faith, Moses maps out the twists and turns of what comes next: the demanding road of discipleship.

A Respectful, Theological Approach

Readers may not know what to make of a modern commentary that pursues a respectful, even appreciative presentation of Deuteronomy. Questions may abound about my goal of a constructive, theological reading of the book. Why pursue such a reading? Is such interpretation even legitimate, something more than subjective piety?

God save us from all subjective sugarcoating of the Scriptures. Striving for an authentic reading, I aim to lay bare the *inherent* vitality of this book.

I have sought to understand the gushing stream of theology that flows through it from sources in Micah, Hosea, and the Asaph psalms and that rushes headlong into later biblical books, such as Jeremiah and Malachi. I have pushed to illumine Deuteronomy's place in a powerful dialogue of voices, a unique conversation between writings that the faithful have recognized as *Scripture*.

I have written this commentary in the hopes of grasping why the faithful have bequeathed us this book, of understanding why they have held it in such esteem and passed it down for generations. What did they hear in this book? Why such efforts to preserve these particular texts, such conviction that God is speaking uniquely *here*?

Deuteronomy was not preserved and bequeathed to the future as a document of ancient religion, projected out of human consciousness, imperfectly disengaged from the polytheism, ethnocentricity, and violence of its times. Rather, it earned a place in the biblical canon for its innate, genuine witness to the real God, who created human beings on the earth (4:32), who spoke from the middle of fire and allowed Israel to live and tell about it (4:33). Thus I offer a theological reading of Deuteronomy, aligning with the book's own intense regard for the divine word that issued from fire, booming forth to grasp the faithful, have its way with them, and bring new reality to life among them.

The Significance of Deuteronomy

Many today have forgotten Deuteronomy's key role in the history of God's people. The book has loomed large at pivotal moments of God's work on earth that Jews and Christians remember and celebrate. When the kingdom of Judah undertook one of the most significant religious reforms in its history, it did so according to the spirit and letter of Deuteronomy (see 2 Kgs 23). When the prophet Jeremiah, suffering and weeping, guided Judah through destruction and exile, he did so with the wind of Deuteronomy in his sail (see the echoes of Deuteronomy in, e.g., Jer 1:9; 2:6; 28:9).

Christians in particular need reminding that when Jesus of Nazareth wrestled to inaugurate the reign of God, his thinking and teaching often came straight from Deuteronomy (see, e.g., Matt 4:4, 7, 10; 5:21-22, 27-28; 18:15-16; 19:19; 22:37). An energized engine of revival and expectation clearly purrs under Deuteronomy's hood. This is go-to Scripture for critical junctures in the progress of God's salvation.

To understand the Scriptures is to turn repeatedly to Deuteronomy. Resonances with the book abound almost everywhere one looks in the

Bible's two testaments, from Hosea, Micah, and the Asaph psalms to Jeremiah and Zephaniah, and on to Jesus and Paul. The book's diction and thinking are particularly evident in a major editorial layer of Jeremiah's book.

Since the 1940s and the work of Martin Noth (1902–1968), scholars have reasoned that an early edition of Deuteronomy must have informed the presentation of history found in the books of Joshua through Kings. This central biblical history evaluates Judah and Israel along the lines of Deuteronomy's teaching. It gives King Hezekiah and King Josiah notable, unreserved praise for enacting major reforms in accord with Deuteronomy's teaching (2 Kgs 18:3-6; 22:2). It presents Josiah as the incarnation of the lofty ideal of Deuteronomy 6:5 (see 2 Kgs 23:25).

We must be wary of harmonizing the Bible's many distinctive voices with that of Deuteronomy, but should also be honest about the book's dominating role in Scripture. It now forms the capstone of the Pentateuch (Latin for "five books," the traditional books of Moses), the culminating presentation of God's Torah. It simultaneously introduces Israel's central history stretching from Joshua through Kings. (Note: I use "torah" in two ways: the *Torah*, the Pentateuch books [capitalized], and *torah* [lowercase], the Hebrew term for "instruction.")

As the Bible's collections of prophecy came together, editors in the camp of Deuteronomy supplied headings, new layers, and other additions. The biblical Minor Prophets collection now begins and ends with Hosea and Malachi, voices aligned with our book. Most strikingly, the final verses of the Prophets collection as a whole look back to no other Scripture than Deuteronomy. A central discipline of the faith, they proclaim, is the duty to remember Moses, to remember Deuteronomy's covenant of Horeb mediated by the greatest of the prophets (Mal 4:4-6).

Literary and Theological Form

The name Deuteronomy is a Greek term meaning "second law," a title taken from the ancient Greek translation of the Scriptures, the Septuagint. The title probably reflects the Septuagint's Greek wording in Deuteronomy 17:18, a wording that might reasonably be read as referring to Deuteronomy as a "second law." That is, the Septuagint may suppose that the verse's Hebrew term *mishneh* ("double," "copy") refers to a "second" (Greek: *deuter-*) "law" (Greek: *nomos*), not to the king's personal *copy* of the law. Translation mistake or not, the idea that Deuteronomy represents a second version of the law of Moses is fitting. As the book presents itself, it constitutes a new, second forwarding of the torah given at Mount Horeb/Sinai.

Immediately, however, various potential misunderstandings arise. Why might Scripture include a "second" torah? Surely the book of Deuteronomy is not merely redundant, simply a repetition of what we already have in Exodus. It must reissue the torah in order to elaborate on it, reinterpret it, or even revolutionize it. I will argue that although Deuteronomy *is* revolutionary in some key respects, its primary aim is to *renew* the torah for all future followers of God.

In the first verse of Deuteronomy, Moses speaks to "all Israel" (cf. 31:11-13; 32:45-46), that is, to the Israel of God across time. Our book addresses the broadest of audiences, straining for all of us to experience the torah as brimming with revival and expectation. This theological shaping of Deuteronomy makes it especially significant for readers concerned with the relevance of Scripture for life today. We may speak of such a shaping force behind our book's composition as a "Bible-building" or "canonical" energy.

Just as the term "second" (*deuter-*) raises questions, so does the term "law" (*nomos*). In English, the word "law" can sound restrictive, domineering, and burdensome. The Hebrew term at issue, *torah*, has a wider range of meanings than the English word "law," however, and it has connotations that are much more positive. The term *torah* encompasses notions of direction, instruction, and teaching. The book of Deuteronomy presents the torah of Moses as teaching that helps build up the people of God.

Properly understood, Moses' role in Deuteronomy is not to impose a deadening conformity to a strict set of rules but patiently to teach God's people a path of human formation that lives into God's freely offered salvation. Deuteronomy is about the formation of renewed persons, newly graced with abundant, God-directed life. There is nothing of any "works righteousness" or "salvation by merit" here.

The lifestyle here advocated molds people so that they embody God's ways. Its rhythms constantly turn people to God's purposes. The type of catechetical writing born in Deuteronomy will mature much later in works such as the Didache, a first- or second-century CE Jewish Christian community rule. The Didache was meant to guide converts to the faith into perfection by "taking on the whole yoke of the Lord," that is, by striving to live out God's teaching.

Shaping individuals and communities truly to embody God's teaching means encouraging changes in overt behavior but also transforming inner lives. On nearly every page, Deuteronomy's literary style aims at the later goal. The book's main audience is not made up of official judges and learned lawyers but of the land's citizenry. It speaks to their heart and will, creating genuine faithfulness that does not require constant enforcement.

Deuteronomy undertakes to teach and to form God's people in the midst of a journey. The book's introduction sets the discourses of Moses in the middle of a great trek: after the experience of slavery in Egypt and the reception of the covenant at Mount Horeb (1:3) but before crossing the Jordan River into the promised land. As the reader begins Deuteronomy, the people occupy a liminal position amid unidentified locales (1:1). They wait "beyond the Jordan in the land of Moab" (1:5).

Deuteronomy's introduction puts readers on the edge of their seats, expectant about God's future work. In a real sense the "law book" of Deuteronomy is a book of prophecy, a literature of expectation about God's reign. Readers of Deuteronomy stand with Moses' audience on the east side of the Jordan, still on the brink of penetrating God's ideal form of life.

Historical Circumstances of Composition

The words of Deuteronomy issue forth from the mouth of the literary figure of Moses (1:1). Moses wrote its torah "to the very end" (31:24). This voice of the book, this stamp of Mosaic authorization, is of real *theological* significance. It speaks to the fundamentally inspired nature of this text as Scripture. Standing in for the people, Moses suffered the deafening roar of God's word on their behalf. Delivering it to them, he blessed them with God's awesome, spirit-enlivened revelation, which laid claim on them, plucked them out of their old existence, and rebirthed them. Moses thereby drew Israel into covenant. In Deuteronomy, Israel confesses, the selfsame revelation confronts and draws in each new generation.

The words of Deuteronomy stem from the literary and theological figure of Moses, not from Moses the historical figure. At the book's very start, its superscription in 1:1 lets slip that the authors no longer stand with Moses in Moab but are now settled west of the Jordan River. The book explains that Moses spoke "beyond the Jordan," that is, on Jordan's *other side* (NJPS)—across the river (cf. CEB) from where the audience is now.

The authors again seem to place themselves in the land of Canaan proper at 20:15. The verse mentions Canaanite cities "hereabout" (NJPS; literally, "these nations here," NAB, CEB), casually assuming that Moses speaks from within Canaan. Moses would instead have pointed to cities across the Jordan, cities "over *there*."

The second half of Deuteronomy 2:12 speaks of Israel already having crossed into Canaan and defeated its peoples. Deuteronomy 3:14 assumes the same perspective. Similarly, a post-Moses time of composition is apparent in 3:11, which declares that the burial slab of King Og "can still be seen." Moses, whose forces had only just defeated King Og, would not have spoken of his slab as an artifact in this way.

A perspective similar to that of 3:11, which looks back on Moses' era as a bygone time, occurs in 34:6. There, the text declares that no one knows Moses' burial place "to this day." Moses did not have this perspective of distance from his own burial. Even more immediately, one strains to consider the narration of 34:5 autobiographical: "Then Moses, the servant of the LORD, died there in the land of Moab" (34:5). Such telling clues, scattered through Deuteronomy, led scholars as early as Abraham Ibn Ezra (1089–1164 CE) to understand the book as likely stemming from well after Moses' era.

Credit usually accrues to the German theologian Wilhelm M. L. de Wette (1780–1849 CE) for pinpointing the actual circumstances of Deuteronomy's first appearance in Israel's history. De Wette, expanding insights already sketched out in Patristic literature and by Thomas Hobbes (1588–1679 CE), discerned that the core of Deuteronomy was nothing other than the book of the torah identified in 2 Kings 22–23.

According to 2 Kings 22, a certain torah-book came to light in the eighteenth year of King Josiah's reign (622 BCE), making quite a stir in Judah. Chief Priest Hilkiah unveiled it to strong reactions of surprise and chagrin. Receiving it from Hilkiah out of the temple's archives, Josiah read the book aloud, adopted it in a public ceremony of covenant-making, and then implemented its programs in a major, society-wide reform. The details of the reform so match the content of Deuteronomy that there is little doubt that the book, in some form, made its first major impact in Israel's life at this time.

Could not the narrative of 2 Kings 22–23 be fictional, concocted at a later time to lend prestige to Deuteronomy's ideology? No, too much evidence would have to be overlooked to conclude that the account in 2 Kings is pure invention. For example, why would an account concocted to elevate Deuteronomy narrate a reform with significant details extraneous to the book (see 2 Kgs 23:5, 6-7, 8b, 10-13)? Why would it depict King Josiah implementing Deuteronomy in ways counter to the book's spirit, for example entangling himself in supervising temple matters (2 Kgs 23:21)?

Again, if there were no major reform along Deuteronomy's lines at Josiah's time, then why is the Judean state's new advocacy of an imageless, jealous Lord attested archaeologically in multiple ways, including in changes in the seals used by state officials and in correspondence between Judean military officials? Why does the prophet Jeremiah later lament the turn of affairs as flighty and short-lived (Jer 3:10)? Why does archaeology attest to a popular backlash against the officially enforced turn to the Lord, unearthing a sudden upsurge in domestic veneration of goddess figurines?

Still more arguments support Deuteronomy's connection with the era of 2 Kings 22. Strong evidence garnered through research done after de Wette connects the book to a larger body of literature that first emerged late in Josiah's reign. A sizeable body of "Deuteronomistic" reflection appears to have crystalized in writing in Josiah's period. His reign was the point at which the theology and language of Deuteronomy flowered. I say more about this below. (The term "Deuteronomistic" refers to those writers and writings of the Bible that emulate the style and thought of Deuteronomy.)

Central ideals and forms of expression in Deuteronomy fit Josiah's times and are hard to date much earlier or later. Before King Josiah's reform, and that of King Hezekiah (c. 715 BCE), Deuteronomy's demand for a single national sanctuary was neither a norm nor an ideal of Israelite practice (see 2 Kgs 18:22; 21:3; 23:5). Furthermore, before 672 BCE, the Neo-Assyrian treaty protocols specifically reflected in Deuteronomy were unavailable for emulation. True, patterns of international treaty-making that inform the biblical presentation of the Horeb covenant were long known. Deuteronomy's specific covenantal language, however, has its most dramatic parallels with Esarhaddon's treaties from right before Josiah's time.

Deuteronomy betrays direct familiarity with the seventh-century Neo-Assyrian treaties known as the "Vassal Treaties of Esarhaddon" (VTE). For example, the deadly earnest policies against insurrection in Deuteronomy 13 strongly echo Assyrian protocols in VTE 108-122. Similarly, specific language of covenantal curse in Deuteronomy 28:27-35, 53-57 powerfully recalls VTE 419-30 and 448-50, 547-50, 570-72. Further, the covenant of Deuteronomy commends itself remarkably well as a live alternative to an Assyrian treaty. In Josiah's era, Assyria pressed to subject Israel to a coercive, violent, and hierarchical rule. The Lord's covenant, by contrast, pressed to nurture Israel as an integrated community of mutual interrelationship and dependence.

De Wette, hung over with Enlightenment rationalism, argued the highly skeptical view that Hilkiah invented the book of Deuteronomy out of whole cloth—that is, concocted it from scratch. In an infamous judgment, the scholar concluded that Deuteronomy was essentially a "pious fraud," a pseudepigraph manufactured for the purpose of advancing the interests of Jerusalem's establishment and central priests. It is now clear that de Wette's "fraud" claim was very much mistaken.

Far from representing the ideology and propaganda of seventh-century priests in charge at Jerusalem, the traditions of Deuteronomy had a long and venerable pedigree. I mentioned above the powerful stream of theology that flows into Deuteronomy from Micah, Hosea, and Asaph psalms and how it rushes out of Deuteronomy into Jeremiah and Malachi. One thing is clear to anyone who reads Hosea and Jeremiah, major known proponents of Deuteronomy's thinking and theology. These anguished, suffering prophets were no spiritual frauds.

Deuteronomy's theology flowered publically in King Josiah's reforms, but long prior it was treasured and honed by groups on the edge of monarchic society. Among such pro-Deuteronomy groups were circles of rural, landed gentry. One such circle of "people of the land" (cf. 2 Kgs 11:18, 20; Jer 26:17) first raised Josiah to power, likely forming him to be receptive to Deuteronomy's theology (see 2 Kgs 21:24). Having made an eight-year-old king, the group could have exercised tremendous influence over the minor in the turbulent period after his father's death.

Another representative of Deuteronomy's interests, the prophetess Huldah, vouched for the significance of Hilkiah's law book (2 Kgs 22:14-20). Huldah appears strongly connected with proponents of Deuteronomy. Her husband Shallum (2 Kgs 22:14) seems to have been a relative of Jeremiah (see Jer 32:7). She lived in Jerusalem's "Second" Quarter (2 Kgs 22:14), an expansion of the city accommodating refugees fleeing the Assyrian destruction of the north. This was surely the living quarters of the Levite associates of Hosea and the authors of the Asaph psalms who bore the traditions mentioned above as key sources of Deuteronomy's theology.

In my view, the most plausible scholarly reconstruction of Deuteronomy's origins traces the book's roots to traditions that rural gentry, Levites, and other marginal groups treasured. In the fifty years prior to Josiah's reforms, a covert coalition of these groups aligned with power holders such as Hilkiah to transform Judah's monarchic society. In the period just after the appearance of the Vassal Treaties of Esarhaddon, a cadre of their scribes assembled and edited the core of Deuteronomy (chs. 6–26, 28). In these dark times, they kept their work under wraps (see 2 Kgs 21:2-9, 20-22).

Village Israel versus the Royal Court

Scholars commonly misread Deuteronomy as the royal propaganda of Josiah's palace and temple. De Wette's work, developed later by Julius Wellhausen (1844–1918 CE), has profoundly marked subsequent research. This interpretation cannot sustain itself. The book does not speak from a settled position oriented on Jerusalem but from a stance of freedom and movement. God's people have not "dug in" at Jerusalem, but are pursuing a trek of discipleship.

To listen to Moses' words in Deuteronomy is to hear from outside the establishment. Moses is beholden to no one. He has no established wisdom to offer but only God's hand-delivered words. A *wild card,* he symbolizes divine freedom. Texts such as 18:6-8 threaten set privileges and security systems. They undermine the security of Jerusalem's central priests by demanding that they share work at the temple with Levites from Judah's countryside.

Deuteronomy understands the entire land of Israel, not just its privileged capital, as God's sacred territory. Everywhere God's people must observe the Sabbath day and other sabbatical breaks. Worship at the central shrine must hallow God's name (12:5), but so must the utterance of every oath throughout the land (6:13). Across the range of daily life out in the towns and country, from the preparation of food to practices of mourning the dead, Israel must set itself apart as "a people holy to the LORD" (14:21).

The likeliest bearers of the precursor traditions of Deuteronomy are found not within the royal court but among elders and Levites, representing Israel's premonarchic, village-based way of life. Deuteronomy 31:9 names precisely the elders and Levites of old Israel as those best entrusted with Deuteronomy. The development of Israelite society as a centralized monarchic system worked against the orientation and values of these bearers of Deuteronomy's thought by centralizing and stratifying authority.

Deuteronomy re-empowers village Israel's local elders in its instructions concerning ideal leadership structures. It references these traditional, local leaders in the phrase "judges and officials" used at the start of its leadership section (16:18). Deuteronomy 1:9-18 uses the same Hebrew terms, directing that Israel's judges be selected specifically from among tribal lineage heads. Other texts in Deuteronomy emphasize the traditional Israelite pattern of the local elders' judicial authority (e.g., 21:1-9, 19; 22:15; 25:7).

Like Israel's elders, its priestly line of Levites was rooted in the decentralized, lineage-based culture of premonarchic times. Deuteronomy goes out of its way to safeguard the Levites' welfare (e.g., 12:12, 18-19; 14:27-29; 16:11, 14; 26:12). What is more, the book invests them with service at the land's central altar and with judicial responsibility at the highest level (10:8; 17:8-12; 18:3-8; 21:5; 24:8; cf. Jer 33:18). They enjoy close connection with Moses (himself a Levite; see Exod 4:14; Ps 99:6), who entrusts them with preserving God's teaching, God's new torah scroll (17:18; 31:9, 25-26; 33:8-11; cf. Exod 32:25-29). Notably, Jeremiah belonged to a family of Levites resident in the town of Anathoth that traced its ancestry to the officiants of the ancient sanctuary of Shiloh (cf. Jer 1:1; 1 Sam 2:27-28; 22:20-23; 1 Kgs 2:26-27).

A Flowing Stream of Theology and Tradition

The substance of Deuteronomy represented an early, minority perspective from outside the central state culture presided over by kings, royal officers, and official priests. This perspective developed in clarity and expression over time, but had stable, enduring emphases defended by groups on the periphery of society. Across many centuries, various Israelite groups with multiple agendas preserved and passed along its substance.

Why expend the time and effort to elaborate on Deuteronomy's venerable roots and antecedents? Why clutter the text of a commentary on Deuteronomy by marking scriptural cross-references with monikers such as "E" or "Asaph Psalm"? I believe it is a matter of the intellectual and moral credibility of the book.

If Deuteronomy's substance cannot be reduced to an ideological product of its authors, if instead it antedated them, creating and molding their religious perspectives, then it retains credibility, integrity, and currency. If a stream of tradition lies behind Deuteronomy, then one cannot claim that the book is nothing more than a mere product of its times and circumstances. If its precepts were received as authoritative, with due anxiety about their status as revelation, then the book cannot be misconstrued as a piece of royal propaganda or some other ideological expression. Then the book can speak with clear conscience of the divine word as something awesome, uncontrollable, and unattached to any given systems and authorities.

Various, heterogeneous Israelite literatures advocated the theology that eventually flowered in Deuteronomy. This commentary will frequently cross-reference these significant exemplars of early (i.e., "proto-") Deuteronomic religion. The curators of the Horeb covenant behind Deuteronomy cut across Israel's society, geography, and history. They included priests and laypersons, northerners and southerners, both folks fighting the Philistines for their lives and folks facing the wrath of the Assyrian empire.

Hosea and Micah were eighth-century prophets of the covenant of Mount Horeb. They operated in the northern kingdom and in Judah respectively. Both figures have social roots in Israel's premonarchic, genealogically organized way of life. Hosea appears to have been a member of the traditional Levite priestly lineage. Micah was likely a traditional clan head within kinship-based, village-based society.

HOSEA

Hosea's career spanned a few decades beginning after the mid-eighth century BCE. He was active at the time of the Assyrian Empire's conquest of the northern kingdom, which culminated in the fall of Samaria, the capital, in 722 BCE. Hosea proclaimed that Israel's coming destruction by Assyria resulted from its abandonment of the covenant. The centralization of society had led to state priests perverting worship and to self-absorption and satiety as the effects of the generation of new wealth.

MICAH

Micah, some of whose early prophecies assume that the northern kingdom has not yet fallen, was a near contemporary of Hosea. A village elder from the southern town of Moresheth in the agriculturally fertile "Shephelah" lowland region, he combated social injustices perpetrated by the monarchic center of society in Judah. He traveled from the countryside to Judah's capital, Jerusalem, where he prophesied that God would put a stop to the betrayal of the covenant by bringing the menace of Assyria down on Judah.

Twelve psalms carry the name "Asaph" in their titles, Psalms 50, 73–83. The shared superscription of these texts corresponds to a shared tradition, language, and theology. Scholarly detective work has uncovered strong indications that as a body these psalms originated in the northern kingdom's worship among a subgroup of Levites. The prophet Hosea is directly indebted to them.

The Asaphite Levites behind the Asaph psalms kept their traditions alive despite the apostasy of the official, royal worship system. They may have functioned as a minority group within the system, since King Jeroboam I's removal of the Levites from state sanctuaries (1 Kgs 12:31-32; 13:33; 2 Chr 11:14-15) may have been only partial. Alternatively, the Levites may have maintained their own group worship communities at northern sites such as Shechem.

The "E" or "Elohist" strand or source is one of four principal written sources of the Pentateuch posited by modern biblical scholarship (since the work of Julius Wellhausen). This source derives its name from its preference for using the simple, generic Hebrew term Elohim, "God," in referring to the deity. Some complex critical scholarship beginning in the 1970s has doubted the existence of the Elohist source (e.g., John Van Seters, Erhard Blum), but this seems too easily to abandon many hard-won results of critical spadework. For surveys of recent trends in Pentateuch criticism, see the articles by Hagedorn and Stern (in Works Cited at the end of this commentary). The powerful arguments in the books by Graupner, Coote, and Jenks make it hard to deny the facticity of an E source of some type.

The E materials emerged in the period from 922 to 722 BCE, most likely prior to the eighth-century careers of Micah and Hosea (who are both concerned with increasing threats to E's ideals). The circle preserving and transmitting E texts likely updated and adapted them over time, so that E contains both earlier and later faces (thus, e.g., Exod 18:13-27 and Num 11:14-30 represent two stories from different eras that promote the same line of thought). The book of Deuteronomy may directly re-present E or E-related source material at places such as Deuteronomy 31:14-15, 23; 34:5-6.

E-Source [margin annotation]

There are compelling indications that Levites had a strong presence among the E strand's circle of authors. They are certainly the heroes of Moses and God at Israel's paramount betrayal of the covenant (Exod 32:26-29 E; cf. Deut 33:9). Perhaps Levites descended from the priests of Shiloh are particularly responsible for preserving and handing on the traditions and theology behind E. If the group went on to help compose Deuteronomy, they had a precedent in Shiloh for our book's emphasis on Israel having a great focal shrine. Shiloh had singular status as the home of Israel's tent shrine in the premonarchic period. The fall of Shiloh certainly had a powerful impact on the Levitical authors of documents akin to E (see Asaph Psalm 78:60-64; Jer 7:12).

Literary History

Deuteronomy's first incarnation, which Hilkiah brought to Josiah's attention, appears to encompass Deuteronomy 6:1–8:18; 9:1–11:32; 12:1–26:15; and 28:1-35, 38-46. (The actual law code proper of Deuteronomy occurs in 12:1–26:15.) Later materials have now taken root within these chapters, but by and large it is impossible to convincingly isolate hypothetically expansive layers from the genuine Hilkiah-edition material in this key span of text. When one deals basically with clarifications, interpretations, and efforts at buttressing, it is hard to separate the "original" from the "secondary."

JOSIAH [margin annotation]

While secondary additions are generally difficult to pinpoint in this span, the texts of 8:19-20 and 28:36-37 are widely judged to be secondary, and I have excluded them above from my delineation of the Hilkiah scroll. Beyond these texts, there is hardly a consensus about what might be supplementary material, although commentators frequently mention Deuteronomy 11:26-30; portions of chapter 12; and 14:4-20. This commentary will mostly refrain from the temptation to identify possible secondary material within chapters 6–26, 28 of Deuteronomy, unless a good reason is obvious for making the distinction.

The original "Hilkiah" edition of Deuteronomy quickly proved seminal. Within a single generation, the scroll spawned a significant body of related literature. As scholars have realized for over sixty years now (since the work of Martin Noth expanded an insight of de Wette), Deuteronomy was destined to become the introduction to an entire history of Israel, a "Deuteronomistic" history. This history runs from Joshua through 2 Kings, and is narrated in the idiom and thought of our book.

Scholars continue to diverge on the dating of the Deuteronomistic History, but in my view its first edition was certainly preexilic, culminating in Josiah's reign. The history assumes the present relevance, at the time of writing, of God's covenant with David. It stresses the importance of the Davidic covenant in preserving sinful Judah until the coming of Josiah. There was no sacral Davidic kingship after the exile; the theme is only at home in preexilic times. What is more, unless we assume a preexilic edition of the history, it is impossible to account for the text's innocent statements that various realia extant only in preexilic times can still be seen at the time of writing. If these realities remain "to *this day,*" then this day (i.e., the time of writing) must be preexilic.

Finally, only a preexilic edition of the history explains Josiah's ideal, culminating role in the narrative. The history prophesies Josiah's coming three centuries in advance, it presents his reign in an extraordinarily expansive treatment, and it gives the figure himself a singularly positive evaluation. It places him on a par with Moses himself.

The authors of the history in Joshua through 2 Kings produced a new edition of Deuteronomy near the end of Josiah's reign. Their expansions of the book seem visible in many of the following texts: Deuteronomy 1–3; 26:16-19; 27; 28:38-46; 29:2-21; 30:11-14; 31:1-13, 24-27; 32:45-47. Of course, not all scholars agree that all these texts in their entirety come from as early as the end of Josiah's era.

History proved that Josiah, great reformer though he was, was no messiah. He died a tragic, senseless death at the hands of the Assyrians, and his nation quickly lapsed into covenantal apostasy. Judah fell to the Babylonians in 586 BCE, seemingly demonstrating the collapse of the Davidic covenant and the permanent dashing of the Josianic dream. Deuteronomy now reappeared substantially expanded, shaped to account for the death of the nation and to explain how the covenant would nevertheless triumph.

It is impossible to isolate with assurance all the exilic-era additions to Deuteronomy. Certain passages, nevertheless, strongly suggest a setting in exile, with an attendant contemplation of the meaning of Judah's destruction and with powerful efforts to help readers imagine a restoration. These texts include portions of Deuteronomy 4, especially 4:25-31, and portions of chapter 8, particularly 8:19-20 (see also 28:36-37, 47-68 [especially vv. 63-68]; 29:22-28; 30:1-10, 15-20; 31:16-22, 28-30; 32:44).

Deuteronomy's literary history did not end even with its exilic edition. Scholars have found clear signs of the work of editors to incorporate Deuteronomy within the Pentateuch. For these editors, at least, Deuteronomy had a greater role to play than merely introducing the Deuteronomistic History (Joshua through 2 Kings). Late in its history, the book also became the fifth book of Moses, the capstone of the Torah.

Editorial work placing Deuteronomy as the Torah's culmination occurs in places such as Deuteronomy 1:3; 32:48-52; and 34:7-9. In 32:48-52, late editors have resumed and repeated non-Deuteronomic material from Numbers 27. The present effect of this on the reader is to restart a story that was paused back in Numbers. The pause allowed Moses to deliver Deuteronomy's speeches.

The present-day reader of Deuteronomy finds its speeches enmeshed in the Pentateuch's story but now must grapple with an interpretation of Moses' death foreign to the rest of the book. The new language of resumptive repetition in Deuteronomy 32:48-52 introduces the alien idea of Moses' fate as a punishment from God (Num 27:14; cf. Num 20:12).

Structure of the Book

Discerning the details of Deuteronomy's literary organization is no simple task. An initial challenge is that the chapter divisions of modern translations do not reflect the actual boundaries of the book's sections. Even more difficult, a long literary history and an interplay of perspectives have added complexity to the book's structure. Editors of Deuteronomy have surely worked artfully to produce the book's final form, but the subtle intricacies of their work do not always come into focus easily.

Despite the challenges, most scholars agree that Deuteronomy has four major parts. Three substantial discourses of Moses (1:1–4:43; 4:44–29:1; 29:2–30:20) are followed by an ending narrative section with still more Mosaic speech (31:1–34:12). Even this large-scale division of Deuteronomy, however, is not without ambiguity.

A massive central legal corpus, 12:1–26:15, appears in the midst of the second discourse, expanding its size well beyond the dimensions of the other Mosaic speeches. The presence of this textual "elephant" somewhat weakens the impression of a well-balanced four-part structure. It does make obvious, however, the book's emphasis on hard-nosed structures of discipleship.

Disagreement persists on the precise demarcations of the Mosaic discourses. For example, should 29:1 end the second discourse, as I hold, or begin the third discourse? If the latter is the case, as many interpreters think, then the verse introduces a second, separate "Moab" covenant. But this idea is problematic, since Moses has been clear that the present generation he addresses is bound to the original "Horeb" covenant (see, e.g., 5:2-3). Further, the third discourse lacks the core elements of a standard ancient Near Eastern covenant. It is best, then, to take 29:1 as a colophon to what precedes or as a transitional verse. The Hebrew text numbers it as verse 69 of chapter 28.

Given the weightiness of the central legal code, one might approach Deuteronomy as a detailed presentation of torah (chs. 12–26) surrounded by a framing prologue (chs. 1–11) and epilogue (chs. 27–34). The framing chapters themselves may be subdivided into an outer frame (chs. 1–3 and 31–34) and an inner frame (chs. 4–11 and 27–30).

The organization of the central legal core of Deuteronomy continues to be a matter of interpretation. Is this immensely varied collection of instructions ordered and shaped according to definite principles? Insightful students of Deuteronomy have observed that the general flow of chapters 12–26 mirrors that of the Ten Commandments. The view represents a long tradition in scholarship, supported by the careful study of figures such as Martin Luther, John Calvin, Stephen A. Kaufman, and Georg Braulik (for bibliographic notes, see Miller 2007, 24–26 notes 20, 25, 26). The research behind this commentary confirms the approach.

The core's initial chapters can fairly easily be seen to reflect the first two commandments, which demand that Israel worship the Lord alone. Subsequent sections of the core align with commandments 3 through 10. The precise workings of the alignment are often far from completely obvious, however. Instead, we see the Deuteronomic authors' sometimes subtle interpretations of the themes of the various commandments.

The commandment about keeping the Sabbath day, for example, extends into a discussion of various sacred "interruptions" to be practiced in Israel's life. An orientation on Sabbath means the relief of debts every seven years and the sacrificing of firstborn animals to the Lord. Similarly, the commandment about honoring parents extends to encompass respect for much wider circles of authority. Indeed, it becomes a rubric for discussing the entire leadership and polity of God's people (16:18–18:22).

Following is a detailed listing of the major sections and subsections of Deuteronomy. The five underlined headings divide the book according to its central legal core and its beginning and ending framework. The alphanumeric, hierarchically organized outline divides the book according the major Mosaic discourses and their topics and subtopics. As will be apparent, these two literary organizations of the book overlap and do not fully cohere with one another.

<u>Deuteronomy's Prologue, Part I, 1:1–3:29</u>
I. The First Discourse of Moses, 1:1–4:43
   A. Israel's Past at Mount Horeb and at Kadesh-barnea, 1:1-46
      1. Introductory Note, 1:1-5
      2. The Tradition of Mosaic Judges, 1:6-18
      3. Israel at Kadesh-barnea, 1:19-46
   B. Israel's Journey from Kadesh to Moab, 2:1–3:11
   C. The Allotment of Transjordan, 3:12-29
      1. Distributing the Land, 3:12-22
      2. Moses' "Gethsemane" Prayer, 3:23-29

<u>Deuteronomy's Prologue, Part II, 4:1–11:32</u>
   D. Israel on the Plains of Moab, 4:1-43
      1. A Call to Obey Moses' Teaching, 4:1-40
      2. Appendix: Cities of Refuge in Transjordan, 4:41-43
II. The Second Discourse of Moses, 4:44–29:1
   A. Introducing the Torah, 4:44–5:5
      1. Introduction to Moses' Second Discourse, 4:44-49
      2. Actualizing the Covenant, 5:1-5
   B. God's Revelation of the Decalogue, 5:6-33
      1. The Ten Commandments, 5:6-21
      2. The Mediator of the Covenant, 5:22-33
   C. The Command to Love an Integral Lord, 6:1-25
   D. The Command to Show No Mercy, 7:1-26
   E. The Rejection of Dependence on Self, 8:1-20
   F. The Rejection of Self-Righteousness, 9:1–10:11
   G. A Summative Call to Commitment, 10:12–11:32

<u>The Central Legal Corpus of Deuteronomy, 12:1–26:19</u>
   H. A Central Sanctuary, 12:1-32
   I. A Command to Resist Sedition and Insurrection, 13:1-18
   J. A People Called by God's Name, 14:1-29

1. Choose Holiness, Choose Life, 14:1-2
2. Ritual Requirements for Table Fellowship, 14:3-21
3. Tithes and Firstlings, 14:22-29
K. A People of Sacred Interruptions, 15:1–16:17
   1. The Relief of Debts, 15:1-11
   2. The Release of Debt Servants, 15:12-18
   3. Sacrificing Firstlings, 15:19-23
   4. Concerning Festivals, 16:1-17
L. Leadership and Polity for God's People, 16:18–18:22
   1. Judges, 16:18–17:13
   2. Kings, 17:14-20
   3. Altar Ministers, 18:1-8
   4. Prophets, 18:9-22
M. Protecting Innocent Life: The Public Order, 19:1-21
   1. Cities of Refuge, 19:1-13
   2. The Boundary Mark, 19:14
   3. Witnesses, 19:15-21
N. Protecting Innocent Life: Warfare, 20:1-20
O. The Confrontation of Life and Death, 21:1-23
P. The Obligation to Protect Life, 22:1-8
Q. Exposition of the Commandment against Adultery, 22:9–23:18
R. Exposition of the Commandment against Theft, 23:19–24:7
S. Exposition of the Commandment against False Witness, 24:8–25:4
T. Do Not Covet Your Neighbor's Wife, 25:5-12
U. Do Not Long for Anything that Belongs to Your Neighbor, 25:13–26:15
V. Conclusion to the Legal Corpus: A Mutual Covenant, 26:16-19

Deuteronomy's Epilogue, Part I, 27:1–30:20
   W. Ceremonies at Shechem, 27:1-26
   X. Covenant Blessings and Curses, 28:1–29:1
III. The Third Discourse of Moses, 29:2–30:20
   A. Ratification, Part 1: Review of Israel's History, 29:2-9
   B. Ratification, Part 2: A Reciprocal, Immutable Commitment, 29:10-29
   C. Ratification, Part 3: Assurance of the Future, 30:1-10
   D. Ratification, Part 4: A Word Very Near, 30:11-14
   E. Ratification, Part 5: A Necessary Choice, 30:15-20

Deuteronomy's Epilogue, Part II, 31:1–34:12
IV. Epilogue: The Death of Moses and the Torah's Formation, 31:1–34:12
    A. Transferring Leadership and Depositing Witnesses, 31:1-29
    B. The Song of Moses, 31:30–32:47
    C. Moses Commanded to Die, 32:48-52
    D. The Blessing of Moses, 33:1-29
    E. The Death of Moses, 34:1-12

Deuteronomy's Theology and Message

The book of Deuteronomy brims with expansive beauty and deep insight. Its meaning bursts beyond the limited consciousness of its ancient authors. It points beyond its circumstances of origin to a reality that remains true today: human fulfillment comes through a relationship of non-reductive dependence on the Lord. Such dependence should be the lifeblood of the faithful of all generations, and Deuteronomy's purpose is to move imperfect human beings toward this form of life.

The book of Deuteronomy positions its message as unfettered, forward looking, and pressing truth. Characteristic of the book is the immediacy of its challenge to the reader: Commit now to the God of the covenant! Over and over again—more than sixty times—Moses puts the emphasis on "today." By "today" he means the present moment as the time for decision and alignment with God. Moses virtually reaches out from the hoary past to speak with persuasive urgency to present-day readers.

Deuteronomy presses for decisive decision and commitment, but is interested in far more than a one-time "altar call." You do not sign on to the covenant of Horeb and then proceed on your way. Deuteronomy presses its audience to leave all self-directed paths and choose God's singular path of lifelong journey. Having been found by God, the text assumes, the reader will yearn for an ever fuller immersion in God's way of life. Here is where some get confused, objecting that God should be offering up grace, not rules and strictures. But God's grace is *not* opposed to effort, only to all thoughts of desert and self-justification.

"Effort" does not mean "earning." Deuteronomy knows of no other possible God-attuned life than life characterized by sacrificial transformation into God's likeness (8:6; 10:12; 11:22; 19:9; 26:17; cf. Exod 33:13; Mic 6:8). This is a book of "costly grace," of persistent, dogged discipleship. Dietrich Bonhoeffer, German theologian and martyr (1906–1945 CE), spoke in the spirit of Deuteronomy when he wrote of the *cost of discipleship*.

Deuteronomy addresses Israel collectively, as a community, in its call to decision and discipleship. It advocates a *communal* process of formation in God's ways. Thus, its torah aims at shaping the entire body of God's people in God's likeness. As noted above, a core meaning of torah for Deuteronomy is catechesis. I would characterize the book as a communal catechism focused on the molding of Israel as "children of the LORD," "a people holy to the LORD," "his treasured possession" (14:1-2).

Collective religious formation will doubtless be an unfamiliar concept to many readers of this commentary. For Israel, essentially, formation is to be a process of demarcating covenant life as set apart, trenchantly life-affirming, and hallowing of the name of the God of blessing. It is about interconnecting with the God of awe, standing apart, becoming "other." Israel is to make the effort to become a distinct people, differentiated in life from those who are non-covenantal or even anti-covenantal.

As Deuteronomy presents it, the means of striving to be a holy people are wide ranging. The book has commands about remembering God's acts, about studying God's teachings, about ethical behavior, about observing sacred interruptions of life's flow, about structuring society, about worship, sacrifices, and fellowship, about ritual and ceremonial practices. Together, these commands transform ordinary life entirely, turning people's focus away from fear, self-concern, pride, and ambition. They direct the community to a fuller experience of life in God's intimate presence, in sacred freedom.

Deuteronomy has much to say about human leadership and teaching in the process of Israel's communal formation, but believes the force that actually transforms lives is God's word. God's word, preserved in Deuteronomy, has issued from the midst of Horeb's fire (Deut 4:33, 36; 5:24, 26). Even in the present, far removed from the fire atop Horeb, the word of God burns with fiery potential when publically read, privately embraced. It interconnects Israel with God's otherness, evoking awe, human mutuality, and yearning for morality. Through the word of God, Israel of all generations learns "to fear/revere the LORD" (31:12, 13).

Previous studies of Deuteronomy have not always kept in focus the key role of Israel's land, God's promised territory, in Israel's communal formation. An excellent metaphor of Deuteronomy's ideal Israel is a branching tree planted on fertile soil. The tree's twigs and leaves represent families and family members, its limbs and branches represent lineages and tribes, and its trunk and roots are the people as a whole. The life-giving sap of community flows throughout the tree, cutting across all levels of society. The tree's flow of "sap" interconnects the living and their ancestors, reinforcing the solidarity of generations.

Just as the tree depends on the soil for its life, so Israel's covenant derived its power from vesting kin groups with inalienable ancestral land. Inherited farmlands sustained clan families, tied them to their buried dead, and allowed the clan to extend support to those in need. Bounty flowing from the land gave the covenant power to support the bonds of community.

Deuteronomy's concern extends beyond Israel's tree to encompass the wider forest world. For this book other nations, such as Edom, Moab, and Ammon, also claim a God-given homeland. God cares about the nations, and molds Israel through covenant as an example to them of the glory possible for earthly community at large.

Using this Commentary

This commentary steps back from Deuteronomy's details and minutiae to focus on the large, coherent passages of the book. At many places it steps back to gain theological perspective from a vantage point even outside of Deuteronomy itself. Where Deuteronomy's meaning is ambiguous or puzzling, the reader may often gain clarity through a look at comparable language and symbols in sibling Scriptures. Some may object that Deuteronomy should be allowed to speak for itself. Deuteronomy's emphasis on reengaging past revelation, however, means the spirit of the book is antagonistic to any artificial insistence on a closed, bounded interpretation.

A theological reading of Deuteronomy should be eager to listen in on the dialogues that Deuteronomy has provoked, especially its inner-biblical conversations with family-member texts. The book is part of something larger than itself, a flowing stream of tradition, an expansive revelation. Its authors bore fertile ideas, bearing fruit in later texts. What better way to gain traction on what the community of faith has heard in Deuteronomy over time than to step back and reflect on its echoes in kindred Scriptures?

The treatments of individual passages here are not necessarily linear, and I hope that this will not frustrate readers. I do not intend this commentary to be a plodding, verse-by-verse treatment of Deuteronomy. Instead, I want to encourage a dynamic conversation with the book's passages. I want to interact with the book's vibrant, integral units.

If a unit's closing verses are part of a framing structure, for example, I might well treat them first, before getting to earlier verses. Although this lively conversation with the Scripture may jump around a bit, along the way the commentary will cover all essential details of each text. I do, however, try to avoid tangential information and long digressions. This is a focused, accessible commentary, not an encyclopedic tome.

Eschewing reliance on any single English version, I often cite a variety of modern translations of Deuteronomy. Taking an eclectic approach, I select translations that best render the sense of the text. This bucks a common trend to make things easier on readers by linking a commentary to a single translation such as the NRSV or the NIV.

No one translation can perfectly convey the meaning of Deuteronomy every time. The sense of the Hebrew is best captured by different English versions at different places. What is more, one must often hear from two or even three translations to grasp a biblical text's full meaning. A cross-reference may be most apparent in one translation, a play on words clearest in another. In some instances (e.g., catching an allusion, grasping a poetic structure), understanding depends on a tight, word-for-word rendering of the Hebrew. In other cases, the passion, humor, or spirit of the text can only be appreciated by a flexible, dynamic rendering or even only by a paraphrase.

A few sample cases where consulting multiple translations proves helpful demonstrate the point. As trustworthy as the NRSV is, it proves inadequate at Deuteronomy 33:16. The NRSV has the verse call God "the one who dwells on Sinai," but the Hebrew actually speaks not of "Sinai" but of a *seneh*, a "thorny shrub." The verse plays on the sound of "Sinai," the mountain of the covenant, but also echoes a rare Hebrew term in Exodus 3:2-3. It thus conjures up the image of God's fiery manifestation to Moses in the burning bush.

Clearly, one must look beyond the NRSV at Deuteronomy 33:16 to appreciate the full sense of the verse and to catch the occurrence of a repeating theme of Deuteronomy. The book continually returns to a stress on God's fiery, imageless, immediate *presence* to Israel. In this book, the people of Israel are blessed with the favor of God speaking to them directly and personally out of the divine fire (cf. Deut 4:33, 36; 5:24, 26), a mode of communion already experienced by Moses in Exodus 3. The NJPS does better with this verse of Deuteronomy, speaking of "the Presence in the Bush."

The NRSV, along with most English translations, again seems insufficient at Deuteronomy 10:16. Here Moses commands the people to "circumcise, then, the foreskin of your heart." This rendering is fine as a literal translation, but the meaning is lost on today's average reader. The NJPS works harder to draw out the actual sense of the metaphorical language: "Cut away, therefore, the thickening about your hearts." With this translation the reader can understand that Moses is asking people to cast off all that constrains and numbs their spirits. Willing to drop the language of circumcision, *The Message* is even more insistent on sounding the core point: "Cut away the thick calluses from your heart."

Another feature of this commentary that may strike readers as unusual is the regular use of source designations, such as "E," "D," or "Asaph Psalm," when citing Scriptures echoed or cross-referenced in Deuteronomy. I realize that to many readers these labels will seem technical, jargon-like, and otherwise unfriendly. I use them very deliberately, however, in order to spotlight Deuteronomy's noble pedigree.

As I have explained above, Deuteronomy's moral authority relates to the authenticity and depth of its background. This background also contributes greatly to the book's literary richness and theological profundity. The theology that surfaces in this book has proved adaptable for the life of faith across changing times and challenges. Allotting source tags to Deuteronomy's cross-references helps us keep this in mind.

In these and several other ways, I have aimed for this commentary to offer a distinctive and insightful new presentation of the book of Deuteronomy. My efforts pale, of course, in comparison with the great strength and majesty of the biblical text itself. Read alongside of the text of Deuteronomy, however, this commentary should prove newly illuminating of the form, theology, and significance of this monumental Scripture.

THE FIRST DISCOURSE OF MOSES

1:1–4:43

Israel's Past at Mount Horeb and at Kadesh-barnea

Deuteronomy 1:1-46

The book of Deuteronomy consists of three great speeches or "discourses" of Moses plus an epilogue. The first major speech comprises 1:1 to 4:43. It is backward looking, reprising the story of Israel's past. It begins in 1:1-46 with an introductory note (vv. 1-5) and a historical recapitulation of Israel's wanderings that brought them to the brink of settling the promised land (vv. 6-46).

Introductory Note, 1:1-5

The reader learns upfront—from the book's initial verse—that the substance of Deuteronomy will consist of recorded speech, "the words that Moses spoke." Moses, the book's orator, is extraordinary—the daring mediator of God who risked his life to enter God's blazing presence and receive God's will for God's people. The name "Moses" is prominent in the first clause of v. 1, occurs again in v. 3, and rounds off the introduction in v. 5. It is hard to miss this structural emphasis on Moses. There is no naïve historical claim here, nor is this "pseudonymity," slyly lending the book legitimacy. Rather, as Arnold (2010, 73) explains, the authors pressed to sound Moses' very voice (*ipsissima vox*) and strove to continue an activity of exposition that he once "began" (1:5 CEB).

Who would not want to hear and understand this voice/*vox*? The Old Testament celebrates the foundational, incomparable character of Moses' discourse from start to finish. The Pentateuch concludes by exalting Moses: "Never since has there arisen a prophet in Israel like Moses, whom the LORD knew face to face" (Deut 34:10). The last of the prophetic books echoes the theme. The prophet Malachi urges as central to faith the injunction to "Remember the teaching of my servant Moses" (Mal 4:4).

Moses does not speak his mind; he speaks God's mind (v. 3). Deuteronomy's heritage of tradition held as fundamental that Moses was

God's intimate, personal representative. Unlike other prophets of God, be they visionaries or dreamers, Moses was God's unique channel of revelation—God's covenant mediator. God communicates with Moses "face to face—clearly, not in riddles" (Num 12:8 E). Jeremiah, the great prophet and proponent of Deuteronomy, will later bear the mantle of this unique relationship. According to Jeremiah 1, the Lord stretched out the divine hand, touched Jeremiah's mouth, and inserted the divine Word (v. 9). Mirroring Moses' precedent, Jeremiah directly receives God's revelation—*hand delivered* (see Deut 18:18).

Mosaic discourse is uniquely, singularly God-inspired. Is not this claim to qualitative difference from other discourse intolerably narrow and chauvinist? Does not God have many channels of communication—many prophets and truth-tellers? A modern question to be sure, but also an ancient cause of consternation. Already in biblical times, heartfelt objections to this very theology sounded forth. Some Israelites became willing to ask questions: "Has the LORD spoken only through Moses?" (Num 12:2).

Such questions are misplaced. Many brave prophecies may inspire the reader; Deuteronomy in no way denies their validity and usefulness. But Mosaic discourse is unique: it lays before the reader the very Word of God that has gone forth to accomplish the world's salvation. This divine Word tears down all opposition to salvation and creates covenantal community. Receptive to God's word as teaching, as "catechism," the community of faith opens itself to initiation and formation in a new, God-inspired way of life (see the discussion of Deuteronomy as *catechism* and *formation* in the Introduction).

In accomplishing salvation, establishing the divine sovereignty, and laying out the path of formation in the faith, God has acted decisively, completely, and adequately. As the great twentieth-century theologian Karl Barth has emphasized at length, there is a *yawning gulf*, with no fellowship or comparison possible, between the Word of God that has wrought such wonders and all other words. No other utterance, however spiritual, can compete with such a word or really even supplement it.

The reader begins Deuteronomy expecting great things to come but also encounters a lightly veiled note of caution and pessimism in vv. 2-3. The NET rendition of the verses captures the subtle yet sharp critique of Israel's waywardness: "It is ordinarily an eleven-day journey from Horeb to Kadesh Barnea by way of Mount Seir. However, it was not until the first day of the eleventh month of the fortieth year that Moses addressed the Israelites." Because of Israel's rebellion (cf. 1:25-40; 9:8), it has taken the people almost forty years to get to the promised land. There is something wrong with this picture, and the problem is worth the reader's reflection.

The reader will encounter a similar realism, even skepticism, about human nature throughout Deuteronomy. It is a simple and natural choice to follow God's teaching for authentic, abundant life, the book avers, yet people seem unable to do so. In Hosea's prophecy, antecedent to Deuteronomy, God puts it this way: "My people are bent on turning away from me" (Hos 11:7). Hosea's Hebrew verb literally describes the people as having a "hang up." Deuteronomy forwards the same dim view of humanity's apparent moral inability to detach itself from unfaith (see 1:32; 9:6-17, 22-24; 31:27).

The writers of the pessimistic words of vv. 2-3 of Deuteronomy's introduction probably just lived through an experience of Judah's propensity toward rebellion. In the era immediately before the religious reforms of King Josiah, King Manasseh had undone many of the significant reforms of his father King Hezekiah (2 Kgs 21:9-15; 23:26-27). At a later date, the prophet Jeremiah will confirm that the apostasy under Manasseh was far from isolated. Even Josiah's reforms promoting Deuteronomy's vision of a faithful people prove unable to stick (Jer 3:10; 22:15-17).

Whereas historians sometimes dismiss the biblical evaluation of Manasseh as revisionist, Jeremiah's sorrow at Judah's ongoing, chronic apostasy is almost certainly authentic. He despairs that nothing seems able to turn God's people permanently around. The final editors of Deuteronomy share his view (cf. Deut 4:27-28; 28:36-37, 63-68).

The book of Deuteronomy will handle the problem within human nature in a number of ways. Alongside its ideal blueprint for the good life, it will introduce notes of sober realism and highly pragmatic regulations (e.g., 4:41-43; 15:11; 17:16-17). It will impress its vision upon the reader, literally drilling in God's instructions (see, e.g., 6:7; 11:18-20). Finally, in a startling move that is really more akin to prophecy than appropriate for a body of law, it will look ahead to a future ("eschatological") saving work of God that will permanently transform the bent human heart (see esp. 30:6, 8).

The Tradition of Mosaic Judges, 1:6-18

After the brief introduction, Moses plunges the reader into a historical review of Israel's wanderings in the wilderness after the exodus from Egypt. The review occurs in 1:6–3:29 and has several sections, the first of which recounts events at Mount Horeb (Deuteronomy and its antecedent traditions call Mount Sinai "Horeb"). The focus is on one particular experience: Moses' organizing of judges to help administer the covenant.

Singling out this event fits Deuteronomy's overall vision; it sounds a theme of ideal leadership of society to be taken up in more detail later (see 16:18–18:22). Deuteronomy envisions an ideal social organization, where Israel can experience authentic formation as God's holy people. It insists on a *communal* catechesis.

Deuteronomy's ideal polity, which foreshadows the reign of God on earth, entails people living as co-vassals under the divine suzerain. God's reign, the book avers, is nothing more and nothing less than a brotherhood and sisterhood of human beings living in mutuality under God and inter-connected with the natural environment. God's covenant is grounded in the arable land: "See, I have set the land before you" (v. 8).

The scriptural sources underlying Deuteronomy describe the inevitability of God's people and God's land joining in intimate relationship with each other and with God's self. Grasping this key thematic trajectory helps us avoid misapprehending the text out of misplaced political suspi-cions. The settlement of Canaan is no land-grab by xenophobic opportunists, as modern readers not attuned to Deuteronomy's spirituality too often suppose. It is the fulfillment of a long-range *theological* plan of God.

For Deuteronomy's sources, the land of Canaan is God's sanctuary, God's holy territory for nurturing and forming an elect people of God's special choosing (see Deut 32:13-15; Exod 15:17 E/D; Ps 78:54, an Asaphite source of Deuteronomy). God's people will not develop in a vacuum but in this special territory of the Lord. Deuteronomy 1:8 picks up on source texts describing the land as promised to Israel's ancestors long before the time of the exodus (see Gen 15:16 E; Exod 13:5, 11 E; 32:13 E; Num 11:12 E). God's chosen people have had to wait 400 years since the ancestors' era, until God's patience with the land's preceding occupants reached its limit (Gen 15:16). The reader will encounter the theme of God's ancestral promise repeatedly (see 1:35; 4:31; 6:10, 18, 23; 7:13; 8:1; 10:11; 11:9, 21; 19:8; 26:3, 15, etc.; cf. Mic 7:20).

Although God's people read in v. 8 that God has "set the land before you," they also immediately learn that they have significant responsibilities to uphold if the ancestral promises are to be realized. God does God's part, but it is up to Moses' hearers to "go in and take possession of the land" (v. 8). This will hardly be a matter of merely taking up residence there but of grounding a lifestyle of covenantal mutuality in the land.

Good social institutions, leveraged by the covenant, will be crucial for this to succeed. Everybody—not just rulers—must be responsible for the success of Deuteronomy's ideal communal structures. Moses insists on collective responsibility when he reminds readers that the entire people promised their support. "The plan you have proposed is a good one," they declared (v. 14).

Those living the covenantal lifestyle will have to share God's sacred land equitably and use its agricultural produce to sustain and nurture the lives of all inhabitants. Moses' proposed cadre of "wise, discerning, and reputable . . . leaders" will guide them (v. 13). Such "Mosaic" judges are to administer the covenant, giving community members a truly fair hearing when disputes arise. They are to "judge rightly between one person and another, whether citizen or resident alien" (1:16).

The Hebrew term "brother" appears twice in v. 16. The NRSV loses something of the force of this diction in speaking instead of community members and citizens. In Deuteronomy's covenantal society the land's inhabitants are not merely its citizens. All inhabitants, whether Israelite or alien, treat each other like immediate family. They guard each other's dignity and right treatment as if they were brothers and sisters.

Johannes Pedersen captured the power of this theology in describing the covenant that David made with Jonathan, the son of his rival, King Saul. David showed particular loving kindness (Heb., *khesed*) to Jonathan's son when most monarchs would have had him killed (2 Sam 9:1). Pedersen comments, "The friendship between Jonathan and David shows us the covenant of unrelated persons in its strongest form. Here the community of soul is whole, as strong as that of kin, nay, kinship must give way to friendship. 'My brother' David calls Jonathan (2 Sam 1:26), as if they were of the same kin" (284).

The authors of Deuteronomy knew exactly the sort of judicial abuse to be guarded against in proposing an ideal form of human community. In the preceding century, the prophet Micah had railed against the monarchy's new centralized judicial system for failing to ensure the security of Judah's farmlands. By Micah's eighth-century times, state officials clearly no longer respected traditional covenantal protections.

Instead of protecting the hereditary lands of Israel's families and kingroups, Micah charged, the state's appointed officers "give judgment for a bribe" (Mic 3:11). They "abhor justice and pervert all equity" (3:9). As a result, the land-grabbing lords of Jerusalem were beginning to put pressure on the latticework of God's covenant. "They covet fields, and seize them; houses and take them away" (Mic 2:2). The same Hebrew word for Israel's judges, the Hebrew term "heads," appears in both Deuteronomy and Micah. Deuteronomy insists that these "heads" of the people live up to covenantal standards, that they disavow the behavior for which Micah had castigated them.

Deuteronomy 1:9-18 echoes two E passages, Exodus 18:13-27 and Numbers 11:14-30, which both affirm the traditional judicial role of tribal Israel's elders, its lineage "heads." Exodus 18, the later of the two texts, appears particularly aware of the Israelite monarchy's dangerous innovations: extracting the "surplus" yield from people's farms, centralizing and stratifying the judiciary, taking justice out of the hands of local tribes, clans, and families and vesting it in state hierarchies. The language of vv. 21 and 25 tempers the monarchy's power by specifying that judges be chosen from among those already pretested in the covenant role of local judge.

Israel at Kadesh-barnea, 1:19-46

Moses now recounts the fateful events that occurred after the people moved from Mount Horeb up to Kadesh-barnea, a wilderness oasis south of Canaan selected to be the staging ground of the land's settlement. Despite forceful reminders of God's grace and of God's promises to the ancestors (v. 21), the people revolt. They insist on having scouts reconnoiter Canaan (v. 22) and then, having received their report, prove unwilling to enter the land (v. 26).

Eugene H. Peterson's translation powerfully captures the people's frenzied emotional and spiritual state:

> You complained in your tents: "GOD hates us. He hauled us out of Egypt in order to dump us among the Amorites—a death sentence for sure! How can we go up? We're trapped in a dead end. Our brothers took all the wind out of our sails, telling us, 'The people are bigger and stronger than we are; their cities are huge, their defenses massive—we even saw Anakite giants there!'" (Deut 1:27-28, *The Message*)

In response to the mutiny, God gives up on the exodus generation and turns them away from the land. The decision shocks the reader, but arguably represents an appropriate judgment. By their words and actions, the people block divine grace and exclude themselves from relationship with God. Their insane outcry "the LORD hates us" (v. 27) effectively annuls their election by God, the basis of God's granting them the land (see Deut 7:6-8).

In Hebrew parlance, talk of God's "love" and "hate" represents language of covenantal relationship (on God's "love," compare 10:15; Hos 11:1; Mal 1:2; on God's "hate," compare Hos 9:15; Mal 1:3). Thus, v. 27 actually has the people declare themselves on the outside of any vassal relationship with the Lord. They have kicked out from beneath them any basis for proceeding into the promised land.

Even worse, the people's frenzied terror (v. 28) places them in the shoes of God's adversaries, whom 2:25 declares to be the ones to feel dread at the prospect of God-initiated war. Finally, to top everything off, the people exhibit the exact opposite of the *teachable* spirit on which Deuteronomy predicates all of its catechesis (see Introduction). They are unwilling to receive any lessons about God's care either at the exodus (v. 30) or during their trek through the wilderness (v. 19).

Despite the dark mood of this part of Moses' story, his speech at this juncture is meant as constructive. It contains deep, positive insights about God's ways with God's people. The point of recalling the story of the older generation's failures is to allow the present generation, including all future readers of the book, to learn from their mistakes.

Moving through the account of this outrageous give-and-take between the people, Moses, and God, the reader perceives a caricature of un-faith so gross as to bring into relief the marks of a genuinely intimate, transformative walk of discipleship. Hearing the ludicrous claim of God's "hate," one finds oneself marveling at the diametrically opposite facts on the ground. What an unspeakable gift for God's people to be the cherished, personal treasure of God, when all of us really have nothing to offer God (Deut 7:6-7; cf. Exod 19:5 E).

How the entire world waxes and wanes when one experiences the intimate care of God, offered out of sheer love and commitment to age-old promises (Deut 1:31; 7:8; cf. Hos 11:1, 4; Exod 19:4; 32:13 both E)! How ridiculous to melt in fear before frail, human enemies when before you marches one whose visage must be shielded by cloud and fire lest, apprehending it, onlookers lose their very lives (Deut 1:33; 4:12, 33; cf. Exod 19:9; 33:9, 20 E; Judg 13:20-22)! When such a deity intends to move "in the midst of you" (Deut 1:42; cf. Exod 33:14 E), who would presume to enter the fray independently? Trembling overtakes any who have felt the presence of Deuteronomy's God. They soon discover any foolish presumption snuffed out (see Exod 33:15 E).

Deuteronomy has its own distinctive portrayal of God's presence with God's people, which this passage begins to reveal. It is very different from what we find in Leviticus and Ezekiel, for example, and is even more different from what we find in the Psalms and Isaiah. Attention to this portrayal helps us more fully appreciate some of Deuteronomy's profound theological contributions. It is rather more complex than scholars commonly contend (see the discussion in Vogt 2006, 192–93).

In particular, Deuteronomy's presentation does not mesh well with interpreters' commonplace idea that the book, in a mode of demythologizing, offers a rather rationalistic notion of divine self-revelation, in which the divine "name" serves as a sort of proxy for God. The divine self, in this view, always remains fully transcendent and intangible. God only puts God's *name* on earth, not God's physical presence (see esp. Deut 12:5). By this move, Deuteronomy supposedly repudiates earlier, more primitive, "anthropomorphic" conceptions of God.

The passage at hand, however, clearly does not back away from belief in God's real presence with God's people. Apparently, its authors "missed the memo" on the need to become more intellectually refined. Deuteronomy regards the idea of an ongoing, tangible presence of God as anything but primitive. The God of Deuteronomy manifests the divine self visibly and incontestably (v. 30), gets involved with the people's lives practically (v. 33), and yearns to express love tangibly (v. 31). Verse 42 baldly states God's hope to be "in the midst" of the covenant people, establishing their identity and success (cf. 4:7).

The language of God being "in the midst" (v. 42; cf. Hos 11:9) is distinctive, strongly resonating with Exod 33:12-23 (E/D), a Deuteronomy-related text about Moses and God wrestling over issues of presence and relationship. That passage, akin to Deuteronomy, describes God securely attaching the divine presence to Israel. In Exodus 33, Moses insists on getting God's commitment to accompany stiff-necked Israel, just as God promised at the burning bush (Exod 3:12 E). Moses reminds God repeatedly that the nation consists of "your people" (Exod 33:13, 16), whose special character depends entirely on the Lord's accompaniment (cf. Deut 4:7). God takes Moses' pleas to heart and promises that God's own presence will in fact personally accompany God's people (v. 14; see NJB, NLT).

God's personal presence, to which God refers in Exodus 33:14, is much more than a proxy-like phenomenon issued by a "demythologized" God— much more than some secondary manifestation of God's involvement, some divine *hypostasis* (a divine name or attribute come alive as God's stand-in). If Moses had been willing to settle for some sort of proxy or hypostasis, then the angel of God would have sufficed (see 33:2-3, "I will send *an angel* . . . but *I* will not go"; cf. Exod 14:19; 23:20; 32:34, all E). Clearly it did not suffice, even though God's name is "in him" (Exod 23:21).

Moses bravely declared God's angel insufficient: "If you do not come yourself," he tells God, "do not make us move on" (Exod 33:15 NJB). The Hebrew idiom in 33:14-15, employing the noun "face," signals the very presence of God's person. Deuteronomy 4:37 quotes this idiom.

Immanence and intimacy characterize God's presence according to Deuteronomy—that is, Deuteronomy properly understood (and not taken as a "demythologizing" work). This characterization, however, tells only half the story. God offers loving intimacy to be sure (Deut 1:31), but the divine presence should not be regarded as something familiar and safe. Rather, it is potentially lethal! That is why God seriously hesitates to attach to Israel in Exodus 33—out of fear of consuming a stiff-necked, faithless community! Note the Lord's initial concern, as communicated to Moses: "I will not go up among you, or I would consume you on the way" (33:3).

Deuteronomy echoes the theology of Exod 33, recalling images of fire and cloud concealing God's scorching reality (Deut 1:33). Even Moses, who enjoyed a singular intimacy with God (Exod 33:11), always required such shielding (and, indeed, a layer of tent-covering besides). Screens had to protect him from God's true visage (Exod 33:9; cf. vv. 21-23). Moses must never take in a direct view of God's self. As God puts it, "You cannot see my face; for no one shall see me and live" (Exod 33:20; cf. Gen 32:30 E; Exod 24:11 E; Deut 4:33; 5:24).

Rudolf Otto apprehended something of the mystery at the heart of Deuteronomy's theology of God's presence. He carefully described the widespread human experience of divine holiness as mysteriously double-sided. The paradox of the Holy, he argued, is that it is simultaneously magnetic, drawing one into intimacy, and threatening, causing one to cringe in terror.

In Otto's language, the Holy (the *numinous*) is something both fascinating (Latin: *fascinans*) and terrifying (Latin: *tremendum*). The deity before whom the camp at Mount Horeb trembles (Exod 19:16 E) is the selfsame being who later on the mountain draws Moses and seventy elders into intimate table fellowship (Exod 24:11 E). The reader of Deuteronomy will encounter this double-edged quality of holiness repeatedly. Like a parent or mate, God truly belongs to us; yet God's inner being is dangerous and strictly off-limits to us, belonging to God alone (Deut 29:29).

In Deuteronomy 1:37 we encounter Moses taking on and somehow absorbing the Lord's dangerous, numinous anger on account of the people's sin. His death on others' account is somehow a bridge to survival and new life for the Israelite people, particularly for the next generation (v. 39). This mysterious release of Israel from judgment is remarkable, and pushes readers to reconsider commonplace prejudices against Deuteronomy. There is no ironclad law of retaliation in Deuteronomy, but some mysterious grace of God! Robert Frost was highly unfair in his long poem "A Masque of Reason" to have God thank Job for stultifying Deuteronomy's theology (Frost, 374).

The book's vision of justice is anything but a closed system of rewards for obedience and retribution for sin, all enforced by a rigid deity.

Lest we are tempted to dismiss the reference to Moses' innocent suffering in v. 37 as casual and insignificant, we shall see it reiterated again at 3:26 and 4:21. Lest we imagine there can be no thought of vicarious atonement here, we find Moses himself suggesting the idea earlier in the E strand.

At the sin of the golden calf, Moses approached God and offered to be *blotted out*—to die—with the thought, "perhaps I can make atonement" (Exod 32:30-32 E). God's intention at that point, however, was to blot out only those who had sinned, not the sinless, however willing to sacrifice themselves they might be (see Exod 32:33). The people as a whole were to be spared, and a self-offering in atonement was *not yet* necessary from Moses (see Janzen, 241–42; Fretheim, 290; Olson, 35).

Israel's Journey from Kadesh to Moab

Deuteronomy 2:1–3:11

Deuteronomy now turns in an upbeat, encouraging direction. Moses drops the story of past failures and launches the story of Israel's forward thrust into God's promises. With God among them and before them no obstacle can prove too much, no citadel can prove too high (2:36; 3:5). Gone are the years of endless wandering in and around the hills of Edom, south of the promised land ("Mount Seir," 2:1-3). The torch has now passed to a new generation (2:14-15). Israel finally moves into the Transjordan, the lands on the eastern side of the Jordan River. These lands are a gateway into the heart of Canaan, and their northern sections are an area where some of Israel's tribes will permanently settle.

As the ascent to the promised land begins, God gives a warning. Israel must dismiss any thought of grabbing land from Edom, Moab, or Ammon (2:4-5, 9, 19). This is not because the biblical writers believed that these nations belonged to other gods (see 4:19 and the NRSV's translation "the gods" in 32:8). Rather, Deuteronomy understands that God is about to reveal a new form of communal life on earth (Deut 2:25; 4:6-7; 26:19; cf. Exod 19:6 E). Such life will not form in a vacuum or in a world of diffuse pantheism, but will take shape and grow within a bounded sanctuary-land, God's holy territory for nurturing a holy people (see Deut 26:19; 32:13-15; 33:28; cf. Ps 78:54, an Asaphite source of Deuteronomy, and the E strand at Exod 15:17; 19:6).

Deuteronomy is clear that the Lord is sovereign over heaven and earth. The thought that foreign gods have bailiwicks of their own is ludicrous in this theology. Rather, the Lord controls exactly which people will live in Edom, Moab, and Ammon (Deut 2:5, 9, 19). The underlying assumptions behind this assertion are rooted in Deuteronomy's theological sources (Exod 9:14, 16, 29; 19:5 all E; Asaphite Ps 50:12) and are unambiguous in Deuteronomy itself (see Deut 4:32, 35; 10:14; 26:19; 32:39).

God's followers should be humbled to learn that there is nothing special about a homeland from God (cf. Amos 9:7). God has graced other nations with lands in the identical manner that Israel is about to experience. According to 2:9, God gave Moab its land as a God-gifted "possession." Similarly, 2:21 asserts that the Ammonites had God's help in clearing their territory of aboriginal inhabitants. Further, Edom's conquest story exactly parallels that of Israel (2:12). What is special—what distinguishes Israel from the nations—is to receive God's unique election as a *covenantal* people. God is forming God's beloved people into a unique community of mutuality on earth.

Eventually, God's covenantal election will make a substantial difference in Israel's history on its land. Taking up the theology of Deuteronomy, the postexilic prophet Malachi will insist that God's love (Hos 11:1; Deut 10:15) has a significant impact. By Malachi's time, Edom, the land of Jacob's twin Esau, lay in ruins. Malachi could see that the "Esaus" of the world—profane and without covenantal tutelage and discipleship—have no good future. The "Jacobs," in contrast, are fast-tracked for the reign of God, not via worth or merit (see Deut 7:7-8) but due to God's summons. The realization should turn earth's nations toward the true God, the God of covenant.

After passing through the lands of Edom, Moab, and Ammon (2:1-23), Israel stands on the brink of launching the conquest of their newly gifted land (2:24-25). "Begin to take possession," God orders (v. 24). The people must clear out the inhabitants of the transjordanian kingdoms of Og and of Sihon and occupy their territories.

Problems of interpretation immediately arise. The story of Israel's journey through Transjordan depicts a conquest, a divinely initiated incursion of armed forces. It would be hard to underplay the strong negative reaction of many readers. Value judgments flow like torrents of water, objections like a stream that never dries up.

Who can condone notions of holy destruction, with no sparing of women and children (2:34; 3:6; cf. 7:2)? Could God ever be behind such merciless aggression? How does this differ from United States history, in which a doctrine of manifest destiny wreaked a horrific toll on Native American populations? Did the biblical conquest story not inspire Dutch-origin Afrikaners to expel "black Canaanites" from desired lands in South Africa? Is not what we need now, in the twenty-first century, a universal disavowal of all ethnocentric assertions of privilege, of all chauvinistic military campaigning?

Before jumping to embrace such a hermeneutics of suspicion about Deuteronomy's conquest passages, recall the facts on the ground. Unlike most modern books about the United States and South Africa, Deuteronomy is not political history. Rather, it recounts stories of divine intervention from the Beyond, stories not of human campaigning but of victories of the *divine warrior* (1:30; 3:22; 20:4). In Near Eastern poems and myths, the divine warrior as the heavenly champion musters the heavenly hosts, defeats chaos, and brings order and new life to birth in the cosmos. Stephen Chapman (2013a, 50) has elaborated on how the concept of "holy war"/*jihād*, understood as battling to kill, tax, or convert infidels, "is decidedly *not* to be found in the pages of the Old Testament." Here, God is explicitly *not* aligned with Israel's intentions. Rather, Israel is called to submit to God's numinous work to achieve God's intention.

Deuteronomy takes its cue from its theological source material. The E sources present the conquest story as the victory of God the divine warrior, whose mere presence creates enemy panic and disarray. In E God promises, "I will send my terror in front of you, and throw into confusion all the people against whom you shall come, and I will make all your enemies turn their backs to you" (Exod 23:27 E). Toward the end of the Song of the Sea in Exodus 15:16 (E/D) we read, "Terror and dread fell upon them; by the might of your arm, they became still as stone until your people, O LORD passed by."

True to these source texts, Deuteronomy describes God's terrifying presence personally accompanying the people. This numinous presence (Latin: *tremendum*), not any human prowess, causes all onlookers to shrink in dread (Deut 2:4, 25; cf. 7:23; 9:3; 11:25; Josh 2:9). Because God's people themselves must instinctively shrink as well (Exod 19:16 E), any prideful, chauvinistic appropriation of our passage is ruled out of hand for those who understand it truly. Our text can *never* rightly be co-opted as an alibi for imperialism, intolerance, or genocide. With God's consuming presence attached to a community, a spirit of imperialism is impossible.

As the Scriptures took their present, canonical form, *apocalyptic* literature appropriated the poetic idiom of the divine warrior's victories. This literature commandeered the combat myth to depict Kingdom Come as a new divine defeat of chaos and a cosmic re-creation. This depiction accords with Deuteronomy's canonical role, which projects all appropriation of the promised land into God's promised *future*. The book ends the Pentateuch with Israel still east of the Jordan, still on the brink of penetrating the promised land's core. Readers of Deuteronomy are *en route* to God's reign, in no position to forcibly claim it. Again, a chauvinistic appropriation—that is, a use of Deuteronomy to justify treating Native Americans, Native South Africans, or any other group as "Canaanites"—is excluded. Readers are prohibited from seizing Deuteronomy's conquest stories in support of this-worldly ambitions, whether in North America, South Africa, or elsewhere. Rather, they must wait patiently for the divine warrior's appearance. In God's time, the warrior will usher in history's consummation.

Meanwhile, the community of God's election must maintain a highly *self-critical* stance. Taking up Deuteronomy's language of exodus and conquest, Malachi 3:1-2 describes the divine warrior's epiphany at history's consummation: "The Lord whom you seek will suddenly come to his temple. . . . But who can endure the day of his coming?" Will many *within Israel* be unable to stand on the day of the warrior's appearance?

Far from contemplating violence against external peoples, Deuteronomy avers that the community of faith should be working to minimize inner-communal violence—a very real threat (note the careful injunctions in 19:1-13 to establish "cities of refuge" in Israel to curb the spread of violence). We will see Deuteronomy's aversion to physical violence unfold especially in its handling of the sixth commandment prohibiting murder.

The initial readers of Deuteronomy lived in King Josiah's time, six hundred years removed from the events of Moses' story. The kingdoms of Heshbon and of Bashan described in the present section did not exist in their era. They were of another, near-forgotten world, of primarily *antiquarian* interest. Actual wars of conquest with them are obviously not at issue. Our text can be no literal call to arms, no battle cry of invasion. Strong signals, rather, point to another call—a call to a *spiritual* brand of "warfare."

At key junctures, the text orients the reader away from real military and political dynamics to larger-than-life, transcendent power plays. Far from national and political entities, the enemies against which Deuteronomy's God directs Israel are poetic, mythical, and demonic. Strong hints of this arise already in the text of 2:1-23, where the reader is surprised by striking mythological accents. If the pattern of Israel's settlement mirrors the experience of the other nations described here, they will be up against huge monsters, mobs of hulking giants, and ghosts. Readers of Deuteronomy must grapple with these ghouls, not real populations.

Just as God was about to hand over a promised land to Israel, God had previously cleared out legendary monsters from other peoples' new home-lands. Before God gave ownership of the land of Moab to the Moabites, the Emim ("Terrors") used to live there (2:10). The text describes the Emim as a "race of giants" (v. 10 NLT), as lofty as the Anakim (the huge aborigines of Canaan; see 1:28; 9:2). By the same token, before God gave the land of Ammon to the Ammonites it harbored its own variety of giants, the

Zamzummim ("Barbarians"; 2:20). They too were powerful and legion, like the Anakim.

Fascinatingly, both the Emim and the Zamzummim fall under the umbrella category of Rephaim ("Healers"; 2:11, 20). Elsewhere in the Hebrew Bible, the Rephaim are departed spirits—shades of the living dead (Job 26:5; Ps 88:11; Prov 2:18; 9:18; Isa 14:9; 26:14, 19). Popular religion considered them to possess supernatural healing powers, an idea disputed by the biblical texts (cf. the mocking language of Isa 14:10).

The idea of shades from Sheol surely operates in Deuteronomy 2–3. Like the names Emim ("Terrors") and Zamzummim ("Barbarians"), "Rephaim" is not a normal label for a people (a gentilic name). It is a latter-day, pseudo-ethnic label with paranormal nuances. Deuteronomy must apply the term to the aboriginal giants of the olden days from a vantage of great distance, long after the aborigines were understood to have passed on into the Beyond. Only then would they be considered healing shades.

At King Josiah's time, the Rephaim were considered to be the mighty men of old, renowned warriors (cf. Gen 6:4). They were viewed as extinct but able to interact with the living as ghosts. Venerating them posthumously, some considered them to be healers/protectors of the living (Spronk, 227–31; Rouillard, 697). There are parallels in ancient Greek history, where a hero-cult likewise found an impetus in hoary tales of giant warriors. Similar to what we will see in Deuteronomy 3:11, prehistoric, awe-inspiring grave monuments also inspired the Greek cult.

As we move into Deuteronomy 2:24–3:11, Israel receives its marching orders to conquer the same mythical forces that the Moabites and the Ammonites had conquered. The conflict relevant for readers' lives is not one of military violence, but a rigorous moral contest with dark powers greater than any earthbound army. Deuteronomy would have its readers understand their real enemies to be all dark forces of ignorance, pollution, and evil that battle with them for space in God's land.

As early as 1:28, Israel's scouts had reported "offspring of the Anakim" in Canaan (cf. 9:2; Josh 11:21; 14:12, 15). The Anakim are a race of mythical giants, just like the Emim and Zamzummim (2:10-12). "Who can stand up to the Anakim?" went a popular saying (9:2). Like the Emim and Zamzummim, the Anakim are Rephaim, whose dead spirits haunt the land as revenants (2:11). If Deuteronomy were written today, its authors would probably speak instead of a conquest of "zombies." (I owe this observation to a former graduate student in my Deuteronomy seminar, Josiah D. Rengers.)

A key Israelite victory in the Transjordan was over the armies of Og, king of Bashan (3:1-11). The language of vv. 4-10 echoes the style of

Neo-Assyrian boasts of victory, such as those of the Assyrian monarch Sennacherib. The last verse of the account reveals exactly the being that Israel had defeated in winning this campaign. King Og of Bashan was of preternatural proportions; he was a card-carrying member of the Rephaim (3:11; cf. 3:13; Josh 12:4; 13:12)!

The attention paid to Og's bed in Deuteronomy 3:11 may strike modern readers as unusual, until we realize that a royal bed might be a significant battle trophy (see Lindquist). The bed of the god Marduk of Babylon played a key role in the international politics of the seventh century BCE. In a hugely symbolic move, King Sennacherib of Assyria removed Marduk's bed when he conquered Babylon. Og's bed was like Marduk's, a prized trophy for a force able to bring down a superhuman, supernatural power.

According to 3:11, Og's bed, still extant in the city of Rabbah, was six feet wide and almost fourteen feet long. It was almost certainly a burial slab made of basaltic, iron-colored stone (the reference to a tomb is clearest in the TEV, NEB, NET, and CEV). Large grave monuments ("dolmens") fitting this description lie in the Transjordan. They consist of upright stones supporting large horizontal slabs and date from the late third and early second millennium BCE. The stones formed the inner skeleton of a burial mound of earth or smaller stones. Such megalithic skeletons evoked the awe of later generations, who imagined those who commissioned them to have wielded unspeakable prowess.

Subsequent texts in Deuteronomy reiterate that Israel's conquest of the promised land was directed against such mythic-demonic figures as Og and other Rephaim, particularly the offspring of the Anakim (3:13; 4:47; 9:2; 29:7; 31:4). The book's present canonical shape thus reinforces the interpretation of the conquest offered here, that Deuteronomy's "conquest" is not literal and militaristic but an all-out faith struggle aimed at holiness and the rejection of all underworld forces. Deuteronomy's conquest is a metaphor—a symbolic, nonviolent call to discipleship.

Deuteronomy's choice of a metaphor of violence makes sense given its milieu of horrifying Assyrian military propaganda. The authors offer an action plan to compete with and trump the violent ideology of empire they confronted. The spiritual campaign to occupy an arena of *covenantal obedience*, they argue, is at once more noble and more world-changing than the imperial campaigning so clear round about. The really meaningful human task, they insist, is not grabbing others' territory but pushing out of one's own "territory" all defilement and evil. God is providing a unique sphere for forming a holy people, which nothing must compromise (Deut 2:25; 4:7; 26:19).

Augustine of Hippo (354–430 CE) rightly insisted that Deuteronomy is not first about attacking pagans and smashing their idols. Rather, it is about breaking all the idols of the human heart (Sermon 62.17, *WSA* 3:165). His contemporary John Cassian (360–432 CE) argued that the Canaanites of Deuteronomy are a "figure" for the reader's instruction, not literal people. They are the innumerable vices the faithful must overcome through formation in virtue (Conference 5.16.1-2, ACW 57:196-97).

Deuteronomy's insistence on conquering defilement, even in the Transjordan, speaks against the scholarly misunderstanding that the book's program of centralizing worship (see Deut 12) aimed to *desacralize* the land of Israel. Influential scholars such as Moshe Weinfeld and Baruch Halpern have encouraged a view that Josiah's officers and priests worked to restrict the realm of the sacred to Zion. Hoping to unify the people and concentrate their loyalties on Jerusalem, they sought to secularize existence outside the capital and shift all life's sacral bases to the central sanctuary (see Cook 2013, 127).

It is difficult to see how the passage at hand could fit with any theory that Deuteronomy "desacralizes" Israel. The text's language of holy destruction (Heb., *kharam*; Deut 2:34; 3:6) is *recycled language*, picked up from ancient religious usage (e.g., cf. the Moabite Stone) and redeployed to drive home points about the radical apartness of *all* Israel (see the interpretation of Deut 7 later). Even in the Transjordan, far from Jerusalem, Israel must occupy a holy ground, claimed *in toto* by the divine warrior. The land *as a whole* is to be a place apart, rigorously cleared of all sources of temptation.

The reader will encounter this theme repeatedly in Deuteronomy, which is faithful to its theological sources in this regard. The psalms of Asaph understand Israel as the Lord's godly people (Ps 50:5). The E strand calls them a "holy nation," sacral through and through. Every member of society shares proximity to God and attendant responsibilities of purity (Exod 19:6). God plants the holy nation in God's own highlands, characterized in its entirety as a sacred place, a sanctuary (Deut 32:13-15; 33:28; Exod 15:17 E/D; Ps 78:54, an Asaphite source of Deuteronomy). Throughout the land, one receives *locally* the sacral blessing of the Lord (thus, Deut 12:15 universalizes the language of God's blessing that it finds in the old altar law of Exod 20:24).

Exodus 19:5-6 (E) appears to lie directly behind multiple texts in Deuteronomy, which take up its rare language about Israel as God's "treasured possession" (Deut 7:6; 14:2; 26:18-19; cf. 4:20). Every one of these texts of Deuteronomy understands the entire people to be "holy" in their observable life and work. Moreover, God plans to make Israel a visibly consecrated people, who flourish dispersed throughout the land (28:9-10). Deuteronomy 5:12-15 and 14:21 attest that conduct throughout the land, not just in Jerusalem, is directly pertinent to Israel's sacral status (cf. Vogt, 95; Lohfink, 36). Out in the towns, when giving a tithe to support the landless, the Israelite farmer makes a triple confession of ritual purity (26:13-14). Deuteronomy understands the whole land to have the purity of a holy sanctuary.

Joshua 22:10-34 illustrates well how centralizing worship does *not* secularize Israel's periphery. Brimming with Deuteronomy's theology, the text recounts how tribes in the Transjordan insisted on a symbolic (nonfunctional) copy of the Lord's altar on their territory—a huge altar. They were insistent that their territory, as far as it was from the tabernacle, was still God's land, part of God's unique sanctuary.

The Allotment of Transjordan

Deuteronomy 3:12-29

Moses now completes the story of Israel's movement into the regions of the Transjordan with an account of distributing the lands that Israel conquered there (vv. 12-22). A primary aim of this material is to express the solidarity of God's people. In the second part of this section (vv. 23-29), Moses movingly entreats the Lord to let him live to see the settlement of the promised land. From God's negative response, it becomes obvious that Moses's death outside the land has core theological meaning for Deuteronomy.

Distributing the Land, 3:12-22

Moses summarizes the settlement of the tribes of Reuben, Gad, and half the people of Manasseh in the newly conquered territories east of the Jordan River. Each receives tenure of its own territory, but only in the context of knowing that they are not yet able to settle down. Their lands are the gift of the divine warrior (v. 18), and their success thus far is merely the start of God's larger project on behalf of the entire Hebrew people.

There is more here than a simple appeal to norms of fair play, of reciprocity. The book's Hebrew uses concrete language of kinship. A vision of co-vassals closely bound by family ties—indeed, a true sodality of "Israelite kin"—lies at Deuteronomy's core (v. 18). Only as a tight-knit "kindred" will God's people successfully trek forward (v. 20). Only thus will they begin to savor God's "rest" (v. 20)—"rest" in the sense of freedom to blossom as a covenant people, as free human beings at liberty to encounter God in freedom, a God whose presence is available among them (cf. Exod 33:14 E/D: "My presence will go with you, and I will give you rest").

A mantra at Deuteronomy's core, *one God, one people*, lies embedded in the grammar of the narrative. God (through Moses) addresses Israel in the opening chapters of Deuteronomy as a *singular* (individual) "you." Israel appears as a holistic, individuated body, enjoying an "I-Thou" relationship with God. In this book, the covenant entails a personal bond between two integral partners (see the Hebrew of Deut 1:21, 31; 2:7, 9, 18, 19, 24, 25, 30, 31, 37; and 3:2) As Deuteronomy proceeds, it will often shift between a singular and plural "you" in addressing Israel. This *Numeruswechsel* in the book still awaits satisfactory explanation. It is not always a sign of editorial activity.

Deuteronomy received its ideal of "one God, one people" from its theological sources, which all stress God's vision of one integrated family, "Children of the living God" (Hos 1:10). God addresses Israel as "my treasured possession" (Exod 19:5-6 E), "my firstborn son" (Exod 4:22-23 E; Hos 11:1), my "wife" (Hos 2:20). The people are God's united "flock," destined to pasture on one sacred highland (Mic 5:4). All lost sheep of Israel who become scattered will eventually come home (Mic 5:3).

In Deuteronomy's sources, God refuses to treat the divided kingdoms of Israel separately. In Hosea 6:4, God wrestles with both as though they are still one community (also cf. Hos 1:11). Similarly, Micah 1:5, 8-9 assumes that the northern kingdom's sin will affect Judah. Deuteronomy picks up where Hosea and Micah leave off: all Israel's cohorts together form one assembly of worship (see Deut 1:31; 27:9; 31:11; 32:10; 33:5).

Deuteronomy exhorts its readers to place more focus on their "family ties" of faith. It reminds them of the significant power for living inherent in God's address to them as a *collective* "you." Abraham Heschel, the celebrated rabbi, scholar, and activist, aptly described the spiritual power of this vision: "All generations are present, as it were, in every moment. Israel is the tree, we are the leaves. It is the clinging to the stem that keeps us alive" (Heschel, 424).

The style of chapter 3 drives home Deuteronomy's stress on the solidarity of generations. Creating rather choppy reading, little parenthetical asides repeatedly interrupt the narrative at vv. 9, 11, and 13-14. In each case, the intrusions speak directly to current readers. They show readers how this story's meaning reverberates "to this day" (v. 14). Verse 11 notes how Og's iron bedstead "can still be seen." Verse 14 clarifies that Jair's villages still bear the name that he gave them. The verse also tacitly confesses that the land's settlement ends up being an ongoing process, not a simple, one-time accomplishment of Joshua. The task of "occupying" the land, that is, of blossoming as a community of love, continues for each new generation of the faithful.

Moses' "Gethsemane" Prayer, 3:23-29

Moses briefly turns from the project of conquest to recount an agonizing dialogue that he initiated with God. As at 1:37 we sense a touching pathos as he expresses his personal pain at being barred from ever entering the promised land. Just as at 1:37 and 4:21, Moses specifies that God's anger with him is on the people's account (v. 26). His punishment of going to his death excluded from the land is somehow vicarious, he believes, endured in innocence on behalf of the community of faith. God had turned down his previous offer to die (see Exod 32:31-33 E), but now, here in the Transjordan, God would accept his death as atonement for sin (see Exod 32:30 E).

True to its theological sources, Deuteronomy recognizes that life is often not fair. The wicked may prosper (cf. Ps 73:3, 12 an Asaphite psalm) and the innocent be stricken (cf. Ps 73:13-14). Yet, when innocent sufferers continue to cling to God (Ps 73:26), they may birth a new form of life. Such new life entails a death of all grasping at blessings. The Asaphite psalmist exclaims to God, "There is nothing on earth that I desire other than you" (Ps 73:25); "As for me, to be near God is my good" (Ps 73:28 NAB).

Moses fervently believed the promised land to be his "good," naming it "good" twice in v. 25. Yet God needed him to refocus on a more ultimate "good," to model a higher form of life in which human beings embrace their limitations and let go of all grasping for personal blessing. For thirty-one more chapters of the book, Moses will forward God's purposes for Israel despite himself being left out of them.

As the discourses of Moses continue into the heart of Deuteronomy, readers should not lose sight of Moses' impending death. Its forecast here and its fulfillment in chapter 34 envelop the words of the book. In recurring instances, Moses' sacrifice echoes in reader's ears (e.g., 4:21-22; 5:25-27; 9:18; 18:15-16; 31:2; 34:4). Indeed, as Olson argues, the very *structure and theological movement* of Deuteronomy . . . participate in the theme of Moses' death. . . . In each of the major sections, the experience of God's people moves through death to life. Human limits and the press of death are overcome only through the God who 'kills and makes alive'" (Olson, 21–22).

All this signals the book's aim to foster the selfless, other-centered lifestyle to which Moses' death bears witness. In obedience to this calling, Moses has blazed the way forward. His costly support of the Israel of his day, and indeed of the reader of the book, provides the capital needed to launch God's project of renewing human community. His unqualified gift of love frees the reader to love in return and to spread love. His death thus forms the first link in an emergent, expansive network of selflessness on earth. This is the atoning power of his necessary sacrifice. This is the reason for God's awful demand that he surrender his life.

Israel on the Plains of Moab

Deuteronomy 4:1-43

In this final section of the first discourse, recollection of the past takes a back seat to insistent exhortation. Israel simply must cling to God in loyalty and obedience. No other god, no other relationship, compares to what Israel has within its grasp—a covenantal attachment to an awesome deity of terrifying majesty and intimate nearness. An appendix treats the three "cities of refuge" Moses set apart in the Transjordan.

A Call to Obey Moses' Teaching, 4:1-40

With a call to attention, "So now, Israel, give heed" (v. 1), Moses signals that he is addressing God's people in the here and now. He shifts the focus to "today" (vv. 4, 8, 26, 39, 40), the present moment, with Israel stationed on the plains of Moab ready to enter Canaan. In the beginning and end of this section, its "outer frame" in vv. 1-4 and v. 40, Moses reiterates that the instructions of the covenant, if taken to heart, will mean living long and living well in the land—enjoying truly human living. It will mean blooming as a model human community on earth (cf. vv. 6-8).

Israel observed God's presence "blazing up to the very heavens, shrouded in dark clouds" (v. 11, cf. v. 24). An experience of this kind—an encounter with the *numinous*—overturns the soul, provoking surrender (cf. Gen 22:12 E). The deity's searing holiness draws people in like a moth to the flame. It fosters an intimate bond, a veritable marriage between God and Israel—a marriage that can call forth the people's very best, forming them in true spiritual maturity.

Given the intimacy of Israel's marital bond with God, the people's history of betraying the Lord appears unconscionable. The religious orgies at Peor, to which vv. 3-4 refer (cf. Num 25:1, 3, 5), are a paradigm of their horrific infidelity. There at the last station of the wilderness journey, Israel repaid God's intimate love with fertility religion and orgiastic worship of foreign gods. The people prostituted themselves religiously, just as they would later when settled in Canaan (see Hos 4:11-14; cf. Exod 32:6 E, "an orgy of drinking and sex," GNT).

Some contemporary scholars question whether debauchery was a real part of the fertility religion that infected Israel in biblical times. They point to a tablet from Ugarit about the storm-god Baal in which he appears to disdain, not encourage, lewdness at religious feasts (CAT 1.4 III, lines 17–22). Scholars are justified in skepticism about a hypothetical "cult prostitution" in ancient Canaan. It takes hard work, however, to discount some sort of sex-and-religion mix behind Exodus 32:6; Numbers 25:1; Hosea 4:10, 13, 14; and Jeremiah 3:23-25. It is hard as well to make a dislike of such a mix on Baal's part fit the context of Ugaritic tablet CAT 1.4 III. In this text, Baal is upset over his public humiliation by another god, probably Yamm. His debasement by Yamm much more likely issued in a "whispering" of servant-girls than in their "lewdness." The former translation, "whispering," of the Ugaritic term *tdmm* is fully possible. Baal is stating that he disdains whisperings about his humiliation, not lewdness mixed into religion.

Moses, in Deuteronomy 4, calls those poised to enter Canaan to a truer, more fulfilling relationship than one with the over-sexed fertility deities of the land (the Baals—Hos 2:13, 17; 11:2). The Lord's offer of a covenanted life of intimacy, Moses knew, far surpassed any benefits of fertility worship. Pushing aside the Baals, Israel must cling tight to the Lord, its true husband (Heb., *dabaq*; NRSV "held fast"; Deut 4:4; cf. Gen 2:24; 34:3). This alien God—this Other—a deity specifically *not* "just like yourself" (see Asaphite Ps 50:21), will stretch and transform Israel beyond its wildest dreams.

As the covenant takes root and blossoms in the land, the nations will puzzle over how divinity can be so incredibly intimate with humans (v. 7, cf. v. 37). At the same time, they will marvel at how Israel has survived the roar of God's word issuing from fire (v. 33). God intends Israel's unique experience to do more than merely provoke global envy. Deuteronomy 26:19 declares God to be elevating Israel high above all nations to make them a consecrated, *holy* people. God hopes to form all Israel into "priests" to the nations, commissioned to teach the world God's ways, to place incense and burnt offerings for all peoples on God's altar (Exod 19:6 E/D; see Deut 33:10, 19).

From a perspective immersed in Deuteronomy's thought and language, the prophet Malachi makes inclusive and universal claims about the covenant's expansive goal. At God's reign, he prophesies, the reverence of God will burst "beyond the borders of Israel!" (Mal 1:5). Though God's reign is contested at present (see Mal 1:4: 2:17), sacrifice and pure oblation are "about to be offered" God all around the world (Mal 1:11; my translation). It is a doxological truth, celebrated in worship (cf. Asaphite Ps 76:12), that God inspires *universal* reverence (Mal 1:14).

Moses' teaching in the core of chapter 4 (i.e., in vv. 9-31) assumes the radical truths in the framing sections. Without a grasp of the frames' theme, it is hard to appreciate the obsession of the core with the absolute avoidance of idols. Why this focused prohibition of graven images, when these likenesses cannot actually represent real gods ("there is no other," v. 39; cf. v. 28)? Why focus only on the purest way to worship the Lord, leaving out social ethics and a great many other concerns?

From the discussion thus far, it should already be clear that the mysterious nature of God's presence is far from a petty concern in Deuteronomy. Grasping the stunning nature of God's contact with Israel changes everything for both God's people and for all earth's nations. Awe at God's incomparable nature is the engine behind Israel's entire covenantal response to God's grace. Grasping God's *otherness* from all of creation transforms both worship and social ethics—indeed, everything in between.

The wonder that drives the core of chapter 4 is the mysterious truth that the *numinous*—that which dwarfs and unnerves us—gives rise to ethical growth. The mystery is truly profound. *Awe* before the uncanny provokes in the soul a profound sense of *ought* (morality and obligation to God; see 5:29; 6:2, 24; 8:6; 10:12; 13:4; 17:19; 25:18). At Horeb Israel first experienced God's dizzying otherness. There, Israel shrunk back as the *numinous* descended to earth (4:10; 5:5). Mount Horeb quaked as God came down ablaze (Deut 4:11-12, 15, 24, 33, 36; 5:25; Mic 1:4; Asaphite Ps 50:3). Below, the people cowered, inadequate to cope (Exod 19:16; 20:18-19 both E; Deut 5:26; 18:16; cf. Mark 9:6; Luke 5:8). They learned the *fear of God* (Exod 20:20 E; Deut 4:10; 5:29).

In biblical parlance, to *fear* (or "revere") God is to embrace integrity in relationships (Gen 20:11; 42:18). It is to treat others with justice and kindness. The covenant of Deuteronomy legislates this way of living, reinforcing and regulating the *fear of God* through structures of torah (Deut 4:5). From the experience at Horeb, Israel practiced the *fear of God* by obeying the covenant (Exod 18:21; Deut 6:2, 24; 10:12).

Why should we instinctively embrace the moral in the face of that which is overwhelming? The jump from *awe* to *ought* is mysterious—anything but natural. It is a powerful clue pointing to the reality of God. When God speaks from the fire, all human hierarchies suddenly collapse. God becomes the "I"; humanity becomes the "Thou." God becomes suzerain; Israelites

bond together as co-vassals. With good reason God voices the commandments of Deuteronomy specifically "out of the fire." The phrase recurs here
four times (Deut 4:12, 15, 33, 36; cf. v. 24; 5:4, 22, 24, 26; 9:10; 10:4).

It is now apparent why chapter 4 has such an abhorrence of worship
images. They fly in the face of God's singularity, otherness, and freedom.
Israel must not make a worship form, because they saw no form on the day
that God spoke out of the fire (vv. 15-18). If the Lord were like the creation,
humans could fashion God in a homemade form. They could give their god
a tail and grab her by it. Such gods do not surprise, convict, and stretch but,
like the Baals of Canaan, only confirm the familiar.

Verses 19-20 present a special polemic targeted against any idea that the
sun, the moon, and the stars are animate deities. Very old mythology in
Israel's milieu contained such an idea, picturing the gods of polytheism each
receiving an individual nation as property. Each god shared an "allotment" of
earth's people. Texts such as Psalm 82; Deuteronomy 29:26; and
Deuteronomy 32:8-9 all co-opt this myth and spin it to theological advantage. The present text also critically appropriates the myth. It twists it,
denaturing it.

Deuteronomy 4 admits that for the present, foreign peoples have a raw
deal. They are worshiping the gods of polytheism, not the true God. But this
is the extent of truth in the old myth. The wording of 4:19 makes clear that
the nations' worship objects are not divine beings but mere creatures, on a
par with creeping things and fish (v. 18). It uses deliberate language
rendering the gods of the nations passive and de-animated. It speaks of a
"host of heaven," language different from usages such as "gods" in Psalm
82:1 and "sons of God" in Deuteronomy 32:8 (NAB). This is conscious
demythologizing.

The theology introduced here in chapter 4 will become crucial for
understanding chapter 12 and its radical, innovative insistence on *one sanctuary* (see Deut 12:5, 11, 21; cf. 14:23; 16:2, 5-6, 11; 18:6-7; 26:2). Israel's
one sanctuary, for Deuteronomy, becomes a powerful locale of awe as the
driving engine behind covenantal discipleship. It is at the one sanctuary that
the experience at Horeb can be relived and reinforced. As everyone gathers
together at the shrine, as at the mountain of the covenant, communal
memories of the Lord as a devouring fire well up. By coming together at the
one center, Israel will repeatedly encounter God's "I" as an integral, integrated "Thou," bound together in commitment to one another as a
community of mutuality.

The language of 4:10 is pregnant with meaning, extending dynamically
out into Israel's future. At Mount Horeb, God ordered Moses to "Assemble

[Heb., *qahal*] the people for me . . . that they may learn to fear me" (4:10). This is exactly what is projected to happen in the land, at God's one sanctuary. Every seventh year, the Levites and elders are to "Assemble [Heb., *qahal*] the people . . . so that they may hear and learn to fear the LORD" (31:12). The verbal echo is no coincidence.

With its instructions for celebrating the Passover each year, Deuteronomy again makes the "assembly" of Horeb a recurring event. Deuteronomy 16:7 anachronistically instructs the people to "go back to your tents" after the Passover meal. Thereby, it deliberately echoes God's original command at Horeb recorded at 5:30. Here too, the implications are clear. No anchors should moor the Horeb experience in antiquity.

Deuteronomy intends that the assembly (Heb., *qahal*) that occurred at Mount Horeb should become a central institution of Israel once the settlement is established (cf. 23:1-3, 8). Israel must stand before God again and again, becoming ever reinvigorated as a cohesive network of brothers and sisters. Israel should assemble annually for the Passover to bind themselves together as co-vassals under God (16:5-6). Similarly, they should gather year after year in the presence of God to make their tithes and "learn to fear the LORD your God always" (14:23).

The covenant assembly includes all Israel: "men, women, and children, as well as the aliens residing in your towns" (31:12). Even those on society's periphery draw into communal mutuality. The trick is that the entire body of people confront God's presence together, experiencing collectively their commonality as frail vassals.

According to 4:21-22, Moses will die outside of Canaan; God insists on it. Because of his mortality, God will have to create a succession of prophets like him (18:15-19). These prophets too, in turn, must each die. Nothing must sabotage the great "leveling" dynamic of the awe of God. Everything and everyone must eventually be yanked from intermediate positions between God and Israel, God's vassal people.

Would Israel actually make Moses an idol, take a human being as an object of worship? They might be tempted, given his "signs and wonders" (34:11; language used of God in 4:34; 6:22; 7:19; 26:8; 29:3), his God-like "displays of power" (34:12; language used of God in 4:34; 26:8). As Olson argues, Moses has to die outside the land "as a reminder that he himself was not a god, an object of worship" (35).

Moses dies so that God's word—God's covenantal instruction—can push forward, forming the people into God's ideal community. From now on, there will be only this word of God, not Moses, when Israel assembles at

God's one sanctuary. This word, not Moses, will connect the people with God's otherness.

At Horeb, spastic in shudders, its smoke rising as if from a kiln, God thundered God's word (Exod 19:19 E; Deut 4:12, 15, 33, 36; 5:22; cf. Mark 9:7); by no means did God keep silent (Asaphite Ps 50:3). The real force going forth from God to change and mold history is not a great wind, an earthquake, or a firestorm, but the inspired Word (see 1 Kgs 19:11-12). This "performative" Word confronts the reader with God. As we shall see in detail in interpreting chapter 12, there is an advanced theology of divine presence and absence here. Only by such means as a lone sanctuary and an imageless Word—such disciplines as a *via negativa*—may Israel freely encounter the God of freedom in an intimacy that transforms and leads onward toward the eschaton.

Deuteronomy 4:36 uses the language of parents' intimate teaching and guidance of their children. The NRSV's translation "discipline" is too negative; the Hebrew evokes images of raising and forming a beloved child (see NET, NJB, NLT; cf. the verb's use in Hos 7:15; Prov 31:1). God was present at Horeb, but remains intimately present with Israel through teaching, through catechism. Chapter 4 reiterates this theme relentlessly: Israel must heed *teaching* (4:1); the past has been prologue to *teaching* (v. 5); God's *torah* ("teaching") is incomparable (v. 8); the worship assembly is for *learning* (v. 10); the purpose of Horeb was receiving God's *words* (vv. 12, 15, 33, 36); Moses will *teach* (v. 14), emphasizing the awe of God (v. 15); God's voice teaches and forms (v. 36).

The experience at Mount Horeb was an archetypal event of teaching that will repeatedly manifest itself in Israel's future (cf. Deut 18:15-16; Jer 1:9; 20:9). Back at Mount Horeb, God spoke with a "loud voice" to the whole assembly (Heb., *qahal*) (5:22; cf. 9:10; 10:4). Once settled in the land, all Israel must periodically assemble (Heb., *qahal*) to "hear" God's word, and "learn" (31:12). The Word will place God before them, so that they "fear the LORD." Thus, each generation will "hear and learn to fear the LORD" (31:13).

Verses 25-31 form a later editorial addition to chapter 4 from the time of the Babylonian exile. They reflect editors' efforts to update Deuteronomy in light of the massive failure of the covenantal project. Awe at God's fiery, formless *otherness* had not taken hold in the land. People learned neither to revere God nor to relate to each other in mutuality. Instead, the editors aver, they turned corrupt and worshiped homemade gods. Thus, they found themselves exiled to foreign nations. There, they could worship graven images to their hearts' content.

Deuteronomy's final edition addressed this situation, proclaiming that the exile did not mark the covenant's death. Deuteronomy had always held a dim view of human nature. Well aware of the bent human heart, it had always put the stress on God's grace. It never proclaimed an ironclad system of retribution in which people only receive what they deserve. Rather, it spotlighted the mystery that new life may spring out of death. Moses surrendered his life, in fact, that new life might abound.

Even in exile, God's people can find the God of the covenant. Even there, if they seriously seek God heart and soul, they will find God compassionate. Just as Hosea the prophet was unable to abandon his adulterous wife, God is ever seeking to renew loving intimacy with God's people. God's plan to establish loving community on earth, dating back to Israel's ancestors, is bigger than one era of failure on Israel's part.

The divine project of establishing covenantal life still awaits a faithful generation, still awaits action on the part of present readers of the book of Deuteronomy in its final, canonical form. Deuteronomy is set on the brink of the land's settlement. It invites its readers to prepare symbolically to cross the Jordan River and claim God's promise to the ancestors, which is still in effect today.

Appendix: Cities of Refuge in Transjordan, 4:41-43

Moses ends this section, and his first discourse, by setting aside three "cities of refuge" in the lands of the Transjordan. The idea of "cities of refuge" was aimed to curb the excesses of violent revenge, which unfortunately were not infrequent in tribal culture. In traditional (tribal) Israel, unintentionally killing a person put one's life at risk. The offending party was immediately in grave danger of dying at the hands of an "avenger," a near relative bent on evening the score on behalf of the wronged party.

When accidental manslaughter occurred, a parent or uncle of the deceased might well pursue the perpetrator. The goal was to preserve the honor of his family and clan. Cities of refuge were places where one could flee and save one's life (if the death was truly accidental and there was no history of bad blood between the killer and the victim).

These verses, 4:41-43, fit awkwardly at this point in the book. Readers may well puzzle as to why they are here. Among the various explanations of commentators, two stand out as theologically interesting.

First, it appears significant that Deuteronomy's initial discourse ends on a note of realism and contingency. Moses has been presenting lofty ideals and high standards, and some readers may be on the verge of dismissing him as utopian and otherworldly. This little appendix stands as a corrective. It signals Deuteronomy's recognition that life is complicated. Mistakes occur; bad things happen to good people. God knows that the journey of discipleship is less than an ideal experience, and that God's disciples will have to contend with all manner of breakdowns.

Second, because life is contingent and complicated, even divine torah must not be fixed and rigid. As we get ready to engage Deuteronomy's main body of torah, this text signals readers to prepare for an agile and deft handling of Israel's legal tradition. It points out that even cases of homicide, the most serious crime against a fellow human being, may be murky and gray. Many legal cases are not black and white. The application of torah must be flexible. How responsible is a defendant? Were his actions truly accidental? Is an innovative judgment possible that avoids further bloodshed?

Deuteronomy as a whole will wrestle with such questions on a large scale. In fact, one key aim of the book is to shape the torah of Moses for adaptability and continual reapplication. The attempt to maintain fairness and enforce justice will always encounter new challenges and gray areas. Deuteronomy situates itself at the heart of this challenge, its authors pressing hard to engage and extend earlier "laws of Moses," such as those in the Covenant Code (Exod 21–23), readying them for the here and now.

Treasuring and upholding Mosaic authority, Deuteronomy's scribes strove to continue Moses' witness, to sound his voice for a contemporary audience. "The scribes who gave us the canonical shape of Deuteronomy," Arnold explains (2010, 74), "developed and perpetuated the Mosaic *traditum* ['tradition'] and saw themselves as instruments for the voice of Moses. . . . By understanding Deuteronomy as the *ipsissima vox* of Moses, we acknowledge their self-understanding and honor their work."

THE SECOND DISCOURSE OF MOSES

4:44–29:1

Introducing the Torah

Deuteronomy 4:44–5:5

Deuteronomy's great "second discourse" of Moses is extensive, covering 4:44–29:1. Here, Moses presents the great body of catechetical teaching that forms the center of the whole book. Two short passages introduce this torah. The first, 4:44-49, inculcates a mindset of expectancy and dependence. The second, 5:1-5, pushes the covenant directly into the present, driving it home as personally relevant to the reader.

Introduction to Moses' Second Discourse, 4:44-49

Echoing the start of Moses' first discourse (1:1-5), a new introduction in 4:44-49 sets the stage for the book's second major speech. The second discourse begins by reestablishing where and when Moses is speaking. Specific, particular divine acts have brought Israel to this point. The exodus from Egypt has occurred. Two larger-than-life enemies, Sihon king of the Amorites and Og king of Bashan, have fallen. Their lands are left to Israel.

Despite the progress, however, the people are still on the east side of the Jordan in a valley near Beth-Peor. They must continue to press forward toward God's promises. Just when people feel accomplished and established, the God of Deuteronomy breaks camp and disrupts all that seems fixed and official. Israel's victories in the Transjordan have been just a foretaste of what God will accomplish for them. The mighty victories of God have been a mere prelude paving the way for God's establishment of an ideal covenant community on earth.

The process of forming God's ideal community needs a rule of life, a rigorous structure for the people's growth. The rich legal vocabulary of vv. 44-45 alerts the reader to prepare to learn the structure. Readers are about to receive God's *torah* (v. 44), that is, a catechism for forming persons in the love of God and in true human mutuality.

Actualizing the Covenant, 5:1-5

At Mount Horeb, Israel assembled as a collective whole oriented around God's presence. It happens again now, on the east side of the Jordan. Here and now, in a valley near Beth Peor, Israel takes its place existentially at Horeb, before the blazing mountain of the covenant (cf. 12:7). The *torah* comes to the people "today" (v. 1), in their hearing ("right now," CEB). Moses' striking rhetoric helps Israel viscerally experience a stance before God's presence: "Not with our ancestors did the LORD make this covenant, but with us, who are all of us here alive today" (v. 3).

God becomes present to the people in a thoroughly immanent and deeply personal way, in an encounter that v. 4 describes as "face to face." The expression cannot be literal, for Israel "saw no form when the LORD spoke . . . at Horeb out of the fire" (4:15; cf. 4:33; 5:24). Rather, the wording coveys the immediate and profoundly existential character of God's presence with Israel (cf. 1:31, 42; 4:7, 37; 6:15). God's word issues "out of the fire" (5:4), and, Moses recalls, "You were afraid because of the fire" (v. 5).

As the fear of God washes over the people, it predisposes them for what comes next. As they feel their profanity and brokenness, they yearn for the tools to get right with God. In their vulnerability, they sense their need for each other, and they band together as co-vassals. They become highly receptive to divine instruction.

God's torah binds the people together across lines of gender, property, and even ethnicity. The inclusivity of Moses' audience is clear: "all of us here alive today" (v. 3; note that "all of us" includes non-Israelites, see Exod 12:38 E). All are included in the assembly: "men, women, and children, as well as the aliens residing in your towns" (31:12). The covenantal ties binding the people into a collective whole stretch farther. They reach out not only across all levels of society but also across time. For Deuteronomy, Israel's solidarity is that of a huge branching genealogical tree, planted on the promised land. All generations—even those that have passed on—are as one.

No one is still alive from the generation of the exodus (see 1:35). Yet Moses insists that the present audience was in fact back at Mount Horeb. He assumes that Israel of all generations forms one big branching entity, whose life extends both into the past and into the future. The current living growth of this entity is the group standing before him. "God made a covenant *with us* at Horeb," he says (v. 2).

Readers naturally understand themselves addressed as Moses speaks: "[Open] *your* listening ears *today*. . . . GOD, *our* God, made a covenant *with us . . . with us*, with all of *us* who are *alive right now*. God spoke to *you personally. . . . You* were afraid, *remember,* of the fire. . . . He said: I am GOD, *your* God, who brought *you* out of the land of Egypt" (*The Message,* emphasis added). This intensely personal and immediate language draws in the reader, encouraging her or him to take ownership of the covenantal relationship.

Written at Josiah's time, the original hope of this passage was that Judah would collectively re-actualize the covenant year in and year out at God's one sanctuary. The assembly (Heb., *qahal*) that occurred at Mount Horeb should become a central institution of Israel (cf. 23:1-3, 8; 31:12). There, as Israel cyclically unites for an "I-Thou" encounter, reverence will spread, build, and reach critical mass.

Confronting the Lord's presence at the central shrine (see 12:7, 18; 14:23, 26; 15:20), reverence and humility will wash over Israel, making the people receptive to God's torah. Moses's own model of humility and self-sacrifice paves the way for Israel to embrace their new form of life. At Mount Horeb, Moses risked his life in the dangerous breach lying between the Lord and the people (v. 5; cf. vv. 23-31). Now, he makes his final addresses before laying down his life outside the land of promise.

Moses will not cross the Jordan, will not live to continue to play the crucial role of mediator at God's great sanctuary in the land. In coming chapters, however, the book will make allowance for other significant mediators of the covenant. These will include the Levites, a branch of whom traced decent to Moses. Deuteronomy will also describe and celebrate a line of prophets in the tradition of Moses (18:15-19; 31:9-13).

Levites will be mediators in the same way Moses did.

God's Revelation of the Decalogue

Deuteronomy 5:6-33

The Ten Commandments (5:6-21), spoken by God directly to the people, are foundational divine words. Yet the Decalogue merely prepares for all that follows in Deuteronomy. Israel must not remain tied to Horeb but move forward toward God's reign. Moses, in his role as mediator of the covenant (5:22-33), keeps God's instruction adaptable. He guides Israel prophetically as the people journey to God's ideal world.

The Ten Commandments, 5:6-21

By Hosea's era, the Ten Commandments were already recognized as "the law [Heb., *torah*] of your God" (Hos 4:6). The psalms of Asaph attest that the pedigree of the Decalogue stretches farther back still. Asaphite Psalm 50:16-20 refers to three of the four commandments cited by Hosea and identifies these laws with God's "covenant" (v. 16).

Hosea had charged Israel with ignoring the sixth, seventh, eighth, and ninth commandments (Hos 4:2). At the time of King Josiah, in the seventh century BCE, the first and second commandments were not properly honored (2 Kgs 22:17). Deuteronomy puts the Decalogue again before Israel in a new edition, insisting that it is high time to "observe" it (Deut 5:12, a new wording, different from Exod 20:8).

The full form of the Decalogue appears twice in the Scriptures (Exod 20 and Deut 5), both times bearing obvious signs of ongoing reflection. Deuteronomy 5:16, for example, expands the fifth commandment beyond its simpler form in Exodus 20:12. It recalls the commandment's archaic pedigree. It also sacrifices a straightforward wording in Exodus (about avoiding exile) to make a deeper claim about the joy of the promised land.

Exodus 20 has expansions of its own, including an insertion in v. 11 by editors from the Holiness School (a group of central priests at Jerusalem, the best known of which was the prophet Ezekiel). Using echoes of the priestly creation story in Genesis, these editors have taken the fourth commandment in a very different direction from what the reader will see has happened in Deuteronomy. The complex editorial history of Exodus 20 and Deuteronomy 5 makes the relative dating of the two texts problematic.

Deuteronomy understands the Decalogue to encapsulate Israel's covenantal obligation (cf. Jer 7:9). The inscription of the Decalogue on two tablets (4:13; 5:22; 9:10, 11, 15, 17; 10:1, 3) signals that a covenant *in nuce* lies before us, since ancient Near Eastern vassal treaties had this sort of two-part form: one complete copy for the suzerain and another copy for the vassal people. Lest the reader entertain any doubts that a covenant-summary is in fact at issue, Moses himself declares the Decalogue to be God's "covenant, which he charged you to observe, that is, the ten commandments" (Deut 4:13). Deuteronomy 5:2; 9:9, 11; 17:2-3, and similar texts likewise specifically equate the Decalogue with the covenant (see Levinson, 134–35).

The Decalogue is a direct address of God, transmitted personally (Deut 5:4). It is hand delivered in God's own writing on permanent tablets (Deut 4:13; 5:22; 9:9, 11; 10:4), executed by the very "finger of God" (9:10). Once God spoke the Commandments with a loud voice out of the fire, that was it—no more words of this stature (5:22). Qualitatively different from the rest of God's laws, the Decalogue goes directly in the ark (10:2, 5), not beside it like the larger scroll of God's teaching (31:24-26). The Decalogue even has a special name, the "Ten Words" (10:4). Beyond all this, the Ten Commandments echo down through the remainder of Deuteronomy. In fact, they appear to provide the organizing rubric the book uses to order its laws (Deut 12–26).

Summing up the great significance of the Decalogue, Patrick D. Miller (2009, 4) states,

> Repetition, placement, highlighting, divine authorship—all serve to tell the community of faith that here is the foundational word for your life as God's people. All you need to know is given to you in these Ten Words. They may be summed up succinctly (as in the Great Commandment) and elaborated in great detail (as in the legal codes . . .), but they are a sufficient guide for one's life with God and neighbor.

Deuteronomy makes a distinctive, nuanced presentation of the Ten Commandments, different from that in Exodus. Over against the form of the Commandments in Exodus 20, Deuteronomy shapes the Sabbath rule as the Decalogue's center. Notable expansions lengthen the Sabbath commandment to four full verses (vv. 12-15), creating a strong impression of weightiness. Striking rhetorical features support the impression, including the way the commandment now echoes the Decalogue's beginning and end. Verse 15 echoes the Decalogue's opening in v. 6, and v. 14 echoes the vocabulary of its closing words in v. 21.

By making the Sabbath commandment the focus, Deuteronomy interprets the Decalogue as a rule of life for sanctifying Israel. Keeping the Sabbath "holy" (v. 12) means weekly training in holiness practiced universally. It means forming everyone in the discipline of treating the entire people and land of God as sacred. This is, of course, Deuteronomy's main aim.

Deuteronomy intends to create a new form of communal life on earth (Deut 4:6-7; 26:19; cf. Exod 19:6 E). Its vision is a people of wondrous intimacy with God blossoming within God's sanctuary land (note the bilateral language of covenantal "love" in v. 10). It sees embracing God as something done while eating, working, walking around, and even sleeping. Deuteronomy may want to do away with the land's many shrines (see Deut 12), but this is in no way about desacralizing Israel's countryside.

Week in and week out, out in the "towns" (v. 14), away from the central sanctuary, the people must observe the Sabbath. Such observance will remind them that their sacred intimacy with God must manifest itself across daily life and up and down all levels of society. Verse 14 specifies that the Sabbath includes even slaves and non-Israelites. All classes of people share intimacy with God and must be included as co-vassals, their human dignity respected, their welfare upheld (cf. 1:16; 16:11; 24:17).

Over against the simpler Sabbath commandment in Exodus 20:10, Deuteronomy specifies that at issue is the "rest"—the well-being—of even the lowest of social classes, the "male and female slave" (Deut 5:14b). Verse 14b of chapter 5 is a gift to the most vulnerable members of the working population, a gift probably of broader significance than at first meets the eye. "Rest" is often a pregnant term in Deuteronomy, with connotations of enjoying expansive life from God on God's land (cf. 3:20; 12:10; 25:19).

Deuteronomy wants a clean break from the hierarchy and oppression that was, and is, so widespread in the world. God's people must resist the culture of the nations, which always threatens to drag them down to its level of immaturity. With its attention fixed on God week in and week out, Israel can recognize the kind of human community God wants on earth and, striving for it, develop as God's treasured possession. In God's community, even the slave is understood as a brother or sister (see the Hebrew of 15:12).

As living catechesis, not deadening law, Deuteronomy speaks to the hearer's soul. It persuasively encourages observance of the Torah. Taking a different tack from the Sabbath rule as formulated in Exodus 20:11, Deuteronomy 5:15 reminds the people of their own experience as slaves. Anything else but empathy with slaves is unthinkable given Israel's own suffering in the exodus era: "You were a slave in the land of Egypt." The motivating reminder is characteristic of Deuteronomy (15:15; 16:12; 24:18, 22), which carves out an ideal life of freedom antithetical to Israel's visceral memories of slavery.

Verse 6 begins the Decalogue by recalling God's redemption from Egypt. The act of liberation was no end in itself. God intends to nurture Israel's humanity to maturity. Thus, the verse is a mere historical prologue to the chapter's main business of revealing Israel's core covenantal *obligations*, the Ten Commandments. Israel's real freedom comes not in escaping from the clutches of Egypt but in accepting God's covenantal rubrics for growth and ennoblement. By binding themselves in joyful service to the Lord as their covenantal suzerain, Israel can experience an expansively free life of "enslavement to God" beyond the people's dreams.

Deuteronomy sounds other distinctive notes in its presentation of the Decalogue. Notably, it inserts the clause "that it may go well with you" in v. 16 in the fifth commandment (expanding what we see in Exod 20:12). Here, it again reveals its vision of a redeemed life of expansive freedom enjoyed on God's land.

The suggestive vocabulary of the Hebrew clause "enjoy the good" in v. 16 far outstrips any narrow focus on material success. For Deuteronomy, what is truly "good" and joy filled is a mature, thriving interconnectedness. It is shared mutuality with God, with all one's sisters and brothers, and with the arable land. It is living out the truth that God is all encompassing, that God is "one" (Deut 6:4 NET, NIV).

Micah and Hosea, two of Deuteronomy's precursors, both spoke of the "good" in this way. They identified the "good" with the transformed lifestyle deriving from obedience to the covenant (Mic 6:8; Hos 8:3; cf. 1 Sam 12:23 B-source, a literary strand of 1 Samuel bearing marked affinities with Deuteronomy). Repeating the formula "that it may go well with you," Deuteronomy makes the "good" of the covenant a recurring theme (Deut 4:40; 5:16, 29; 6:3, 18; 12:25, 28; 22:7; cf. Jer 7:23).

It is no coincidence that Deuteronomy inserts its motivating reference to the "good" life of the covenant specifically in v. 16, in the fifth commandment: "Honor your father and your mother." This commandment is less about childhood obedience to parents than about the freedom and good of the entirety of Israel's community. Much more than a "recipe for happy families," it is key to society's covenantal well-being (Wright, 77).

Modern readers rarely grasp the workings of Deuteronomy's vision of society due to unfamiliarity with decentralized societal organizations based on kinship and lineage. Deuteronomy uses Israel's old tribal ties of kith and kin as the physical basis of its communal vision. In this theology, the life of the covenant flows like sap through the many branches of Israel's genealogical "tree" planted on God's land. The fundamental unit of Israel's lineage organization, its "tree," is the extended family of about three generations, the "house of the father." "Honoring the father" means upholding this large household, the basic unit structuring Israel's covenantal network.

An "umbilical" line of life interconnected the generations in old Israel. Children, grandchildren, and great-grandchildren honored and revered fathers and mothers buried on ancestral lands. Farmlands inherited from the ancestors, in turn, sustained the extended family. Inalienable ancestral land granted families the material means of supporting both themselves and larger units of kinship, the clan and the tribe.

The concept of honoring the father and the mother involves preserving lineages on their lands, protecting the economic lines of support that allowed the covenant to have a substantive impact. In the era before Deuteronomy's appearance, prophets such as Micah decried the breakup of precisely these "umbilical" lines of support. Extended families risked losing their inherited lands due to the greed and callousness of Israel's new centralized, monarchic society (e.g., Mic 2:2, 9; 3:2-3). It is no wonder that Deuteronomy strategically inserts the word "field" into the tenth commandment among the items that Israelites must never covet (Deut 5:21; contrast Exod 20:17).

An "umbilical" theology also lies at the heart of Deuteronomy's third commandment on respecting the *name* of the Lord (5:11). In ancient times, one's name marked one's identity, one's kinship relations, and one's rights to inherited land. In old Israel, to respect the *name* of an ancestor was to maintain an "umbilical" connection with him or her, to demonstrate covenant loyalty (cf. Ruth 4:5). Psalm 16:4 thus speaks of binding the deceased with their former patrimonies using the biblical parlance of "lifting up the name" to the lips. This is the same idiom appearing in the "name" commandment, the exact diction that occurs in Deuteronomy 5:11 (in the verse's Hebrew). If the names of the dead are invoked over their lands, how much more should the name of the living God (Deut 5:26), the ultimate landowner, be invoked over the entire territory of Israel?

When Israel settles the land, the people are to "blot out" all other divine names, the *names* of all alien gods from all scattered shrines (Deut 12:3). No alien name will remain anywhere, not "on the mountain heights," not "on the hills" (12:2). Each plot of land shall have only one umbilical connection to heaven—a connection to the Lord alone. Israel must honor only the Lord, who sustains the land, blessing it with fertility.

What is the reader to make of Deuteronomy's references to other gods, to names of other deities? With its worries about blotting out these gods' names, does the text not concede their existence? Does not the Hebrew of the first commandment (v. 7), in fact, speak of removing competing gods from "in front" of the Lord (cf. LXX: "before my face")?

Deuteronomy strove to be relevant and challenging in a real world of contingencies and complications. Addressing the reality of its times, the book acknowledged and pushed back against the polytheistic world of its first audience, a world replete with deities of all forms. Today's reader of the Decalogue lives in a different milieu, but one not without parallels. In a pluralistic society, a plethora of suggested "faces" of God confronts and rivals the Lord's "face." Deuteronomy adjures both ancient and modern readers to have no other "gods" than the Lord. Such "gods" may claim worshipers, but the Lord reigns over every nook and cranny of reality (10:14).

Like the fourth (Sabbath) commandment, the third ("name") commandment inculcates holiness throughout the land of Israel. Israelites of all types and in all locales can both hallow the Lord's Sabbath and hallow the Lord's name (Miller 2009, 67). Israel can uphold the Lord's name at the central shrine (12:5) and at the utterance of every oath invoking heaven (6:13).

Deuteronomy again differs from the Decalogue in Exodus (see Exod 20:16) in repeating the third commandment's vocabulary of "wrongful use" in the ninth commandment (Deut 5:20). The "false witness" of v. 20 (NRSV) is literally "wrongful" or "worthless" testimony. Deuteronomy wants the reader to see the third commandment's force extending to the commandments that specifically uphold the neighbor. Worthless treatment of neighbors in court (5:20) has no place in God's holy sphere marked by God's name. As the prophet Malachi will note, those who revere the Lord and respect "his name" are God's "special possession" (Mal 4:16-17). Such a people know themselves as co-vassals under God, and they treat one another as holy, treasured possessions of God (Deut 7:6; 14:2), not wrongfully or worthlessly.

A final distinctive of Deuteronomy's unique Decalogue is its repeated evidence of respect for women. Here again the book pushes back against the immaturity of its surrounding world, in which patriarchy reigned in many spheres of life. Verse 14 is careful to include the female slave along with the male slave in its admonition to provide Sabbath rest. Although the *"father's house"* was the basic unit of tribal society, v. 16 commands that Israel honor both father and mother. With its unconditional prohibition of adultery, the seventh commandment (v. 18) encompasses the well-being of both husband and wife. The absoluteness of the verse cuts against ancient Near Eastern conventions. In ancient law codes, such as that of Hammurabi (see sec. 129), adultery was a matter of the husband's contractual rights. The woman's personhood seemed to count for little.

Verse 21 again elevates women. It departs from Exodus 20:17 in separating craving for a married woman from coveting material things. Women, in Deuteronomy, are not things but persons. Thus, the text places the wife first, not second (after "house") as in Exodus. It makes the command about her a separate clause; and it makes the verb of that clause different from the one in the following sentence. The ancient Masoretes used a paragraph marker in the Hebrew text to separate the prohibition of coveting a wife from the rest of v. 21. Going even farther in this direction, both Roman Catholic tradition and Lutheran tradition interpret coveting a wife and coveting property as two distinct commandments within the Decalogue (numbers nine and ten).

The elevation of women in Deuteronomy's version of the Decalogue coheres with the overall spirit of the book. Deuteronomy assumes that women, as members of the covenant community (12:12, 18; 16:11, 14), have the status of legal persons. In a spirit similar to that of the seventh commandment, the law of adultery in 22:22 treats women as responsible parties, not as wards of their husbands.

The Mediator of the Covenant, 5:22-33

The people of Israel were unable to endure the encounter with God at Mount Horeb. They realized that ongoing exposure to God's fiery glory and greatness was simply out of the question. They cried out, "Why should we die? For this great fire will consume us; if we hear the voice of the LORD our God any longer, we shall die" (v. 25). God understands. It is okay. Through Moses, God tells them, "Return to your tents" (v. 30).

Questions immediately arise. Why does God respect the people's frailty? Can they not rise to Moses' level? Cannot the role of covenant mediator be a shared enterprise? Should God allow the people to lay everything on Moses: "Go near, you yourself, and hear all that the LORD our God will say. Then tell us . . ." (v. 27)?

Answers begin to emerge when we consider the extremity of what Moses, as God's intimate companion, endured. He gives up his life, dying outside the promised land (1:37; 3:25-27; 4:21-22). In v. 27 the people essentially ask Moses to die for them. Olson writes, "The intimations of the necessity of his death are again clear" (46).

Covenant mediators who follow in Moses' steps make similar sacrifices of the self. Jeremiah, the great epigone of Moses, endures anguish as the Lord's confidant (e.g., Jer 20:14-18). Like Moses (Deut 3:23-25), he balks at the cross he must bear (Jer 20:7-10). Jeremiah's descent to the depths is unique and archetypal. It would be beyond the pale for God to demand that everyone become a Jeremiah.

Knights of faith like Moses and Jeremiah do not mature overnight. That is why God does not coerce the people as a whole to maintain the Horeb experience, to bear up under the great fire and booming voice. That is why there are only individual covenant mediators. The people need toughening up through the dogged trek of discipleship. The journey will transform them, taking them to a place where, like Moses and Jeremiah, they will willingly lay aside all for God, their ultimate good. At journey's end, the people will accept God's overpowering intervention (30:6), which will free them from the bent nature of their existence (see the commentary above on 1:2-3).

Although direct exposure to God is too much for anyone to bear on a continual basis, periodic I-Thou encounters, as a worshiping assembly, are Israel's unique prerogative. Such encounters challenge and fortify God's people, forming them for intimacy with God. Both the E strand and Deuteronomy repeatedly make this point. Both stress that God wills to have intermittent encounters with God's servants and mysteriously preserves their lives through it all. No one sees God and lives; yet God somehow does indeed meet Israel directly, face to face (Gen 32:30 E; Exod 33:18-20 E; Deut 4:33, 36-37 [here, also see BHS n. a-a]; cf. Judg 6:22-23; 13:22-23).

Just as God releases the assembly at Horeb to their "tents" in Deuteronomy 5:30, so also Israel will cyclically return to its "tents" after repeat encounters with God in the promised land (16:7). The deliberate verbal correspondence of 5:30 and 16:7 is one of several indications that Deuteronomy wants the Horeb experience to influence and transform life in the land on an ongoing basis, year in and year out. Periodic interconnection with God as the Lord's worship assembly (5:22, Hebrew *qahal*; cf. 9:10; 10:4; 18:16) will allow Israel to rehearse the rubrics of discipleship that they must practice day by day back at home in the countryside.

With the people backing away from Mount Horeb, Moses stands isolated as God's singular confidant, God's unique mediator. The role was already clear in Deuteronomy's sources in E, especially in Exodus 20:18-21 (also cf. Exod 19:17, 19 E). Deuteronomy 18:15-22 will define the role outright and specify its ongoing nature. Moses, as bearer of the Horeb covenant, is the first in a line of intermediaries—specifically *prophetic* intermediaries.

Upon reflection, it is imminently reasonable to associate Moses and his role with prophecy. Prophets, after all, were essentially messengers or go-betweens who channeled or mediated God's words and will to Israel. This makes them mediators of the covenant. Moses, then, is the original, archetypal mediator who gave his life to bring the covenant down from Horeb—the quintessential prophet. Deuteronomy 34:10 directly affirms the fact: "Never since has there arisen a prophet in Israel like Moses, whom the LORD knew face to face." Prophets such as Hosea naturally look back to Moses' prophetic example: "By a *prophet* the LORD brought Israel up from Egypt" (Hos 12:13).

Once we see Moses as a prophet, we begin to understand the distinction our passage makes between the Ten Commandments and the more adaptable teaching of the rest of Deuteronomy. The Lord spoke the Decalogue to Israel directly (5:4), but the great mass of torah in Deuteronomy will be God's *prophetic* message through Moses (5:5). The laws that Moses subsequently propounds (Deut 12–26) are less like classic stone monuments and more like future-oriented messages from a Hosea or a Jeremiah.

The Ten Commandments are a rock-solid starting point, while the subsequent laws of Deuteronomy, like prophecy, are lively, relevant words, confronting the people where they are, keeping them on God's path. They are words oriented toward the future, guiding Israel on the trek of discipleship, pushing them ahead. The people of God must look to their incomparable foundations but also to God's promised future, a realized salvation where they will willingly lay aside all for God, their ultimate good. Thus, the tradition of Deuteronomy understands the covenant of Horeb to have both a fixed, authoritative yesterday and a prophetic tomorrow.

The book of the prophet Malachi, which is highly Deuteronomic in character, builds on this yesterday-and-tomorrow theme. Malachi 4:4-6, which concludes Malachi, makes pointed references both to Moses, the incomparable mediator of the Horeb experience, and to Elijah, the archetypal prophet in the line of Moses (see esp. 1 Kgs 19:8-9; 2 Kgs 2:8) who takes up the mantle of covenantal mediator for a new age. The point of the ending of Malachi is simple. The ancient experience at Horeb will remain forever foundational, but the covenant has a moving, changing, forward trajectory.

The Command to Love an Integral Lord

Deuteronomy 6:1-25

Chapters 6–11 gear up for the core corpus of Deuteronomy (chs. 12–26) by teaching and interpreting the book's first and great commandment, the command to love the one Lord alone (5:6-7; 6:4-5). Moses begins in 6:1-3 speaking personally and motivationally. He plays the role of an earnest prophet, pushing the people ahead on God's path. Verses 4-5 lay the great commandment before us, presenting it in beautifully concentrated, artistic form. In Judaism, v. 4 is widely regarded as the heart of the faith.

The Hebrew text of v. 4 is compact, and pregnant with meaning. No English translation can really convey the rich conciseness of the original. The Masoretes (the scribes who gave us the Hebrew Bible) have "guarded" its precise, terse beauty using enlarged Hebrew letters at the beginning and end of the verse. Isolating and splicing together the two letters in large script, we get the Hebrew word for *testimony* or *witness*. Deuteronomy 6:4 *witnesses* to the fundamental nature of God, and of Israel's relationship to God.

A literal rendering of the Hebrew of v. 4 would run as follows: "the Lord, our God, the Lord, *one.*" The key Hebrew term is *'ekhad,* "one." Not even a verb is present to distract from its emphatic ring. Referring to a future ideal triumph of v. 4, Zechariah 14:9 repeats *'ekhad* twice: "On that day the Lord will be one [*'ekhad*] and his name one [*'ekhad*]." Here, to say God is "one" is to say something about the *holism* of the Lord's being and sway. Hence, it is to assert the holism of reality itself. God's dominion is all encompassing, and thus each sphere of existence is integral to the whole of life.

The way that Canaanite polytheism associates various names of gods with all sorts of places makes reality look piecemeal and compartmentalized. A Baal is in charge at Peor (4:3); Yarikh, the moon god, is in charge at Jericho ("moon city"); and Shemesh, the sun god, is in charge at Beth-Shemesh. According to Deuteronomy 6:4, this fragmenting of reality distorts the truth and must stop.

Since God's name is *one* (see Zech 14:9; cf. Mal 1:11), Deuteronomy wants the many other divine names of the land expunged: no more names of multiple gods scattered indiscriminately throughout the land (Deut 12:3). God's one name (Heb., *Yhwh*; NRSV: "the LORD") now reigns; 6:4 emphatically presents it twice within in its tight four-word pronouncement. The worship of the Lord will now be focused and coherent—at *one* shrine, vested with *one* name (12:5).

As the reader has already learned (see the commentary on 5:11), to lift up God's name over God's *one* land is essential (see 6:13b). The entire people and every plot of land shall connect with the Lord alone. Antecedent to Deuteronomy, the E source solemnly urged Israel to keep connected to God through God's singular name. Introducing the Lord's name (Heb., *Yhwh*) for the first time, God commends it as an instrument for invoking God's presence: "You are to tell the Israelites, 'Yahweh, the God of your ancestors . . . has sent me to you.' This is my name for all time, and thus I am to be invoked for all generations to come" (Exod 3:15 E, NJB). Abraham Rattner's compelling painting, *Moses Composition No. 2* (1958), aptly inscribes Deuteromomy 6:4 within the burning bush. Deuteronomy 6 and Exodus 3 tightly interconnect.

As the people of Israel remember God's oneness, they find their own community reintegrated. They rediscover themselves as a singular people "called by the name of the LORD" (Deut 28:10). The Lord's oneness encompasses their own divisions and draws them into wholeness. As they remember the name of God, God "*re-members*" them. That is, God re-gathers them as members of a community that belong together.

As the people rehearse God's oneness, they become a singular, unified "Thou," addressed by a singular command: "Hear, O Israel" (Heb., *Shema' Yisra'el*, v. 4a). The second-person-singular imperative, which lends v. 4 (and also vv. 4-9) the traditional name, "the Shema," echoes through Deuteronomy (5:1; 9:1; 20:3; 27:9). This echoing command was likely well known from Israel's worship together as the "people of the LORD" (27:9). It was probably the worship assembly's opening summons (cf. 20:2-3; see von Rad, 63). The worship assembly's togetherness extends to encompass Israel's entire genealogical tree. Moses teaches both for those now alive and for "your children and your children's children" (6:2).

Later, in the postexilic era, the prophet Malachi will cite Deuteronomy 6:4 as a means of "re-membering" the fractured community of his day. At a time of great vitriol within Israel, especially among the priests (Mal 2:3, 8), Malachi will draw on the oneness of God to bring together what belongs together. "Has not *one God* created us?" he pleads, echoing the Shema. "Why then are we faithless to one another?" (Mal 2:10).

Approaching God as Deuteronomy 6:4 would have us do, as an undiminished entirety, means joining the entirety of one's existence in the love of God. This is the force of v. 5. It is the way of all truly existential love, as the Song of Songs knows well. Such love relativizes all one's power and wealth: "If a man offered all his wealth for love, He would be laughed to scorn" (Cant 8:7b, NJPS). It cannot be coincidental, then, that the Song uses the Shema's language of oneness to describe true love's obsession with the beloved: "Only one is my dove, My perfect one, The only one" (Cant 6:9, NJPS). Canticles 6:9 sounds very much like Deuteronomy 6:4 in the NJB: "Yahweh our God is the one, the only Yahweh."

Adam Welch, writing in 1928, memorably captured how God's singular oneness must claim everything upon which a person's life touches:

> Yahweh is one. . . . He has a character which sets Him apart from everything else to which other men gave the title of god. Hence His relation to them is as unique as His nature. He cannot demand a little more or a little less from His worshippers. He claims everything. His jealously is the proof of what He is. To admit the claim of another god is to deny the lonely and sufficient character of Yahweh. He does not demand His rights when He refuses to share His honour [sic] with another; He merely declares what He is. (Welch, 62–63)

Verse 5 commands loving God "with all your heart, and with all your soul, and with all your might." The language of love here is the language of covenant. The parties to ancient Near Eastern vassal treaties—both sovereigns and their subjects—spoke of their binding relationship as "love." The language emphasized the pure devotion and genuine obedience that should characterize covenant loyalty.

One of the Amarna letters between the Egyptian pharaoh and his northern vassals (fourteenth century BCE) uses such treaty language. In the tablet (EA 114:68), the governor of Byblos, Rib-Adda, asks the pharaoh, "Who will love you, should I die" (see Cook 2004, 74). Biblical traditions employ this political language of love as an analogy for Israel's covenantal relationship to God (e.g., Judg 5:31; Exod 20:6), insisting all the while that Israel's political "love" of God must simultaneously be a passionate affair of the heart. The prophecies of Hosea made clear that covenantal love has all of the intensity of a human love affair (e.g., Hos 2:14-23). Bill T. Arnold (2011, 560) has shown convincingly that in Hosea and Deuteronomy alike "the emotive significance of *'hb* ['love'] is primary and is not negated by its political usage in the ancient Near East."

Can passionate emotions be evoked by divine fiat? Can God rightly *require* love from us? In this case, yes! To internalize the relativizing singularity of God (v. 4), as God requires, is automatically to feel the requisite emotions and passions flow freely (v. 5). Consequently, vv. 4 and 5 combine as a dual command within the Shema, a package deal: "Hear . . . and love." To appreciate God's oneness is already to love God with all one has. If one can begin to grasp the character of God, one becomes ecstatic—what a lover, this God (see Cant 6:9, NJPS)! Martin Luther wrote, "When we . . . understand that all things flow from Him alone and that we are in His care, then sweet love toward Him has to follow" (68).

Far from seizing the role of dictator, God's intention for Israel is liberation (see 6:21). The NRSV of 6:25 speaks of putting Israel "in the right," but the Hebrew (*tsedaqah*) equally suggests that Israel will be "set free" (on *tsedaqah* as "deliverance," see Isa 45:8, 24; 46:12, 13; 48:18; 51:6, 8). *Tsedaqah*—liberation—resounds as the verse's first word. The freedom inherent in the covenant even allows Israel to reject God, provoking an intensely emotional divine response. Israel can push God to the wall (v. 16), ignite God's hot anger, and grieve God to the divine core (see 9:26, 29).

Pushing the reader deep below the realm of legal rules and footnotes, v. 5 spells out a covenant of two lives knit together, God's life and Israel's life. Dean McBride describes the three elements of v. 5, "your heart," "your life," and "all your capacity," as three concentric circles. They build on each other, climaxing in an absolutely singular devotion to God. To love with all the heart is to love with all one's intentions (in Hebrew thought, the "heart" controls the understanding and will). More intensively, to love with all the soul is to love with the entire self, even to the point of death (Heb., *nefesh* includes all that makes a person unique). Climactically, to love God with all one's *me'od* (literally, one's "very-muchness") is to love with full gratuity, with total abandon. As McBride puts it, "*Me'od* evokes the fullest 'capacity' of loving obedience to Yahweh which the whole person can muster" (McBride 1973, 304).

Only one person in the whole of Hebrew Scripture is said to have loved God in this way: King Josiah, who embraced the newly discovered scroll of Deuteronomy (2 Kgs 23:25). No wonder some at the time wondered whether Josiah just might be the Messiah. Sweeney (170–84) provides a good scholarly treatment of how the Deuteronomistic authors hold Josiah, the "lost messiah of Israel," to be a super-David.

Verses 6-9 complete the Shema with compelling language about internalizing the covenant. To "recite" God's words (v. 7) is to teach them incisively, to "drill them into your children" (NAB; "drill," the same Hebrew root behind "tooth"!). To have them on hands and foreheads (v. 8), doorposts and gates (v. 9), is to make everyday life a holy business.

Verses 10-15 warn about satiety in the promised land (cf. 8:11-20). The people are walking into houses pre-filled with goods, taking possession of cisterns they did not hew, and beginning to enjoy the fruits of vineyards and olive groves that they did not plant. They will enjoy the fullness of God's land at the risk of excessive satisfaction. Content and self-satisfied, taking it all in, they may well forget how they got there!

Deuteronomy's theological sources share the book's worry about satiety leading to forgetfulness of God. Hosea was shocked that God's marvelous care of Israel met only ingratitude (Hos 4:7; 8:11; 10:1; 13:4-8). Whereas the land's rich fertility should have provoked thankfulness, the bounty had only focused the people on their harvests. As James L. Mays writes, "Israel's true love was the grain . . . no matter whether they thought of themselves as Yahwists, their worship was a fertility cult" (126). Asaphite Psalm 78:29-31 mirrors Hosea's complaint. Israel's satiety yields neglect.

A satisfied people may lose their sense of dependence. Propped up by seemingly firm underpinnings, Israel may develop an attitude of self-sufficiency and entitlement. Believing it has earned its ease and abundance (Deut 8:17), Israel may even come to feel invulnerable to criticism. Hosea puts the following boast in Israel's mouth: "With all my wealth they will not find in me any iniquity or sin" (Hos 12:8, NIV).

The antidote to the vice of complacent ease is the virtue of gratitude. Truth be told, no fixed principle of order props up Israel. The wondrous "good" of the promised land is not innate to it but flows down from its umbilical connection to the Lord whose name is invoked upon it (Deut 6:13; cf. 11:11-15; 33:13-17, 28; Hos 2:8; Jer 5:24; 31:12). This Lord's singular identity claims Israel's wholehearted gratitude and makes forgetfulness of God inconceivable. Lest the people ever be tempted, Deuteronomy adjures them to fix God's words as a sign on the hands and an emblem on the forehead.

Verses 16-19 address a threat closely related to that of self-sufficiency, namely the human craving for *control*. Deuteronomy is keenly aware of the human ego's longing to orchestrate life on its own terms. This is the vice at issue when v. 16 commands, "Do not put the LORD your God to the test, as you tested him at Massah" (cf. Exod 17:2-7 E).

Testing God on *God's* terms is fine, even desirable. God has promised the people a "good land," where covenantal fidelity will bring expansive, savory life (Deut 6:18). The Lord hopes that they will go in, taste that life, and validate the divine promise (cf. Mal 3:10). What will pervert the process, and constitute a forbidden type of "testing," is a spirit of self-centeredness and insistent impatience. In a later era, the prophet Malachi will work out arguments (Mal 3:13–4:3) countering this very brand of stubborn short-sightedness. Many in his audience wanted the covenant of Horeb to be a "prosperity gospel," guaranteeing that each individual adherent would inevitably get ahead. They wanted a "test" that would box God in, forcing God to meet their terms and their timetable (Mal 3:13-15; cf. 1:2; 2:17). Happily, some of Malachi's contemporaries knew a reverent "fear" of God (Mal 3:16; 4:2; cf. 1:14; 2:5; 3:5) and could see a bigger picture in which awe of God evokes the kind of right living under covenant that, in the long run, in God's time, brings spacious, fulfilling life (see Deut 6:18).

As we have seen, the oneness of God means that the whole of life coheres together in a holistic system. Demanding satisfaction on your own terms ("testing God") disconnects you from this larger integrated reality that is not beholden to you. Receiving true, savory life, conversely, entails becoming integral within the system. It means upholding God's name, other community members, and the integrity of the arable land.

In many ways, hewing out their own cisterns, planting their own vineyards, and cultivating their own olive groves would be better for God's people than being handed all these things on a platter. It would afford them a vivid sense of connectedness. They would be splicing themselves into the larger system of life that sustains them. They would feel the system's delicate balance, take responsibility for its maintenance, and internalize a deep gratitude for its wondrous functioning.

Chapter 6 concludes in vv. 20-25 with a return to the theme of teaching subsequent generations of Israel (see vv. 2 and 7 above). The section is composed of a short creedal statement or catechism, summing up why it is that Israel observes God's commandments. The credo answers the basic question, "What is the point?"

The answer returns to the theme of God's identity and the attendant claim on Israel's devotion that holds the present chapter together. The God of the commandments is the one, unique Lord who pulled the people out of slavery in Egypt to integrate them into the holistic life of the promised land. The commandments represent the land's encoded operating system, by which it delivers, according to v. 24, Israel's "lasting good" (NRSV), that is, its "prosperous and happy . . . life" (NAB). With its term "good," v. 24

again signals Deuteronomy's vision of a redeemed life of expansive freedom enjoyed on God's land—a truly human life of mature, thriving interconnectedness.

The Command to Show No Mercy

Deuteronomy 7:1-26

In chapter 7, the reader encounters what many experience as a true text of terror. With this text, the same wrenching questions confront us that arose earlier in the accounts of the defeats of Sihon and Og in Moses' first discourse. How can the Lord command Israel to "utterly destroy" men, women, and children (2:34; 3:6; 7:2, 26; cf. 20:16-17)?

The haunting affront of this command will surely never cease to challenge the community of faith and indeed all readers. There will always be some who consider Deuteronomy 7 to be an ethically and theologically irredeemable passage. Yet, as with the conquest accounts of the first discourse, all is not as it first appears. A flat-footed "bare reading" of Deuteronomy 7 simply does not do the text justice. Radical discipleship, not ethnocentrism and genocide, is the heart of the text's present literary and canonical form.

In its canonical context, Deuteronomy 7 continues Moses' preamble to the laws of chapters 12–26. Throughout the preamble (6:1–11:32), Moses aims not to incite or justify violence but to expound the force of the Shema. He works incessantly to train Israel's attention on the Lord's singular oneness and its attendant, necessary claim to the people's all-encompassing focus. Here in chapter 7, Moses buttresses the Shema and its claims by debunking the counterclaims of fear and panic (vv. 18, 19, 21; cf. 1:29). At Josiah's time, when Deuteronomy first surfaced in Israel, fear and panic had again become live threats. In the face of the violent propaganda of enemy Assyria, their menace was real indeed.

Josiah's reign and Deuteronomy's appearance were six hundred years after the events of Moses and Joshua's time. There were no longer any Canaanite armies to destroy. Instead, the reader confronts a living motif from the poems and myths of the divine warrior: *panic before a swarming enemy*. As we have seen, Deuteronomy drew on the ancient Near Eastern combat myth to communicate its vision of the Lord battling for Israel (1:30, 42; 3:22; cf. 20:1-4). Verse 21 puts chapter 7 solidly within this tradition.

In divine-warrior myth, the Lord and Israel face an inflated, swelling enemy (cf. Exod 15:7; Pss 48:4-5; 76:10; Ezek 38:9; Mic 4:11-12; Hab 3:14). Its soldiers are filled with pride, hate, and ravenous desire. "I will pursue, I will overtake, I will divide the spoil, my desire shall have its fill," the enemy rants (Exod 15:9); "Let our eye obscenely gaze on Zion" (Mic 4:11, NJPS). Reflecting the combat myth, Deuteronomy 7 understands the enemy's numbers to be overwhelming, beyond reason (vv. 1, 7, 17, 22). As in Joel 4:14, there are "multitudes, multitudes, in the valley of decision!" A mob mentality propels the frenzied enemy. The insanity and the hatred of God (see Deut 7:10, NAB, NIV, NJB; also 7:15) evoke the specter of primordial chaos. In the combat myth, the watery abyss of chaos and death, signified by the Hebrew *tohu wabohu* (Gen 1:2), is the true and sole enemy of the divine warrior. Habakkuk 3:8 specifies the "rivers" and the "sea" as the driving cosmic forces propelling the foe.

A number of details in Deuteronomy 7 confirm that chaos and death are God's true enemies, not literal Canaanite armies. According to vv. 25-26, the spoil of the enemy is abhorrent, to be detested (vv. 25-26). Verse 15 associates the foe with "dread diseases." And, as noted, vv. 1, 7, 17 together stress an overwhelming threat that panics Israel. The threat is archetypal, made up of an unholy totality of "seven" enemies (v. 1). One thinks of Sheol (home of the "silent majority"!) as the cosmic power able to muster such numbers. According to Deuteronomy, Israel's "conquest" directs itself against Rephaim (dead shades), particularly offspring of the Anakim (see 3:13; 4:47; 9:2; 29:7; 31:4).

Divine warrior poetry typically describes a stunning reversal of the enemy swarm's intention to instill terror. The panic that the force wields inevitably falls upon itself, resulting in total confusion (e.g., Exod 23:27; Pss 48:5-6; 76:5; Zech 14:13). In their disorientation, brothers end up slaying brothers (for the self-slaughter motif, see Judg 7:22; 1 Sam 14:20; Ezek 38:21; Zech 14:13; Rev 6:3-4; *1 Enoch* 100:1-2).

This is exactly what happens in our passage, as God vows to throw the enemy "into great panic, until they are destroyed" (v. 23). The Hebrew term *tsir'ah* in v. 20 of our text refers to the awful dread associated with the epiphany of the divine warrior in Exod 23:27-28 (E; also see Josh 24:12; Hab 3:5). Disabling panic is almost certainly the threat at issue when Exodus 23 and Deuteronomy 7 use the term (English translations of the word *tsir'ah* range from "hornets" to "pestilence").

In this canonical context, Deuteronomy 7 aims to vindicate the truth of the Shema over against all of Israel's fears about their own internal security. The Israel of King Josiah's day must learn to trust the Lord, not rely on military treaties, strategic maneuvers, and empire building. Israel must not divinize doctrines of national security; the terror of Death must not reign; Assyria can be no cause for fear!

Divine warrior symbolism celebrates the ultimate powerlessness of all deathful, helter-skelter realities over against God's partisanship on behalf of life. As the divine warrior defeats all surging forces of opposition, order and growth emerge on earth. Its life resurrected, nature produces abundant crops, allowing humanity to thrive (Exod 15:17; Deut 33:28; Pss 29:11; 68:9-10). Thus, language of divine warfare in Deuteronomy 7 combines with language about the divine blessings of fertile wombs and a fecund ground (v. 13). This chapter's metaphors of war symbolize God's determination to overturn sterility, barrenness, and death (v. 14; cf. Exod 23:26 E). God's ideal even includes the end of all sickness (v. 15; cf. Exod 23:25 E). The fertility gods of Canaan claimed to have charge over nature and its fruits, but our text exposes these claims as lies. Deuteronomy knows that the path of abundant life is the path of covenantal discipleship. All phallic pillars and other fertility-and-religion worship objects must go (v. 5; cf. Exod 23:24 E).

In biblical theology, holiness stands at an extreme opposite the chaos and uncleanness of Sheol. Sheol's depths, like a watery grave, lie at the cosmos's nadir. They plummet down the ancient abyss, farther than the mind can fathom. But the Lord reigns in holiness high above. Loving the heights, God has established a highland sanctuary at earth's zenith (Deut 33:28; Exod 15:17 E/D; Jer 17:3). Driving out the nations, God planted Israel on this sacred mountain to make them grow as a people set apart (Asaphite Pss 78:54-55; 80:8-9; Jer 50:19).

The idiom of v. 26 denoting the hallowing of God is of great interpretive significance. Again, the reader encounters diction of the divine-warrior tradition. It is the diction of setting apart all spoil for utter destruction (Heb., *kharam*). Deuteronomy does not deploy the language out of a spirit of violence. Rather, it wants to convey God's claim on the promised land as holy territory, a place for sanctifying God's people.

The language around "utter destruction" stems from the hoary past. Chapman (2013a, 58) clarifies that it "predates Israel and is solidly attested in other ancient Near East cultures: e.g., the inscriptions of the Old Babylonian ruler Iddi(n)-Sin of Simurrum and King Mesha of Moab, as well as the Hittite proclamation of Anitta of Kuššar." In the ancient Near East, *kharam* language was another way of insisting that victory belongs to heaven alone. The entire spoils of victory are offered by fire to the true victor in battle. Thus, Micah 4:11-13 has Israel devote to God (*kharam*, v. 13) the spoils of war after God's defeat of the swarming enemy. The nations had massed together to desecrate the land (v. 11), but these blasphemers are turned to plunder, a holy offering to the Lord.

Deuteronomy 7 *recycles* ancient language in a brilliant rhetorical move manipulating two themes. Interpreters have often thought it incongruous that the chapter combines the theme of destroying the Canaanites (vv. 1-3, 6, 17-24) and the theme of not worshiping their gods (vv. 4-5, 7-15, 25-26). They might be correct to view the passage as a jumble, if it were not for the twin valences of the combat myth. The battles of the divine warrior are about *both* destroying the swarms of Sheol *and*, to the shame of the fertility gods, raising up life. The divine warrior constitutes both Israel's source of security and *sole* guarantor of fertility. God's oneness means the fertility idols must go.

The *kharam* language of Deuteronomy 7 about destroying the Canaanites does not fit its context unless it becomes metaphorical hyperbole about God's singular power over both sterility ("the surging waters of Sheol") and fertility ("God's lush highland sanctuary"). If Deuteronomy 7 is not a jumble, then its language of "holy destruction" must be vivid symbolism about putting panic aside and centering on the one God to the exclusion of all hollow gods and images. Radical discipleship, not any literal genocide, is the point of the chapter. Deuteronomy 7, properly understood, is emphatically not a "text of terror."

In a now classic article, R. W. L. Moberly convincingly argued the point that the theme of holy destruction is pure symbolic language in the present literary form of Deuteronomy 7 (124–44). Looking closely at vv. 2-5, he noted that the sequence of thought makes no sense if understood in a bare, literalistic way. Verse 2 commands the total destruction of the Canaanites, but v. 3 then goes on to forbid intermarrying with them. Crudely put, corpses do not make attractive marriage prospects. The reader is signaled that this text cannot really be about killing Canaanites. Rather, it is about avoiding all relationships and practices that threaten the covenant, that beckon one to serve other gods (v. 4). It is about ridding the land of idols (v. 5).

The text as it stands—appearing centuries after Moses' time—must be addressing an Israel far removed from battles with the Canaanites. The assumed reader instead faces a *spiritual* battle over singular dedication to the one Lord. The only literal imperative for this reader is shunning marriage outside the faith and destroying graven images. The taking of human life is not at issue.

One final reflection helps confirm that Deuteronomy 7 has little to do with ethnocentricity and xenophobia on the part of Israel. The chapter is clear that the threat of holy destruction may fall equally upon *any* people who fail to keep God's land sacred—even Israel itself. Verse 10 specifies that God's judgment pertains *generically* to those who "hate" God (see NAB, NIV, NJB; cf. Exod 20:5; Ps 68:1). Verse 26 declares that if Israel ends up practicing idolatry then God's own people may themselves be set apart for utter destruction just like the Canaanites. Deuteronomy's concern is manifestly with people's relation to God, not with ethnicity and nationalism (cf. 8:20; 9:4, 5; 13:15-18).

The Rejection of Dependence on Self

Deuteronomy 8:1-20

In Deuteronomy 8, Moses continues his efforts to buttress the Shema, to elaborate on the full meaning of the exhortation to love God with absolute single-heartedness. The concern in chapter 7 was that Israel might say in its heart, "These nations are more numerous than I; how can I dispossess them?" (7:17). Here in chapter 8, the worry is that as the people of Israel prosper in God's land, accustoming themselves to the good life that the land will support, Israel might say in its heart, "*My* power and the might of *my own* hand have gotten me this wealth" (8:17, emphasis added). The repeated idiom "say in one's heart" (the Hebrew of 7:17; 8:17, see NASB) marks the major threat to true observance of the Shema that each chapter outlines.

The text of chapter 8 conjures up the ridiculous image of the Israelites strutting across the promised land with an attitude of entitlement, confident in their understanding of the land's workings and in their inevitable desert of its bounty. How ludicrous is the mental picture! It would be the height of folly for Israel to presume to hold autonomous control of life and prosperity on the land, and, if one can imagine it, to arrogate to itself control even over heaven itself. The latter eventuality could happen if, abandoning the true God, the people attach themselves to a gaggle of immanent deities closer to home and the forces of nature and experience (e.g., Baal, Asherah, Shemesh, Molech).

Verses 19-20 of chapter 8, which describe Israel's perishing from God's land because of going after other gods, probably stem from the hands of editors in exile. For them, the most egregious means of buttressing self-sufficiency was reliance on the props of mythological polytheism. The phrase "surely perish" found here in these verses occurs also in 4:26 and 30:18, two other texts belonging to Deuteronomy's exilic edition.

In Deuteronomy 6:10-15, Moses had already warned that satiety could lead to loss of the virtue of gratitude. Receiving all the good of the land on a platter was wondrous, but it also put the people's souls at risk. Here in chapter 8, Moses returns to this theme and notes how blessed God's land truly is. It is a place where people can feel that they have truly "arrived" (vv. 7-9), "a land . . . where you will lack nothing" (v. 9). One can easily lose one's sense of interconnectedness and dependence when one feels like an *arrivé*.

God's people must never adopt an attitude of entitlement and pride (8:14). The point of relationship with God is not getting God to serve them, reducing God to something they can use. Rather, the point is finding true orientation and joy in life through submitting unqualified service to God. The order of the day is a focused God-confidence, not a deluded independence and self-confidence.

Deuteronomy's thinking is very much in keeping with its sources here. The book of Hosea, for example, had earlier outlined a program of austerity as the best means of getting the northern kingdom back on track, back in alignment with the covenant. Hosea 3:3-4 had called for a moratorium on a whole laundry list of objects and systems that propped up the people's sense of control. The items listed were an affront to the mysterious otherness and freedom of Hosea's God. They were all tools for placing divine transcendence and numinous mystery at the disposal of the Israelite people, giving them a false self-confidence.

Following Hosea in valuing the lessons of austerity, Deuteronomy 8 calls readers to remember the deprivations and trials of the wilderness wanderings after the exodus. It turns out that the wilderness years were not simply a regrettable experience of punishment. The era was a time of God's patient guidance of the people in the path of discipleship, in the path of formation in the God-directed life. "Yahweh your God was training you [Heb., *yasar*] as a man trains his child," Moses insists in Deuteronomy 8:5 (NJB). The Hebrew verb *yasar* here is not just about discipline in a strict sense but about raising an individual to maturity (cf. *yasar* in Deut 4:36 REB, NJB, NLT, GNT).

The joy of intimacy within a genuinely loving divine-human relationship is what will bring fulfillment and satisfaction both to God's people and to God. Sheer, gratuitous love for God's people is central to who the Lord is for Deuteronomy and its sources (e.g., Deut 1:31; 7:8; cf. Hos 11:1, 4; Exod 19:4; 32:13 both E). That is why v. 5 of our passage pictures God as a patient and loving parent, carefully instilling in God's child the maturity that will allow for genuine relationship.

The God of Deuteronomy draws Israel into intimacy by God's very nature. Intimacy is an automatic reflex of who God is for Deuteronomy, a reflex of the directness of God's numinous presence in the book's vision of Israel's life (Deut 1:42; 4:7; cf. Exod 3:12; 33:14-15 both E; Hos 11:9). The people experience this direct presence of God near them and among them as mesmerizing and magnetic. As Rudolf Otto has put it, the mysterious numinousness of God is "fascinating" (Latin: *fascinans*).

What lessons did the wilderness era hold for God's people? How was this period especially formative for Israel? The answer lies compressed already in the language of v. 2. Here, Moses instructs, "Remember the long way that the LORD your God has led you these forty years in the wilderness, in order to humble you, testing you." The Hebrew verb for "testing" here, *nasah*, is relatively infrequent in appearance and pregnant with meaning. Its significance in the passage is apparent, for v. 16 repeats it.

"Testing"—Hebrew *nasah*—draws people out of a dull acceptance of workaday normalcy and thrusts them before the vastness of God's numinous otherness. It withdraws the calculations and economics that support banal existence, substituting a God-directed wonder and bonding. Thus, testing is one of God's means of catechetical formation of a people who love God intimately with no other motive or basis than the joy of the relationship itself. It is a divine means of refining and proving the people so that they *own*, for themselves, a genuinely other-centered relationship with their divine Lord.

"Testing" drives home to the people that their love of God transcends any economy of interest. It must do so, for genuine love knows no self-interest or desire for reward. (Contrast the skeptical assertion of Job's heavenly accuser, the satan, in Job 1:9.)

The reader must avoid misunderstanding. God's testing has nothing to do with performing a capricious experiment on helpless subjects. The point of God's "testing" of God's people is to establish a solid foundation to relationship. Such a foundation must be devoid of any motives involving the drive to control the other.

Within the E strand, an important source of Deuteronomy, Genesis 22 is perhaps the Bible's most dramatic case of God's "testing." In the ordeal of Isaac's near sacrifice (Gen 22:1-14 E), God proves and establishes in Abraham the power of the human servant of God to transcend the self. The text specifically refers to this act of forming Abraham as a work of "testing": "God tested [Heb., *nissah*] Abraham" (Gen 22:1).

As the awful *via crucis* of Abraham climaxes in Genesis 22:12, God specifies the exact desired outcome of the divinely imposed "testing." Fully satisfied with Abraham's self-sacrifice, God's angel declares, "Now I know that you fear [Heb., *yare'*] God." This is the selfsame "fear" that Exodus 20:20 (E) ties directly to God's testing. Witnessing the thunder, lightning, and smoke of God's presence on Mount Horeb at the giving of the Ten Commandments, the people shrink back in terror. Moses reassures them:

"God has come only to *test* [Heb., *nasah*] you and to put the *fear* [*yir'ah*] of him upon you." At both the binding of Isaac and at Mount Horeb, God came to confront human beings with the numinous quality of God's being, and, by so doing, to evoke as an automatic reflex of the experience their longing for intimacy with God and for morality in communal living.

The "fear" of God, the fruit of "testing," is the means to relax the need for control and self-sufficiency and to center in God. The cultivation of this "fear" lies at the heart of Deuteronomy's program of forming a people truly intimate with God (Deut 6:2, 24). With such "fear" in place, it will go well for Israel forever (Deut 5:29). Deuteronomy 8 emphasizes this "fear" in v. 6, which identifies the fear of God as the desired outcome of God's past dealings with Israel, of God's "testing" of them in the wilderness.

The awful trek up the mountain of sacrifice in Genesis 22 provoked a humble courage in Abraham. It pushed him to focus resolutely on the truth of God's promises of support, despite having nothing to hold on to from the side of normal human experience. The ancestor's radical, fearless trust threw itself upon God's eerie otherness, transcendent worth, and miraculous provision beyond all human calculations. The courage and determination of Abraham allows him to make the prediction of v. 5: "The boy and I will go over there; we will worship, and then we will come back to you." His profound confidence in God's care appears in the dogged resolution behind the repeated phrase, "So the two of them walked on together" (at the end of both v. 6 and v. 8).

God's miraculous care and provision, beyond all human imagining, is the central theme of Genesis 22, emphasized at its turning point in v. 8. There, Abraham assures his son Isaac, "God will see to the sheep for His burnt offering" (NJPS). Abraham's God is a God who, despite all indications to the contrary, "sees to it."

The wilderness generation should have experienced a swelling dependence on the Lord similar to what occurred in the soul of their great ancestor, Abraham, upon the mountain of Moriah. Just as God "tested" Abraham in terrifying Moriah-land, so also God tested them in "the great and terrible wilderness, an arid wasteland with poisonous snakes and scorpions" (Deut 8:15). In the wasteland there was no food and no water, and what food God did provide seemed miserable, even detestable (Num 21:5 E).

Like Abraham, the wilderness generation walked with God through a wasteland of lack and trial. In the arid wilderness of Sinai, one's love of God is genuinely humble, devoid of self-concern and self-sufficiency. One lets go of any thought that one can box God in, can insist that service of God must bring rewards that one defines. When God permits hunger (v. 3) and turns the world upside down (v. 16), God's people do *not* love God for good cause. They love God only for love's own innate rewards.

Like Abraham, the Sinai generation also experienced the Lord's miraculous provision. To deliver them, God worked around humanly impossible circumstances. God saw to their need in unimagined, uncanny ways. The miracle of manna, a substance foreign to their minds, saved their lives (vv. 3, 16). God relieved their thirst through water gushing from hard rock (v. 15). Even their clothing and sandals eerily maintained themselves, fully meeting their needs (v. 4; cf. 29:5). In the desolate badlands, the people experienced the numinous, developed a different imagination about reality, and learned the lesson that complete dependence on God can actually work.

It is worth pausing now to note the radical corrective that chapter 8 mounts against popular misunderstandings of Deuteronomy as a rigid system of rewards for righteousness and punishments for sin. This commonplace view of Deuteronomy as an ironclad system of blessings and curses is rampant. Thus, a recent treatment of "Ethics and AIDS" equates the tradition of Deuteronomy with the perspective expressed by Job's friends! According to the author of this treatment, the friends and Deuteronomy agree that "If a person were experiencing sickness or other trials, then that person must have sinned" (Overberg, 22). Even Northrop Frye, one of the most influential literary critics of the twentieth century, once described Job's friends as having turned up to counsel Job "armed with the Book of Deuteronomy"! Since Job is experiencing grievous trials and sufferings, Frye states, the friends insist that he "must have done something wrong" (Cayley, 197).

Obviously, none of this fits with chapter 8 of Deuteronomy. As we have seen, Israel's experience in the Sinai wilderness reveals that God is no automated system of reward and punishment. God *cannot* be relied on to bring material supports and mastery of the environment to the righteous, while letting sinners suffer just deserts. The Lord is no wishing-well, trading sure prosperity for loyalty. Rather, God has proved God's self to be readily able to push God's people to their limits, letting them taste severe trials and sufferings, "testing" and "proving" them.

Such trials teach and form God's people, helping them learn that the blessings of the covenantal relationship are not primarily material but relational: "One does not live by bread alone" (v. 3). Indeed, God's numinous reality relativizes all materialistic and self-focused preoccupations. One finds true life by attuning one's life path to the movement of this fearsome God in history, to the movement of God's word. Such attunement means dropping self-sufficiency and control needs, throwing oneself instead on the mysterious provision of the God who always "sees to it."

The Rejection of Self-righteousness

Deuteronomy 9:1–10:11

In 9:1–10:11, Moses continues to charge Israel to "occupy the land" (10:11). The charge is not literal, at least not in Deuteronomy's present canonical shape. What follows in chapters 12–26 is not the land's settlement, as a literalist reading might suppose. The settlement finds description only later, in Joshua. Rather, what comes next is Deuteronomy's core law code, toward which the preamble has been building since chapter 6.

For Deuteronomy, in its canonical form, to "occupy the land" is a metaphor for occupying oneself with the implementation of the book's core catechetical code (chs. 12–26). It is a symbolic expression about carving out of existence a dedicated arena for a nourishing interrelationship with God, neighbors, and the natural environment (cf. 33:28).

As Moses' preamble continues to buttress the Shema, it turns to reject another major threat to God's singular claim. Moses marks the threat in Deuteronomy 9:4 using the same idiom "say in one's heart" that occurs in 7:17 and 8:17 (see NASB). In chapter 7, the threat to the Shema was a timid preoccupation with numbers, especially troop numbers. Then, in chapter 8 it was an opposite failing: a misplaced confidence in one's ability to control life. Here in chapter 9, a third threat finds expression. The issue now is false assumptions about moral and religious standing—the threat of self-righteousness.

Verse 4 of chapter 9 reads, "Do not say to yourself, 'It is because of my righteousness that the LORD has brought me in to occupy this land.'" Such a thought is both presumptuous and out of touch with the facts on the ground. Neither moral standing nor ethical merit has brought the people of Israel to their present point of privilege. They have built up no record of God's approval, no spiritual credit balance. Most especially, there is no question of Israel's moral superiority over other groups, not even over the peoples they will dispossess from Canaan. Israel has no ethical advantage. "It is rather because of the wickedness of these nations that the LORD is dispossessing them" (9:4).

The people of Israel are surely graced to stand where they do, led by a God who will cross before them as a "devouring fire" (v. 3). What is more profound, however, is that they are graced to be alive at all given their actions at Mount Horeb. All was almost lost for them there when they ruined everything by making a calf-god (vv. 19-21). A great deal of Deuteronomy 9:1–10:11 devotes itself to rehearsing this haunting event.

Moses had barely ascended the blazing mount of Horeb to receive the covenant from God when Israel had hurried off the Lord's path (v. 16). Repetition of the term "quickly" (Heb., *maher*, v. 12 [2x], v. 16) emphasizes the people's moral disability. Israel's covenant with the Lord appeared to be over before it began, its tablets smashed (v. 17). The people almost met their end at that time, almost found themselves in history's dustbin. Luckily, God moved beyond Israel's "wickedness and their sin" (v. 27).

Making that calf-god left Moses in dread of what God would do, it so provoked God's furious, blazing anger, ready to destroy (vv. 19-20). And the casting of that "work of sin" (v. 21, NJB) was just the parade example, the epitome, of the people's hardheadedness and intractable failing. If more instances are needed to confirm Israel's entrenched waywardness, Moses easily points in v. 22 to the incidents at Taberah (meaning "[the Lord's anger] Burned," see Num 11:1-3 E), at Massah ("[Israel] Tested [the Lord]," Deut 6:16; Exod 17:2-7 E), and at Kibroth-Hattaavah ("Graves-of-the-Overindulgent," Num 11:31-35 E). To top it all off, Moses recalls that most recently the people of Israel had rebelled in yet another climactic way at Kadesh-barnea (v. 23; cf. 1:19-46). Upon reflection, it is impossible to distinguish God's people from the wicked nations they are about to dispossess of the promised land (vv. 4, 5).

The reader now begins to grapple with a theological mystery, a conundrum that has vexed even the best theological minds. Is Israel really this bad? If so, why is the God of all earth's nations (see Deut 10:14-15) so favoring of this peculiar people?

Israel has emerged as "the fewest of all peoples" (7:7), destitute refugees from "the house of slavery" (8:14), a group eerily "quick to turn from the way" (9:12). To know and embrace these facts is to acknowledge one's desperate need of God. It is to abandon all false confidences based on militarism, materialism, and moralism. Yet this negative path to surrender does leave one wondering about God's motivations. If God's people are so undistinguished, how did they ever get God's attention? What was God thinking in committing to them as God's "very own possession" (vv. 26, 29)?

The sobering fact is that God had no morally worthy alternative people to embrace. Israel's experience is representative, revealing a deeply rooted moral distortion occurring across the board in humanity. No nation walks a path of righteousness leading straight out of the wilderness, through the Jordan River, and into the promised land. Some nations may be lucky enough to taste life in God's sanctuary-land, but they inevitably face eviction for lack of fit with the territory (cf. Deut 4:25-26; 8:19-20; 9:4-5). They never take root due to ignorance of the land's core orientation on nurturing a true vassal people of the Lord (see Deut 8:19-20; 9:4b; 12:29-32; 18:9-14).

For virtue to take root on earth, God must form a virtuous people from scratch, taking a people on the "outs" and ushering them into an arena of formation, a holy "sanctuary" (e.g., 11:12; 21:23; 24:4). There, they may live into what God is doing for them by embracing God's ways with their whole lives (e.g., 4:5-7, 14, 40; 5:33; 26:15-19; 30:20). Deuteronomy thus takes seriously how God's promises to Israel's ancestors specifically named and emphasized the significance of just such an arena, a *land* sworn "on oath to . . . Abraham, to Isaac, and to Jacob" (Deut 9:5; 10:11; cf.1:8, 35; 6:18, 23; 7:8; and see Deuteronomy's source texts in E: Exod 13:5, 11; 32:13; 33:1).

Of all earth's unremarkable peoples, why choose Israel? According to Deuteronomy, the basis for God's unmerited choice or election was "love." "It was not because you were more numerous than any other people that the LORD set his heart on you and chose you—for you were the fewest of all peoples. It was because the LORD loved you" (Deut 7:7-8; cf. 4:37; 10:14-15; 23:5).

The term *love* in Deuteronomy is a metaphor for the elective grace of God but is also a richly emotive term. God came to love Israel in a manner comparable to how people fall in love (cf., e.g., Hos 2:24-25). To use a slightly different metaphor, God became attached to Israel in the way that parents grow in love for their children (Deut 1:31; 8:5; 32:10-11; cf. Hos 11:1-11). God remains vulnerable because of this love. When Israel pursues foreign gods, God is heartbroken. The infidelity of Israel is akin to sexual betrayal (Deut 31:16; cf. Hos 1:2; 2:5; 3:3; 4:12).

God's motivation of being love struck over Israel pushes Israel's election beyond any fully rational explication. As Blaise Pascal, renowned French mathematician and physicist (1623–1662), famously said, "The heart has its reasons which reason knows nothing of." A sage in Proverbs similarly admitted that the way of two lovers is a thing "too wonderful for me," something that "I do not understand" (Prov 30:18-19).

The notion of a lovesick God injects a dimension of profound mystery into the logic of Israel's privilege. Who can parse love's propulsions? All around us, we observe human beings, both smart and stupid, placing their affections "unwisely." Some around us even love people they simultaneously appear to hate. Humans love their spouses and offspring despite all idiosyncrasies, quirks, and imperfections. Indeed, we seem to love them all the more because of these things! We sometimes wonder in silence how this or that unattractive and peculiar person ever found love. We cannot account for it, yet that person's lover needs no convincing, and would be devastated to lose his or her soul mate. All these instances reveal love to be an irreducible matter of the heart.

Not all readers of Deuteronomy are exasperated at this realization. For some, it is profoundly moving and transformative to realize that God has fallen in love with them despite, or even because of, their foibles. What a load off one's shoulders to realize that one does not have to prove oneself good enough for God. How freeing and enabling to be accepted as oneself! It is as if the reader has received a unique word that she or he is "peculiarly God's own." The word would be good news indeed, too good to believe.

Such a word from God should dispel our anxieties and objections, freeing us to walk toward God. We would be slothful to take it as a cheap word, licensing our moral complacency. Quite the opposite, to take the word to heart would be to feel worse about our stubbornness and alienation. It would be to thirst for better alignment with God. The upcoming core law-code of Deuteronomy (chs. 12–26) will provide structures for working at precisely such an improved alignment with God's walk.

When read closely, our passage provokes the gratitude and discipleship of the reader, yet it does more. It assures the reader that God's unmerited favor is radically persistent, allowing for radical hope that a future is possible. God will continue to choose Israel out of love even when the people fail to uphold the Shema in the promised land.

When this passage surfaced in Israel at King Josiah's time, all was almost lost again, just as when Israel made the calf at Horeb. The covenant lay smashed once more, right before the people's eyes. Things had so deteriorated in the era preceding Josiah's ascension that God had said, "I am bringing upon Jerusalem and Judah such evil that the ears of everyone who hears of it will tingle. . . . I will wipe Jerusalem as one wipes a dish, wiping it and turning it upside down" (2 Kgs 21:12-15).

Josiah's reform, as radical and sweeping as it was, may well have come too late. The king himself is aware that the reformation will be akin to locking the barn doors *after* the horses have run away. The covenant curses in the newly discovered code of Deuteronomy were already zeroing in. Even as the words of the newfound book were beginning to sink in, God was declaring, "I will indeed bring disaster on this place and on its inhabitants— all the words of the book that the king of Judah has read" (2 Kgs 22:16).

Aware of the danger of a new failing of the covenant, our passage has a specific literary and theological shape that confronts the possibility and insists that the mystery of God's love will still triumph. Although God's patience may exhaust itself, this need not spell the end. The covenant's curses may strike with seeming finality, but even this will not doom Israel's relationship with its Lord.

Truly, Deuteronomy's vision far exceeds any mechanical understanding of the covenant's workings. Deuteronomy makes no common cause with the simplistic theology of Job's friends, with its easy linkage of human righteousness and divine favor. Repeatedly, Deuteronomy resists any branding as a book of moralism and legalism. What can be legalistic about God's love continuing beyond the covenant's collapse?

According to Deuteronomy 9:1–10:11, God appeared finished with Israel when the people cast their calf image. "Let me alone," God requests, "that I may destroy them and blot out their name" (9:14). Moses accedes to God's request. In the manner of King Josiah, he accepts the finality of what has transpired. He knows that the proverbial horses have already fled the barn; they are gone whether the doors now be barred or not.

In a major departure from the Exodus version of the golden-calf story, Moses does not now entreat God's mercy (contrast Exod 32:11-14 E). Rather, leaving God in God's anger (Deut 9:15), he allows the covenant to screech to a halt. Turning to the people, he flings the covenant tablets from his hands, smashing them (9:17). Even so, he is not done with this people. The covenant is in pieces, but the story is not over. A completely new beginning is possible for Israel and God: a *new covenant*. It is hard to miss a prophetic, even eschatological, promise for Israel's future here (cf. Jer 31:31).

The text's rhetoric repeatedly impresses upon the reader the possibility of a genuine second chance for Israel, a fresh covenant created from scratch that exceeds the greatness of the first. Just as Moses fasted and prayed before receiving the first set of tablets (9:9), so he abstains from food and drink in preparation for a brand new set (9:18, 25). Just as God wrote on the first two tablets (9:10), so God inscribes a fresh stone pair (10:1-4). Perhaps most striking, the text describes Moses coming down from Horeb with new tablets using the exact Hebrew phraseology with which it described his descent with the initial set: "So I turned and came down from the mountain" (9:15; 10:5).

Despite its emphasis on a distinct new start for Israel, the text reveals that God's new covenant will not come cheaply. The costliness of God's love and grace—the cost of discipleship—remains a vital truth. Deuteronomy has already insisted that suffering and death on the part of Moses are instrumental in Israel's entrance into the promised land. The theme resurfaces here strongly.

Moses lays his life on the line to brave God's mountain, a mountain "ablaze" with God's fiery otherness (9:9, 15). Moses suffers without bread and water as he awaits the stone tablets—suffers not merely for one forty-day period, but as a double (or even triple?) trial of self-denial (9:9, 25; cf. 10:10). Strikingly, the passage speaks *five* times of a trial of forty days (9:9, 11, 18, 25, 10:10).

Moses' self-sacrifice waxes nearly complete in our perception when we find him spending his second forty-day fast "prostrate before the LORD" (9:18). This posture, flat on the ground, is of great symbolic significance for our text. Verse 25 doubles back to the same rare, intensive verbal form in v. 18. It repeats it twice. The Hebrew rings with connotations of falling down in death.

As Moses suffers and symbolically dies, he births a new spirit of self-abnegation within Israel, a fresh lifestyle awash in surrender. Amazingly, he turns down God's offer to "make of you a nation mightier and more numerous than they" (9:14). The false gods of numbers and self-sufficiency cannot ensnare him. Instead, he finds his true self and deepest purpose in a personal embodiment of God's message for Israel.

This lifestyle of service and sacrifice spreads immediately to Moses' extended kinfolk, the Levites. Near the end of the passage, God sets the Levites apart for a life-risking role in God's hazardous presence: "to stand before the LORD to minister to him" (10:8). They will have "no allotment or inheritance" of land like the rest of the tribes (10:9). They will base their lives on relationship with God, not on bread alone.

A Summative Call to Commitment

Deuteronomy 10:12–11:32

Issuing a rich and comprehensive call to commitment, Moses draws to a close the preamble (6:1–11:32) that has been leading up to the core legal code of Deuteronomy (the central law code of 12:1–26:19). He beautifully sums up what covenantal loyalty truly looks like, and he presents Israel with a crucial decision, the choice between blessing and curse. The passage begins in 10:12-22 with a beautifully written précis on the scope of Israel's commitment to God. In the spirit of Hosea 6:6 and Micah 6:8, key sources of Deuteronomy, the text deftly encapsulates the essence of fidelity to the divine suzerain.

Verses 12-13 of chapter 10 string together five verbs that encompass Israel's obligation to God. Israel is to "fear," "walk," "love," "serve," and "keep." Echoing the imperative of the Shema in Deuteronomy 6:5, the central verb of the series is "love." The most centrally important thing in the world is for the love of God to sink deep roots in human hearts, so that it occupies people's minds constantly and nothing else matters but this love (Maimonides, see *Mishnah Torah, teshuvah,* x, 6).

Although all nations and, indeed, all existence ("heaven and the heaven of heavens," v. 14) belong to God, and although God is completely impartial (v. 17), God has mysteriously "set his heart in love" only (Heb., *raq*) on the small, peculiar people of Israel (v. 15). God, Moses tells Israel, has chosen "*you yourselves*" (v. 15, NJB). What other response to this mysterious, deeply personal election can Israel contemplate but to knit its life together with God's life in an all-encompassing, integrated love? What else is conceivable, save to "hold fast" (Heb., *dabaq*) to God in intimacy (v. 20), just as lovers cling to each other (cf. *dabaq* at Gen 2:24)? Israel's love must issue in a giving up of one's self to God with "all your heart" and "all your soul" (v. 12).

God wants an exclusive commitment of love, a love backed up by everything one has within oneself. God is not asking for any obsessive and deadening observance of page after page of legal footnotes. The Hebrew

Bible knew it long before the apostle Paul! What God wants is to see God's reflection on the pages of people's lives. Living such a life requires one to "circumcise . . . the foreskin of [the] heart" (v. 16, NRSV), that is, to commit to a heart sculpted to love God passionately, purely, and unqualifiedly.

Physical circumcision was a radical symbolic act: an invasive and bloody rite performed on the youngest of infants. Deuteronomy's new "circumcision" has an even more visceral and transformative impact. To enact such a "circumcision" is to cut away all cumbersome, numbing thickening about the heart (NJPS), to excise "the thick calluses from your heart" (*The Message*). God wants people inwardly open, pliant, and available to God (contrast the emphasis on humanity's entrenched stubbornness at 9:7, 24).

God's torah aligns Israel with God's living, personal presence, not with stiff, cold rules. Thus, Deuteronomy insists that its imperatives cohere with God's person, with God's very identity. The ethic and spirituality of the book is a veritable *imitation dei*, an imitation of God—an aspiration to act as God acts. To keep the commandments of God, for Deuteronomy, is to "walk in all his ways" (v. 12; cf. 11:22). Just as in Micah, it is to "walk humbly with your God" (Mic 6:8). It is to have a "walk"—a relationship—with God of such respect and intimacy that one unconsciously emulates one's partner.

Abraham Joshua Heschel poignantly described the Torah's commandments as acts of *communion* with God. He insisted that they are expressions of *togetherness* with God, a means of aligning with God's own sacred interests. Heschel wrote,

> The Torah is primarily *divine ways* rather than *divine laws*. Moses prayed: "Let me know Thy ways" (Exodus 33:13 [E-source]). All that God asks of man was summarized: "And now, Israel, what doth the Lord thy God require of thee . . . but to walk in all His ways" (Deuteronomy 10:12). . . . As [God] clothes the naked so do thou also clothe the naked; as He visited the sick, so do thou also visit the sick; as he comforted mourners, so do thou also comfort mourners (*Sotah* 14a). (Heschel, 288)

Verses 17-19 of our passage reiterate the theme, commending the imitation of a God who "is not partial and takes no bribe" (v. 17), who "executes justice for the orphan and the widow, and who loves the strangers, providing them food and clothing" (v. 18). The verses insist that this emulation of God's disinterested love, which extends even to the most unlikely of recipients, must arise from deep within one's heart and one's identity: "Love the stranger [NET: 'the resident foreigner'], for you were strangers in the land of Egypt" (v. 19).

To emulate God's own lifestyle is to embrace free, expansive life, not constricted, diminished life. Deuteronomy refers to this new, liberated life of Israel as that which is "good" (v. 13, Heb., *tob*). Commitment to the covenant is literally "for good to us." The NRSV understands the Hebrew expression about "the good" of the covenant to relate to the people's general "well-being," but we have already seen in discussing Deuteronomy 6:24-25 that the idiom connotes more than people's ordinary welfare. Beyond well-being, the "good" of the covenant entails a life "set right" by God (6:25), a life where everything is right with family members, with the community, and with people's interconnection with nature.

Deuteronomy 10:12-13 and Micah 6:8 both raise the rhetorical question, "What does the LORD require?" Both texts are sure about the answer: a committed covenantal attachment to God that will issue in "what is good [Heb., *tob*]" (Mic 6:8). Along with texts such as Hosea 8:3 and 1 Samuel 12:23 (B source), both understand "the good" as a code-term or cipher for the covenant's new God-bundled, set-right life. This new enduring, savory life of blessing is the necessary fruit of torah observance.

This commentary's introduction noted Deuteronomy's commonalities with ancient Near Eastern vassal treaties, international covenants sworn by oath and guaranteed by sanctions. Comparing Deuteronomy 11 with these vassal treaties proves highly illuminating. Such documents typically ground their corpus of stipulations in a historical prologue, which rehearses the suzerain's gracious acts of beneficence on behalf of the vassal. In like manner, Deuteronomy 11:1-7 recalls God's saving work at the exodus and in the wilderness to elicit Israel's gratitude and response of covenantal obedience.

Two memorable saving acts encapsulate the mighty deeds of the Lord that form the prologue to Israel's covenant. Both show God's power over history and nature alike. First, defeating Egypt, the great external enemy, God buried its army in the Red Sea's waters. Second, putting down the rebellion of Dathan and Abiram (see Num 16), God rescued Israel from the ever-present internal threat of sin.

As elsewhere, Deuteronomy uses potent existential rhetoric to create a sense of direct relevance and immediacy in the reader. Like all good liturgical celebration, it evokes powerful communal memories to bring the spiritually significant past alive for the present. Although not literally factual, Deuteronomy 5:3-4 had inscribed the present generation into the Horeb experience: "Not with our ancestors . . . but *with us*, who are all of *us here* alive *today*. The LORD spoke with *you face to face* at the mountain." Present readers must come to "own" the covenant experience, the text insists, and respond to its call.

Such a rhetorical move of inscribing the present into the past is both anthropologically and theologically legitimate. Deuteronomy retains old Israel's conception of itself as a living genealogical tree, the roots of which remain vital and integral to its present branching growth (cf. 29:4-15). The text assumes the natural solidarity of branches and roots.

As in chapter 5, Deuteronomy 11:1-7 projects the contemporary generation back in time once more. It does so to put the living, breathing world of the present front and center. The God of Deuteronomy is the living God (5:26), and the Lord's pressing concern is with the progress of the physical world in the here and now. A tree's budding branches draw their life from deep roots, but they—not the roots—represent the present flowering of the tree's life that makes a difference in the world.

Just as the people's ancestors take a back seat in the crucial choices of Israel's present (ch. 5), so also do their children and grandchildren (11:1-7). "It was not your children . . . but it is you," Moses charges in our text (11:2). "It is your own eyes that have seen every great deed that the LORD did" (v. 7). The urgent responsibility of commitment pertains squarely to the living, breathing hearers and readers of the present, of the now. Remembrance and obedience is an immediate task in Deuteronomy's view; each generation must own an authentic response (or lack of response) to God's grace.

Deuteronomy 11:8-17 moves from the importance of the past to discuss the relevance of the future. It elicits the people's commitment to the covenant by explaining the unique and intricate workings of the land that they are about to enter. God is one. Israel must approach God's land as a holistic system, as an integral arena of covenantal discipleship. If they do, they will enjoy its good—its savory, expansive life. The text drives home the uniqueness of God's sanctuary land as a holy arena of spiritual formation with language of God's personal pride. Canaan is "a land that GOD, your God, personally tends—he's the gardener—he . . . keeps his eye on it all year long" (v. 12, *The Message*).

The interconnectedness and holism of life in Canaan lends itself perfectly as a metaphor of the well-oiled covenantal life. Unlike in Egypt, where irrigation and cultivation require human ingenuity and effort, life in Canaan flows smoothly and naturally from God's care in the form of seasonal rainfall (cf. Deut 33:28). Existence there entails gratefulness for God's nurture and humility about who is in control. Inhabitants must set aside their control needs and align with the ebb and flow of the environment, the flow of "milk and honey" (v. 9). They must become interdependent with one another in dealing with naturally occurring challenges.

If communal, covenantal life breaks down in the land, the environment itself will suffer and groan. If the people betray their suzerain, God will "shut up the heavens" and "the land will yield no fruit" (v. 17; cf. Hos 2:8-13; 1 Kgs 17:1). Modern readers may jump to assume that this view (viz. that calamities of nature may reflect divine retribution) is simplistic or primitive. If they can suspend their prejudices for just a moment, however, some profound truths quickly emerge.

One is that despite the claims of all immanent deities, such as Baal and Mot, only the Lord is sovereign over nature, death, and life. "The LORD kills and brings to life; he brings down to Sheol and raises up" (1 Sam 2:6; cf. Deut 32:39). The faith that God has ultimate sovereignty over nature and biology abounds with suggestiveness. It points to the power of God to move humans through disability, failure, and the death of exile into a resurrected future.

Many factors will surely affect the life and health of Israel's genealogically constituted "tree." It seems certain, however, that this living growth will never flourish apart from the solidarity of its constituents and their humble respect for the holy ground that nourishes their roots. Deuteronomy knew the truth, which modern "green" thinking is now recovering, that communal health and natural health are deeply interrelated. Today we recognize that when conflict and violence become endemic to a country, its topsoil inevitably declines. Our daily papers shout a message akin to that of Deuteronomy, that human selfishness and pride issue in nature's collapse (oil spills; toxic waste; the loss of whole species). The end result is the dehumanizing of populations.

Ancient Near Eastern vassal treaties typically concluded with a section of blessings and curses that flowed from obedience and disobedience respectively. Covenantal blessings lavished benefits on obedient vassals, but those who concluded a covenant on oath also assumed liability for sanctions if they violated their treaties. Echoing the form of the suzerainty treaty, Deuteronomy now sets before Israel "a blessing and a curse" (v. 26).

Once Israel has entered the land, the people must symbolically enact the two ways of vv. 26-28: the ways of curse and blessing, of death and life. They must pronounce the blessing on Mount Gerizim and must rehearse the curse on Mount Ebal (v. 30). During their ceremony, the words of blessing and curse will echo down from the heights into the valley below as if into a great amphitheater.

This language of two antithetic ways, symbolized by two mountains, is another means of confronting present hearers and readers with an immediate crucial choice. Deuteronomy again insists that its audience commit itself in the here and now. People cannot go on vacillating and hopping between options, but must take up ownership of their response to the covenant. The prophet Elijah, taking on the role of Moses, will echo the sentiment: "If the LORD is God, follow him" (1 Kgs 18:21).

The theme of the covenant's curse introduced here in Deuteronomy is elaborated later in the book in chapters 27–28. In fact, chapters 11 and 27–28 form a sort of literary "envelope" around Deuteronomy's core legal code in chapters 12–26. Why this unsettling emphasis on curse? Why this exhortation to keep the curse in mind as one ruminates on the covenant's details?

Most likely, the book's rhetorical emphasis on curse witnesses to the high stakes involved in a binding, committed covenantal relationship. To enter deeply into a relationship with one who becomes the love of your life is to expose yourself to the risk of great pain and even trauma. Divorce has effects far more dire than the minor repercussions involved in breaking up with someone after only a few dates.

Divorce, however, is only the most extreme and regrettable outcome of God's activation of the covenant's curses. All sides would view such an outcome as the mother of all tragedies. Before that stage was reached, Deuteronomy believed, the curses of the covenant had a much more constructive role to play in the life of Israel. In this theology, pain has a purpose and judgment must be interpreted as grace.

A physician would show her patient no kindness in sparing him the amputation of a hopelessly gangrene limb. To use Deuteronomy's own metaphor, a parent would show his child no love in sparing him or her rigorous discipline. "Know then in your heart that as a parent disciplines a child so the LORD your God disciplines you" (Deut 8:5). Deuteronomy's curses are first and foremost an instrument of discipline.

This, then, is the spirit in which Deuteronomy affirms the value of the covenantal curse. And there are biblical texts that bear witness that Deuteronomy's thinking here is neither primitive nor misguided. Jeremiah 31:18-19, for example, attests that God's painful discipline is potentially effective. Having received and borne the Lord's discipline "like a calf untrained" (v. 18), Israel repents in this text and strikes the thigh in mourning and regret (v. 19).

A Central Sanctuary

Deuteronomy 12:1-32

Lodged within Moses' second discourse is Deuteronomy's great legal corpus (12:1–26:15). Forming the core of the book, this body of law contains the essentials of Deuteronomy's communal lifestyle of discipleship. Among the major concerns are the details of Israel's collective worship, the organization and offices of Israel's ideal society, the judicial principles by which the people are to live, and the liturgical supports of their covenantal identity. These chapters had their first public impact in King Josiah's royal capital (2 Kgs 22:8), but had earlier origins outside the Jerusalemite world. Their concerns are alien to all royal ideals and protocols.

The general flow of chapters 12–26 arguably mirrors the sequence of the Ten Commandments. Thus, the core's initial chapters reflect the theme of the first two commandments, which demand that Israel commit to worshiping only the Lord. Deuteronomy 12 makes an all-out effort to eliminate random, indiscriminate worship from Israel. In place of worship "on the mountain heights, on the hills, and under every leafy tree" (12:2; cf. Hos 4:13), Israel is to worship at one central sanctuary, associated with the Lord's name alone (12:5). Deuteronomy proscribes any imitation of Canaanite worship (12:29-32).

Chapter 12's limiting of worship to a chosen sanctuary was revolutionary. Earlier eras knew no such restriction. A structure on Mount Ebal appears to be an early Israelite altar, perhaps a site of seasonal pilgrimage during the early Iron Age. Similar structures seem evident at Giloh (Iron I era) and at Horbat Radam (a small Iron II site). The gate precincts of settlements appear to have had shrine areas (cf. Deut 16:5; 2 Kgs 23:8, "high places of the gates"). A late tenth to early eighth century BCE altar is extant at Beer-sheba. The key sites of Arad (ninth to eighth centuries BCE) and Lachish (late tenth to eighth centuries BCE) have royal shrines of the Jerusalem establishment, shrines for worship of Israel's Lord. King Solomon sacrificed at Gibeon (1 Kgs 3:4); Elijah did not hesitate to repair an "altar of the LORD" on Mount Carmel (1 Kgs 18:30); a variety of sacrifice sites appear in texts such as Judges 6:24-27; 13:15-20; 1 Samuel 7:17; 10:5, 13.

A major complication resulted from Judah's centralization of worship, and much of chapter 12 is occupied with it. In ancient Israel, the slaughter and cooking of domestic animals was a sacrificial ritual (cf. 1 Sam 14:31-35; Lev 17:3-7). It entailed taking one's animals to a local sacred precinct for slaughter. But local altars would not be available after Deuteronomy's revolution. There was now a real problem for those living far from the newly envisioned central shrine. How would they eat meat (see Deut 12:21)?

Making provision for the new situation, chapter 12 allows for a "profane" slaughter of animals. That is, it now permits animals to be butchered and consumed without the event becoming a religious sacrifice. "Whenever you desire you may slaughter and eat meat within any of your towns," v. 15 declares (cf. vv. 20-22). Care must simply be taken never to eat any animal's blood. Blood was fraught with deep significations in this culture, and must be treated with respect (vv. 16, 23-25).

The revolution of Deuteronomy 12 raises questions of motivation and strategy. What compelling theological motivations could justify the daring innovations at issue? Could not the transformation of butchering into something profane make everyday life in Israel feel less holy? Might not centralization of worship in the capital bolster the authority of Jerusalem's rulers and priests, who would now become guardians of a central national shrine? If so, this would cut against Deuteronomy's ideal of a covenantal community of interdependent siblings (Heb., *'akhim*, 1:16), free from all artificial hierarchies.

The Levites were one key group that might suffer under a centralizing program. They had the Lord alone as their special "portion" (v. 12; cf. Ps 16:5; Deut 10:9). God and God's sacred offerings were their sole "heritage" (Ps 16:6; Josh 13:14; cf. Judg 18:30). Would we not expect Deuteronomy to safeguard the Levites by permitting ongoing worship at the multiple shrines where they received their contributions and portions of sacrifices? Instead, the present chapter proceeds in a different direction.

Despite first impressions, Deuteronomy's centralization theme does not support a Jerusalem power play. Power-craving officials would want people thinking of God tangibly present in Jerusalem, stabilizing the power center. Commonplace biblical scholarship, however, understands Deuteronomy to imagine only the Lord's "name" (Heb., *shem*), not the divine self, as present in the capital (see Deut 12:5). Stephen A. Geller puts the position powerfully: "That God shuns the earth to remain forever enthroned in His heavenly abode is the universal belief of Deuteronomic thinkers" (Geller,

39). Benjamin D. Sommer (62) baldly states that for Deuteronomy, "God dwells in heaven and nowhere else . . . the *shem* ["name"] is only a sign of divine presence [i.e., a token of divine attention], not a manifestation of God Himself."

Geller, Sommer, and like-minded scholars are both right and wrong. Close study of Deuteronomy 12 reveals that it *does* resist notions of a stable divine indwelling of Jerusalem. Deuteronomy has no part in any monarchic or priestly power play. Chapter 12, however, does *not* chase away God's presence.

For Deuteronomy, the wonder is that Israel has thus far survived its exceptional *proximity* to God: "Has any people ever heard the voice of a god speaking out of a fire, as you have heard, and lived?" Deuteronomy asks (4:33; cf. 5:26). With their fiery God "present" in their midst, each day could be this errant people's last (6:15; cf. Exod 33:3, 5, 15, a text related to Deuteronomy). The radical nearness of God distinguishes Israel from all other people upon the face of the earth (Exod 33:16). As Israel occupies the land, God is present (Deut 1:30; 7:21; 9:3). God had brought Israel to Mount Horeb "with his own presence" (4:37) and would "himself" cross over before Israel into the land (Deut 31:3; the Hebrew parallelism here makes God just as proximate to Israel as Joshua is; see the discussion in Knafl, 6). Israel will live in a territory under God's personal care and protection (Deut 11:12; cf. 8:7-10; 26:15; 33:28). There, God is nearby, always close at hand. "What other great nation has a god so near to it as the LORD our God?" Deuteronomy queries (4:7; cf. Exod 33:16).

The Hebrew idiom "stand before [God]" signifies presenting oneself before God's very presence, ministering in close proximity to God. Israel stood before the Lord at Mount Horeb (Deut 4:10); so did Elijah, on the same mountain. As Elijah stood there, God's actual presence passed by (1 Kgs 19:11). Such close encounters with God are to be a repeating experience for Israel. Thus, Deuteronomy 29:14 has Moses use the idiom of "standing before God" as he addresses the people of Israel in Moab (cf. 29:10). Having occupied the land, the Israelites again present themselves before the Lord each time they appear at the central sanctuary (Deut 19:17; Jer 7:10; cf. Deut 12:7, 12, 18; 16:16; 26:5, 10; 31:11).

Deuteronomy understands the Levites and certain other groups to have particularly close proximity to God (Deut 10:8). Some among the Levites will "stand . . . before the LORD" at the central sanctuary (Deut 18:7). But service in God's presence need not entail a station at the shrine. Jeremiah 35:19, in the spirit of Deuteronomy, assures a family line of laypeople known as the Rechabites that for all time they shall stand before God as they go about their lives at home. Within Deuteronomy itself, even the common Israelite farmer, serving the Lord by presenting the triennial tithe *in the hometown*, stands and confesses "before the LORD" (Deut 26:13).

God's presence in Deuteronomy, nevertheless, is mysterious. The book emphasizes a striking presence *and absence* of God. God's people at no time see God's form, but hear "only a voice" (Deut 4:12). "The revelation there [at Horeb] was exclusively auditory" (Sommer, 63). Words and instruction are, for Deuteronomy, the means of encountering God at the central shrine (see, e.g., Deut 17:10-11; 33:10). Deuteronomy 16:16 does not belie this point, as some critics suppose. There is neither good linguistic cause nor any support from ancient versions (such as the Septuagint) to justify repointing of the Hebrew to say "your males shall see the face of the LORD."

Elijah, returning to Mount Horeb, learns that the vital presence of God is missing from wind, earthquake, and fire—the standard trappings of divine appearance ("theophany"; cf. Judg 5:4-5; Ps 28:10-15). God decisively absents the divine self from all such traditional manifestations, restricting all self-revelation exclusively to God's still, calm voice (1 Kgs 19:12, cf. NET). When one hears that voice, however, one had best shield one's eyes. Elijah did, for God was at hand (see 1 Kgs 19:13)!

The Hebrew phrase for what Elijah hears signifies an "irrepressible whisper." In this case, the traditional rendering of the KJV is not at all bad. God encountered Elijah through language, in a "still small voice." The phraseology cannot denote "silence" (NRSV)—this would not fit the idiom's use at Job 4:16 (see NJPS, NET).

Deuteronomy holds divine presence and absence in radical tension. The two tensive truths lie juxtaposed in 4:36-37. Other texts emphasize one or the other truth. A forceful "voice" at Horeb signaled God was there (5:22). Moses is able to "go near" God (5:27, 31) and receive directly what God writes (4:13; 5:22; 9:10; cf. 10:4). God speaks "immediately and personally" (Deut 5:4, my paraphrase). The Hebrew *panim bepanim* ("face to face") signals direct encounter, but encounter lacking literal sightings of God's real self (see 4:12, 15). Israel must never contact God's inner, private actuality, lest the people die (cf. Gen 32:30 E; Exod 33:20 E/D; Judg 6:22; 13:22). The simple hearing of God's words is barely sustainable and threatens the people with death (Deut 5:24, 26). As discussed below, it was Deuteronomy's apprehension of these truths in tension that led directly to its revolutionary insistence on a single chosen sanctuary.

The divine voice, the inspired verbal revelation of God, is certainly no God-empty, deity-devoid phenomenon. Instead, it is the instrument of presence and relationship. Exodus 19:19 (a text in the D family) reads, "Moses was speaking and God was answering him *with a voice*" (NET, emphasis added; cf. NIV). Hosea envisions the Lord restoring Israel through the "sweet talk" of courtship. God will "speak tenderly" to Israel as on a first date (Hos 2:14). Like Exodus 19:19 and Hosea 2:14, Deuteronomy avers that the verbally rooted relationship transcends the sighted one.

Those who have known forms of human intimacy are familiar with this profound truth. There is a mode of personal contact that probes deeper than the visible surface, than the merely skin-deep. What kind of lovers keep their eyes open at a time of "whispering sweet nothings"? Deuteronomy knows, as Geller (53) rightly discerns, that "the ear supersedes the eye as religious organ."

True intimacy requires an unpredictable meeting of souls interacting free of all masks and cosmetics. God's "one-of-a-kind-ness" in Deuteronomy eludes all inclinations towards typecasting, domestication, and idolatry, instead confronting humanity with a genuine *other* able to draw us into closeness.

Intimacy with this God is fully wondrous, for the Lord is utterly free. As God presents God's self to Israel, the syntax rings with the sound of pure freedom. God says, "I will be-there howsoever I will be-there" (Exod 3:14 SCHOCKEN BIBLE); "I will be gracious to whom I will be gracious"; "I will show mercy on whom I will show mercy" (Exod 33:19).

Radical freedom is a hallmark of the *verbal* revelation of Israel's Lord, and constantly a cause of offense. It infuriates Joshua (Num 11:29 E); it drives King Balak to rage (Num 24:10 E). A God who creates Israel's salvation and propels earth's history must speak *freely*, for creation by definition is an act of pure liberty. As literary critic George Steiner (b. 1929) argues, the wordsmith produces executive forms via a "supremely free act." "The poem . . . could very well *not* be" (Steiner, 152–53). (I have found the reflections of Steiner, a brilliant philosopher, helpful in wrestling with Deuteronomy's theology of God's gift of real freedom for intimacy; see Cook 2013.)

Deuteronomy drops all ideas of God's self-revelation through worship images and indwelt shrines. Intimate response to God's mystery and summons must entail God's "real presence" *and* "real absence" (Steiner, 38–39). There is, to Deuteronomy's way of thinking, no element of "absence" in an engraved idol or a traditional shrine. There is no signification of *otherness*, no offer of radical communion between utterly free souls. To encounter God, Israel must turn away from "localized" worship and make pilgrimage.

Acknowledge *one* sanctuary, God demands, and *one* divine name. Remove the lands' plethora of shrines and the gods' many names, thus establishing divine otherness and the offer of true intimacy. Establish one shrine, distant from most hometowns, requiring Israel's worship life to entail constant pilgrimages to a site where all assemble together to hear God as at Horeb. Pilgrims' ears will tingle in unison at God's voice there.

Deuteronomy's one sanctuary in no way "houses" God, but God has placed the divine name there. The name of God at the central shrine represents God's tangible exposure of God's own openness (12:5, 11, 21; cf. 14:23-24; 16:2, 6, 11; 26:2). Samuel Terrien (146) argued that Exodus 33:23 understands the *name* of God to be a veritable self-exposure of the deity. He viewed the name as the divine "back" that is "seen" by Moses at Horeb. Let there be no sabotaging of God's gift of self-exposure. Let there be no other gods' names anywhere—not "on the mountain heights," not "on the hills" (12:2-3).

In the ancient Near East, one's name marked one's identity, one's kin relations, and one's rights to land or territory. Thus, ancient rulers used the Semitic idiom "place one's name" to assert their sovereignty over a domain (cf. Deut 7:24; 25:19). Canaan's diplomatic correspondence acknowledges how Pharaoh has laid claim over local cities where Pharaoh has "placed his name." When Israel carried out Deuteronomy 12:3, every parcel of the promised land would forever be the Lord's domain, the perfect zone for forming a spiritually mature people.

The significance of there being only *one* sanctuary, however, is greater still. Where God is truly encountered, the human soul must perceive the presence of the remote, of the *foreign*. To meet God one must head out away from the familiar, launch out on pilgrimage in search of the mystery behind the divine name. A remote locale of divine encounter—a unique, singular sanctuary—coheres with God's strangeness, which presents itself most powerfully only in language—God as *wordsmith*. Linguistic revelation is paramount, for language shows no visual image of God, thus preserves God's "real absence," God's complete freedom. The verbal encounter, the confrontation with God's word, propels humans into what is undefined, unpredicted.

At the chosen shrine, Israel gathers to hear once again the words that were spoken by the voice through the fire (cf. Deut 27:8; 31:9-13; Josh 8:34-35; 2 Kgs 23:2-3). There, through the medium of linguistic revelation, that is, through the fire from which the wise hear the voice of the unseen God, freedom is enabled to meet freedom. The free human soul is enabled to feel in the guts the "absolutely alien which we come up against in the labyrinth of intimacy" (Steiner, 66, 140).

To welcome the stranger is to take risks, to open oneself to a new horizon of possibilities, an utterly transformative experience. As Steiner explains (188–89), "The 'otherness' which enters into us makes us other. . . . It is via language that we are most markedly and enduringly 'translated.'" In this vein, Steiner can claim that words, unlike those idols that sit in their many shrines, have the potency of both matter and antimatter: "[Two parties], when facing each other in exchange of speech, are at ultimate risk. One word can cripple a human relation, can do dirt on hope. The knives of saying cut deepest. Yet the identical instrument, lexical, syntactic, semantic, is that of revelation, of ecstasy, of the wonder of understanding that is communion" (Steiner, 58).

To bar the door to the stranger, to exercise one's liberty to ignore all verbal summonses, all invitations to pilgrimage, is to become unfree. In refusing the encounter with linguistic forces of creation, we push freedom out of reach. As Steiner (154) puts it, "It takes, as it were, two freedoms to make one." True freedom emerges only where "seriousness meets with seriousness, exigence with exigence"; it occurs only where poetics meets "the receptive potential of a free spirit." In such meeting "there takes place the nearest we can know of the existential realization of freedom."

Deuteronomy 12:5 assures the reader that when the people obliterate the names of ephemeral, narcotic deities from the land (see 12:3), the Lord's name can become their focus. Freedom can be theirs. Again, the "name" appears to be everything. In the biblical world, names are central in relationships.

On Horeb, Moses reminded God of God's attachment to him: "You have said, '[Moses,] I know you *by name*'" (Exod 33:12, cf. v. 17). In turn, Moses requested to know a *name* (cf. Gen 32:29 E; Exod 3:13 E; Judg 13:17-18). In response, the divine presence passes before Moses and the divine name rings (Exod 33:19). Using a rare Hebrew syntax that mirrors the name's earlier unveiling (in Exod 3:14 E), God expounds the name's meaning in a manner expressive of God's radical freedom ("I will be gracious to whom I will be gracious"). Latched on to the alien heart of intimacy, Moses feels full attachment to God.

Elijah, a new "Moses" (see Deut 18:15-19), found himself in Moses' shoes. Desperate for attachment to God, he fled to Mount Horeb. Finding Moses' "cave" (1 Kgs 19:9 speaks of "*the* cave"), the same cleft in the rock where Moses stood (Exod 33:22), he awaited encounter with God. Just as with Moses, the Lord's presence tangibly passes before him (Heb., *'abar,*

1 Kgs 19:11; Exod 33:19, 22). Neither God's angel (1 Kgs 19:5, 7; cf. Exod 33:2-3 E) nor the accoutrements of theophany (1 Kgs 19:11-12) suffice to renew Elijah. He needs the sound of God's intimate, alien voice.

Only a direct encounter with God's felt presence in God's voice, God's "irrepressible whisper," meets the prophet's deepest needs (1 Kgs 19:12; the similar theophany in Job 4:15-21 likewise climaxes in verbal revelation). Upon hearing God's voice, Elijah shields his face. Just as with Moses, he is up against impenetrable otherness, and it draws him out of his cave (1 Kgs 19:13; cf. Exod 34:8). In 1 Kings 19:11-12, the verses in which Elijah comes up against God's very presence, the divine name *Yhwh* occurs an amazing six times. Surely, to know the name is to know relationship.

Given the parallelism with Exodus 33, there is little doubt as to the content of God's articulate murmur heard by Elijah. The name of God, the name *Yhwh*, must have rung in the prophet's ears. Once again, as when the Lord first passed by Moses, the proclamation goes forth: "Yahweh, the one, the only Yahweh; he will be-there howsoever he will be-there" (see Exod 34:6-7 [paralleled by Deut 5:9-10]; Deut 6:4, NJB).

The sanctuary's *oneness* is a driving engine recreating the experience of Mount Horeb, of Moses and Elijah, in Israel's collective life. In gathered oneness, as a united worship assembly, Israel catalyzes the beckoning, summoning verbal revelation of Horeb anew. The people's gathering in unity becomes an act of *re-membering*, of re-creating Horeb's encounter with God's otherness and its community-forming power.

The people of Israel reunite at the central shrine to recapitulate God's binding them together as an integral, integrated "Thou." Forming this "Thou" afresh, they invoke the "I-Thou" encounter between themselves and God that stands at the heart of Deuteronomy's covenant. The single shrine of Deuteronomy furnishes Israel with a staging ground for an event, for the performance of a word-act of divine encounter. In this space, on this stage, Israel acts in freedom and power, re-creating itself as a "Thou" who invokes the Lord. It acts to *re-member* itself, inclusive of all members of its entire populace, so as to summon forth God.

As the covenant community re-members itself at the central shrine, the availability of the divine *name* there suddenly becomes crucial. Now is the time for remembering the name, thus "re-membering" God amid the community's members. Now is the time for communing with God.

Since God is other—alien, outside the mundane—the people must concentrate and welcome God's presence. This phenomenon is known from 1 Kings 8:12-62, a text brimming with the name theology of Deuteronomy 12. Repeatedly in 1 Kings 8, Solomon avails himself of the divine name at the chosen shrine in summoning God. Solomon acknowledges the name, confesses it, and uses it to invoke the Lord (see vv. 23, 25, 28, 33, 35). The name has become Israel's means for perpetuating covenantal relationship.

Remembering the name—taking the name of God on their lips—the community welcomes its most important member, its suzerain. Deuteronomy 12:5 does not focus on God's *name* as a token of a distant God's attention. It does not think that only the name, not the Lord, descends to the temple. Much to the contrary, the verse understands the name to be the means of communion, of connecting with God's presence.

In Israel, respecting the *name* of an ancestor maintains an "umbilical" connection with him or her (Cook 2013, 142). It heightens ongoing relationship (see the importance of the invoking the name at Ruth 4:10; Job 18:17; Pss 34:16; 109:13). God made God's name available to Israel for the same purpose (cf. Pss 30:4; 97:12; Isa 26:8). Possession of the name allows God's people to attend to their relationship with God through public worship, recitation of God's beneficent acts, and invocation of God. Like Absalom, God attaches the name to a specific site (see 2 Sam 18:18), a visible focus of commemoration and a locus for rites of communion.

God revealed the divine name at the burning bush of Horeb with motives not unlike those of Absalom, desiring ongoing presence with Israel. God tells Moses in E, "Yahweh . . . is my name for all time . . . thus [with this name] I am to be invoked for all generations to come" (Exod 3:15, NJB). The key Hebrew word here is "invocation name" (*zeker*). The term's use in this sense of an instrument calling forth God's presence is known from texts such as Hosea 12:5; Isaiah 26:8; Psalms 102:12; 135:13.

The authors of Deuteronomy had a legal text before them bearing precisely this thinking. The passage must have powerfully influenced them. Its wording assured that God would associate God's name with God's shrine for the purpose of invocation. When the divine name was invoked at the one sanctuary, Israel would encounter God.

The specific cross-reference at issue is Exodus 20:24, a law about the altar of the Lord found in the Covenant Code's preface. Deuteronomy 12, particularly vv. 13-15, cites and reworks this verse (see Levinson, 33–34; Cook 2013, 143). In researching his seminal dissertation, biblical scholar S. Dean McBride (1969, 209) discovered that Deuteronomy's "name formula," that is, the phrase "the place which the LORD will choose to establish His name," was modeled on the text.

In the altar law, God promises, "In whatever place [Heb., *maqom*] I choose for the remembrance [Heb., *zakar*] of my name I will come to you" (Exod 20:24, NAB). Deuteronomy embraces wholeheartedly the notion of

Exodus 20 that God's choice of a specific *place* (*maqom*) of encounter is highly significant, that little is of more importance than God's coming to Israel at a place of sacrifice to which God attaches God's name.

As in Exodus 20:24 so in Deuteronomy 12, altar building, placement of the divine name, and the sure prospect of divine presence all adhere together. God elects and appoints such a "place" of encounter with Israel in pure divine freedom (see Exod 20:24; 21:13-14; 23:20); icons imaging God's presence have no place there (Exod 20:23); divine blessing flows through such a locale only insofar as the divine name continues in remembrance and use there (*zakar*). For both Exodus 20:24 and Deuteronomy 12, remembrance of the divine name constitutes the true and effective shrine.

At the chosen *place* of God, Exodus 20:24 states, God causes God's name to be *remembered*. A clear and usual meaning of the Hebrew idiom here is the audible "invoking" of God, the calling upon a deity for help or blessing or as the guarantor of oaths. The verse insists that at God's place of worship the Lord's invocation name must replace all other names. As Exodus 23:13 clarifies, at such a place one must no longer invoke (*zakar*) the names of other gods (cf. how Deut 12:5 contrasts with 12:3).

Exodus 20:22-24 aims to bring God near God's worshipers, as the end of v. 24 reveals: "I will come to you and bless you." Wielding the name accomplishes the goal, for the name has everything to do with the divine presence (Exod 23:21; cf. Isa 30:27). When God appears in Exodus 33:19; 34:5-6; Deuteronomy 5:5-6; and Psalms 50:7; 81:10, God has the divine name on the lips. When God's worshipers invoke God through the name, they implore God's free coming in their midst (cf. Deut 4:7; Pss 20:9; 73:28).

When the people assemble at God's one sanctuary, they come "before the LORD" (see Deut 14:23, 26; 15:20; 16:11, 16). Deuteronomy 12 speaks of eating and rejoicing *in God's presence* at vv. 7, 12, and 18. Surely, God joins with the body of Israel at the central sanctuary. God completes the circle of covenantal fellowship, thus realizing Deuteronomy's ideal of each person's spiritual unity with God and neighbors.

King Josiah, his administration, and his priests doubtless held that God's name belonged under their care, at the temple. Harmonizing Deuteronomic law and the interests of the crown, the king entangled himself in Jerusalem's worship and capped his reforms with a heavy-handed supervision of a Passover held in the capital (cf. 2 Kgs 23:21). Deuteronomy, however, never authorizes any such royal power play. Rather, God's unique form of *verbal* self-disclosure in Deuteronomy precludes any particular faction, even the royal establishment, from ever using God's choice of one sanctuary to personal advantage. God's verbal mode of revelation entails both real presence and the real absence of that presence (thus, God is "numinous"). Israel can never pin down Deuteronomy's God like an idol tethered to a shelf in an immovable shrine.

The "assembly" of Israel, associated with God's worship, is mobile. It can move out as a camp, with God in accompaniment (Deut 23:14; cf. 1 Sam 4:3-4). God's name resided at such sites as Ebal, Gilgal, and Shiloh long before it came to land on Jerusalem (Deut 27:4-8; Josh 9:27; Jer 7:12). All such evidence bars Jerusalem from claims to permanently possess God's name. Deuteronomy simply does not allow that. If it did, would it any longer be a book in which catechetical formation is a *journey*?

The Levites, a tribe of special concern in Deuteronomy, can take heart. If God chooses to place God's name at Jerusalem for a time, Levites will surely be welcome there. They may even choose to exercise their traditional prerogatives in the capital (see esp. Deut 18:1-8). God can enforce their customary rights. Most definitively, God can remove the divine name from any worship site—even Jerusalem!—where people do not honor the Lord's claims and the Lord's covenantal programs.

Jeremiah, proclaiming God's judgment on Jerusalem, conveyed God's exhortation to "Go now to my place that was in Shiloh, where I made my name dwell at first, and see what I did to it for the wickedness of my people" (Jer 7:12; cf. Ps 78:60). The implication is unambiguous: God's name has no more permanently attached itself to Jerusalem than it did to Shiloh (and to Ebal, Bethel, and Gilgal before that).

Deuteronomy 12 associates yet more themes with its command limiting Israel to one sanctuary. Starting in v. 7, the chapter repeatedly encourages a radically inclusive, hospitable fellowship at the central shrine. All Israel's "households" should come "together" there. Verse 12 removes all doubts. The shrine's welcome must pertain to all genders and classes: "your sons and your daughters, your male and female slaves, and the Levites who reside in your towns." Verses 18-19 are parallel.

This theme of an all-encompassing welcome will sound again throughout Deuteronomy (see 14:26-27; 15:20; 16:11, 14; 26:11). Some texts specify that the hospitality of the shrine must even include strangers, orphans, and widows. This inclusivity is revolutionary. Earlier texts had spoken only of Israel's "males" making the required annual pilgrimages to worship God (Exod 23:17; 34:23).

God seeks out and summons all souls open to the workings of God's free and creative word (the "divine *poesis*"). Their welcome of God's word naturally interrelates with a more general stance of welcome. Steiner aptly observes the interconnectedness of hospitality on the one hand and openness to the transcendent on the other. He refers to a widespread "intuition that the true reception of a guest, of a known stranger in our place of being, touches on transcendent obligations and opportunities" (Steiner, 155).

Deuteronomy 12 associates the theme of "rest" with the command to worship at a central shrine (cf. Cook 2004, 31). In vv. 9-10 of the chapter, God speaks of giving Israel "rest" (Heb., *nuakh*), of bringing Israel into a place of "rest" (Heb., *menukhah*). With rest established, the people can finally worship God as God intends. God had promised this very "rest" in a passage recently referenced. Dialoguing with Moses on Mount Horeb, God had assured him with the words, "My presence will go with you, and I will give you rest [Heb., *nuakh*]" (Exod 33:14).

As with the theme of hospitality, the theme of rest partakes of the ethos of Deuteronomy's central shrine. The shrine is a place where liberty springs to life as the free divine word meets the receptive spirit of the free soul. Deuteronomy's concept of "rest" can be interpreted as God's gift of adequate security and sufficient inklings of freedom to make free, receptive souls available for pilgrimage to the central shrine.

Nurtured by God's presence and ensconced in "rest," souls have appetites whetted for encounter with God at the sanctuary. They are living expansive lives on God's land, and hungering to deepen their experience. God has blessed them with what Steiner (154) calls the "freedom of the city." They have been "invited to enter its gates in order to be pre-eminently at home, at liberty."

A Command to Resist Sedition and Insurrection

Deuteronomy 13:1-18

Continuing to illuminate the Decalogue's first two commandments, chapter 13 bans all seditious rebellion against the covenant. No one and nothing must subvert Israel's covenantal bond with its Lord. Even miracle workers must die if they urge mutiny against God. There can be neither excuses nor compassion even for family members who try to turn others traitor.

The deadly severity of the chapter has firm roots in the ancient context in which Deuteronomy emerged, a milieu that furnished the book with key language and symbols. Ancient Near Eastern treaties, which provide Deuteronomy its model of "covenant," require vassals to report instances of political conspiracy, which are then to be punished as capital crimes. Like Deuteronomy 13, the vassal treaty of the Assyrian ruler Esarhaddon (seventh century BCE) specifically mentions prophets and close relatives as potential conspirators. About three decades before King Josiah's reign, the treaty demanded vigilance against "your brothers, your sons, your daughters" and close monitoring of "the mouth of a prophet." Similarly, the Sefire inscription (an Aramaic treaty text from the eighth century BCE) voices the concern that entire towns might break away (cf. Deut 13:12-18).

In today's United States and in many other democracies, citizens live with the separation of church and state. What is the relevance in these societies of Deuteronomy's language about severe and violent sanctions for spiritual crimes?

I trust no readers of the present commentary will execute anyone for spiritual transgressions! What readers *are* called to "execute" is a trek of radical, God-oriented faithfulness. Deuteronomy 13 has lifted language about sanctions from the political realm of ancient treaty-making and applied it as part of a carefully constructed catechesis, a well-planned discipline of religious formation. It puts the language to a new use, shaping readers' *theological* imaginations. It invites readers to convert their minds.

Such conversion of the mind is not without challenges. Can today's readers any longer speak in dead earnest of a coming divine reign in which the Lord is sovereign over every sphere—private and public? Can we grasp this chapter's *eschatological* hope for a break with mundane, secular existence? The vision here is of a new world, where "every man, woman, and child" will know true spiritual "awe," a Kingdom Come where no resident will even think to entertain thoughts of betraying their Lord (Deut 13:11).

The values of God's reign sometimes depart sharply from those of modern secular culture. How hard might today's readers need to work to recover this alien value scale? What would it take for them to appreciate Deuteronomy's utter rejection of all enslaving idols—even that most relevant of modern false gods, the preservation of human life at all cost? What is of unrestricted value for the book of Deuteronomy is not biology's life-breath but following the one true God who both kills *and resurrects* (Deut 32:39), holding on to the God of resurrection cost what it will (Deut 13:4-5).

The language of Deuteronomy 13 is outrageous, "either-or" language of radical discipleship (Luke 14:26 is a relevant parallel). It is costly language of giving up an old world and embracing an alien one. It is "warfare" language, pitting the new world of God against the old world of Egyptian bondage. In a time of "war," all stakes are high, the costs total, and people's guts tell them that traitors must die. The total response of devotion required by this chapter only makes sense as a rally cry to "troops" preparing to cross over a liminal divide and mount an "occupation" of God's ideal world.

On close inspection, chapter 13 is consumed with renouncing an old world, "taking up arms" against it, and embracing God's new salvation. To make such moves is to carry out the first commandment of the Decalogue: "I am the LORD your God, who brought you out of the land of Egypt, out of the house of slavery; you shall have no other gods before me" (Deut 5:6-7). Both v. 5 and v. 10 of our passage echo the commandment, using the self-same phrasing: "the LORD your God"; "brought you out of the land of Egypt"; "the house of slavery." The commandment rejects "the house of slavery" as alien and false. Its decisive "no" to the Egypt of the past (and to the Assyria of its present) is an act of world renunciation. Thus, Deuteronomy's talk of traitors and their execution is meant as morally challenging language, depicting the trek with God as the arduous work of beating a path out of falsehood and violence.

But not all ancient readers of chapter 13 rightly appropriated its costly language of world renunciation. Brushing aside the thought of communal catechesis, some used the chapter as a down-and-dirty weapon. I refer to the foes of Jeremiah. When the prophet dared to indict the temple establishment, his enemies schemed to denounce him, to turn him in as a traitor (Jer 20:10; 26:8). In this they proved false to the spirit of our text, which pushes to prevent, not encourage, retaliatory accusations against the vulnerable.

Even in imagining a coming world where the awe of God is everywhere tangible, chapter 13 backs off more than once from *ideal* vision in order to recognize *real* challenges. The text and its later editors were well aware that in the real world, this side of Kingdom Come, people must exercise extreme caution about dangerous "either-or" language. Such language is arguably crucial in opening eyes to see ultimate reality (again, cf. Jesus' words at Luke 14:26), but it is notoriously vulnerable to abuse.

The real world of moral duplicity comes to the fore in 13:12-18. In dictating the destruction of cities enticed to idolatry, the section insists on preventing any headlong rush to judgment. The text proscribes precipitous action by rival cities; reports of mutiny must never be taken at face value. Verse 14 insists that Israel exercise suspicion, ask questions, probe: the people must "inquire," they must "make a thorough investigation." What is more, the colorful wording of v. 17 seems at least partially aimed at scoundrels, who might try to grab a city's wealth through trumped up charges. The wealth of renegade cities must not stick to anyone's fingers in the wake of battle.

The real world also emerges in 13:9-10. At first blush the text of v. 9a seems to allow, and even promote, immediate and perfunctory executions of traitors. There was some precedent for this in Israel's traditions—cases of instant killings when the covenant was in clear and present danger (Exod 32:27 E; Deut 33:9). In addition, the language sounds a lot like the Vassal Treaty of Esarhaddon, noted above, which encourages a person uncovering a plot against the king's life to execute the perpetrator on the spot (if possible). The editors of Deuteronomy 13 immediately reverse the first impression. Those vulnerable to false accusation, such as Jeremiah, must be protected.

Immediately following the command of v. 9a to kill traitors, vv. 9b-10 introduce powerfully loaded language about casting the first stone. This idiomatic language echoes Deuteronomy 17:6-7. It evokes all of the key presuppositions in Deuteronomy 17 about due process (also cf. 19:15). No individual or clique, our text avers, is licensed to kill. Such licensing is much too dangerous; the world remains mired in moral ambiguity.

Chapter 13 employs the rhetoric of extreme cases, driving home the requirement of single-mindedness. Verses 1-5 insist that the people ignore anyone advocating other gods, even people wielding "omens or portents," that is, the "terrifying displays of power" that God unleashed at the exodus (Deut 4:34; 6:22; 7:18-19; 26:8; 29:2-3; Ps 78:43). God set such powers in the hand of Moses himself (Exod 4:21 E; Deut 34:11). Israel would certainly need to exercise great resolve to turn its back on someone the likes of Moses! Such is the intensity of determination that our passage enjoins.

Teaching the word of God remains central in the spiritual formation of the community (13:4). Over against such instruction, other accoutrements of prophecy, such as seeing visions and performing signs, take a back seat (see Num 12:6-8 E; Jer 23:25; 27:9). The essential prophetic role, for Deuteronomy, is to bring people and word into contact, binding people and God in freedom and closeness.

A second hypothetical scenario of temptation, vv. 6-11, shows that people must resist even clandestine incitements coming from intimate companions. Even the dearest of human bonds must not subvert the total love of God. The Hebrew of v. 6 singles out the full brother (it lacks the NRSV's phrasing, speaking only of "your brother, your mother's son"). This focus on the full brother (cf. Gen 43:29) reinforces how even the closest of relationships must not conflict with covenant loyalty. In like manner, the sensual Hebrew phrase "wife you embrace" betokens the most intense of intimacies.

Does Deuteronomy's passion about *total* allegiance, even in the most private of realms, smack of *totalitarianism*? Are not paranoid tyrants the ones whose tentacles extend into bedrooms and whispered conversations? The modern reader's mind jumps to George Orwell's imagined worlds in *Animal Farm* and *1984*. Recollection of the wider context of chapter 13, however, reveals such comparisons to be misguided.

We just observed in interpreting chapter 12 that Deuteronomy's God grants vassals the "freedom of the city," putting them at home and at liberty in God's land. Far from an interest in total control, this God beckons Israel on a pilgrimage away from all that is fixed and established toward God's radical otherness and its horizon-opening, community-ennobling power. A glance at chapter 12 is fitting, since chapter 13 as a whole may be viewed as a detailed elaboration of Deuteronomy 12:30, "Do not inquire concerning [alien] gods, saying, 'How did these nations worship their gods? I also want to do the same.'"

The final scenario of incitement, which vv. 12-18 describe, entails an entire city of Israel turning away from the Lord. Picking up on how v. 8 already echoed the divine-warrior tradition (cf. Deut 7:2), this section contains striking language of utter destruction (Heb., *kharam*). Verse 15 speaks of "utterly destroying" (*hakharem*) the offending city. Verse 17 directs the total transfer to the Lord of all spoil, the entirety of which is "devoted to destruction" (*hakherem*).

Deuteronomy has used this language before (2:34; 3:6; 7:2, 26), and we have found that interpreting it as "primitive violence" simply will not do. Deuteronomy's language of divine warfare is not about bloodshed and genocide, but about the divine warrior's victory over chaos and defilement. God's goal is forming a land set apart (Deut 2:25; 4:7; 26:19), a place to establish divine otherness and God's offer of true freedom and intimacy (see ch. 12). In direct line with this theme, 13:5 presents the reader with language of purging evil from Israel's midst. The theme will recur often in our book (17:7, 12; 19:19; 21:21; 22:21, 22, 24; 24:7), reinforcing the need to "sweep out evil" from Canaan's every nook and cranny (NJPS; cf. 1 Kgs 14:10). This clean sweep is crucial. In a land claimed *in toto* by the divine warrior, a land dedicated to the awe of God, an ideal Israel can branch and flower as a model of the ennobled human life. Israel may become a people bonded in community and relating directly to God.

The holism of Deuteronomy—its felt need for a community-wide approach to discipleship—is almost impossible for the modern age to grasp. Yet in Deuteronomy God wills to encounter God's people in communal solidarity, up and down all levels of society and across daily life. The society-wide assembly of the people at the central sanctuary catalyzes the encounter, but Israel's growth to maturity must be integral to daily life: something to accompany eating, working, walking around, and even sleeping.

A People Called by God's Name

Deuteronomy 14:1-29

Deuteronomy 14 finds a number of practices especially symbolic of living as a people of God's name, a privilege that the Decalogue's third commandment vests in Israel (Deut 5:11). How the chapter's detailed ceremonial rules connect with honoring God's name, however, is not immediately obvious. Chapter 14 requires readers to enter into thoughtful reflection on the true significance of Israel's traditional ritual requirements.

Choose Holiness, Choose Life, 14:1-2

The initial two verses of Deuteronomy 14 form a superscription, presenting two central themes of the chapter. Immediately, the reader encounters the thrust of how Deuteronomy wants to understand the third commandment. First, to bear God's name means to be God's own "children," to be "holy to the LORD your God." Second, the divine name links up with God's valuing of life, God's identity as the "living God" (Deut 5:26; cf. Hos 1:10).

"You are children of the LORD your God," v. 1 declares. The theme comes from Deuteronomy's sources (Exod 4:22-23 E; Hos 1:10; 11:1), and the book has sounded it before (Deut 1:31; 8:5). Later Deuteronomic texts will again draw on it (Jer 31:9; Mal 1:6; 2:10). Here in chapter 14, the theme becomes a ramification of the third commandment, a stipulation of the ideal character of all who bear God's name. Some in Israel would have felt stretched by this view. The traditions of Zion applied the theme more narrowly, stressing the king as God's true son (Pss 2:7; 89:26-27; 2 Sam 7:14).

For Deuteronomy, *all Israel*, up and down the gathered assembly, must wield God's name to invoke God's presence. With God's name upon the lips, Israel reconstitutes itself in binding communion. In using the name solemnly in oaths, the body of Israel defends social justice in God's land. In multiple such ways, God's name becomes the "umbilical" connection between God,

God's people, and God's land. To wield the name aright is to become a faithful child. God wants Israel as this child.

God, for Deuteronomy, is both intimate and dreadful, both parental sponsor and alien other. God proclaimed the divine name to Moses atop Mount Horeb as part of a near lethal self-revelation (Exod 33:18-20). Before that God had preserved the intense mystery enshrouding the name (Gen 32:29 E). Moses found himself privileged to wield God's personal name, but knew from the start its singularity and absoluteness (note the striking idiom in which he received it at Exod 33:19, as also at Exod 3:13 E). Humans will always find the name unnerving, in a category of its own: "it is unknowable!" (Judg 13:17-18, NJPS), "a name of wonder" (idem, NJB). The name's mystery and otherness mean that God can never attach it permanently to any particular sanctuary (Jer 7:12).

God's name thus marks God's child as interconnected with otherness, with apartness (14:2). Deuteronomy 14:21 echoes this sentiment: Israel's ceremonial rules set it apart as "a people holy to the LORD." Both v. 2 and v. 21 resonate with Deuteronomy 7:6, which makes the same declaration (cf. Exod 19:6 E/D), a declaration pertaining to all Israel. Ideally, the entire divine estate of Canaan should know the name of only one God, the Lord (Deut 12:3). Israelites of all types and in all locales should hallow the name.

To bear the divine name is to be God's holy child and also to uphold the wonder of life. Israel's holiness links up with the celebration of world-affirming, festive life. The theme is already clear in 12:7, 12, 18, and it comes back in the spotlight in vv. 23 and 26 of the present chapter. For this book, the ideal Israel is a community of festal *rejoicing* before the Lord (12:7, 12, 18; 14:26; 16:11; 27:7), a people embracing a ritual and existential stance antithetical to the deathly realm of mourning, corpses, and decay. Chapter 14 is all about symbolic expressions of Israel's ideal communal existence in purity and praise on earth. It is about stressing Deuteronomy's God as a partisan of life—full, expansive, rejoicing life (cf. Deut 4:1, 40, 42; 5:33; 8:1; 30:6, 19-20).

Addressing the people of God, Moses specifies in 14:1 that "You must not lacerate yourselves or shave your forelocks for the dead." Commentators commonly see v. 1 as an injunction against Canaanite practices, but this move is wrongheaded. Rather, Deuteronomy is being revolutionary again. It is legislating transformation, in the spirit of chapter 12's innovative demand for a single sanctuary. Laceration and shaving appear to be normal Israelite rites of mourning in Deuteronomy 21:12; Isaiah 22:12; Jeremiah 16:6; 41:4-5; Amos 8:10; Micah 1:16; 5:1 (see NJPS, NET). No pagan practice lurks behind Deuteronomy 14:1-2, just a standard (if extreme) part of Israelite mourning that the book wants halted.

No call to avoid a Canaanite rite, Deuteronomy 14 calls rather for an end to ritual actions that plunge too deep into the realm of death. Israel must practice the symbolic affirmation of robust, God-praising life. It must avoid funerary stubble, scabs, and scars, which are extreme, lasting signs of descent into death. Funerary acts such as tearing the garments, disheveling the hair, descending to the dust, and other common behaviors of Israelite mourning express identification with the plight of the dead, but only go so far. They assure the dead of honor and evoke their support of the living, but are easily reversed. The careful mourner can soon wash and dress and rejoin Israel's chorus of festive praise (Ps 115:17-18). Not so with shaving and laceration—acts that by contrast take time to reverse. They more lastingly and strikingly link an individual's body with the realm of death—the unclean, irrational enemy of God and God's people.

When persons with lasting funerary marks rejoin the community and its worship, they present a visual confusion of rejoicing and mourning. They combine incompatible categories, creating a mixture abhorrent to Israelite ritual symbolism. This symbolism upholds the value of living praise by isolating rejoicing from mourning in any given person or group (see Isa 22:12-14; 35:10; Neh 8:9-12). As Saul M. Olyan (2005, 122–23) writes,

> Once shaved, the hair of the head or beard grows back only gradually over an extended period of time. Similarly, lacerated body parts take time to heal, and laceration may leave permanent, exposed scars. . . . In a word, shaving and laceration have the potential to become mourning markers "out of place," visible tokens of mourning on the bodies of those who have abandoned the mourning ritual stance and shifted to a posture of rejoicing.

Prior to this chapter's composition, central priests responsible for Leviticus 21:5-6 sought to prohibit funerary shaving and laceration for officiants at the temple's altar. Subsequently, Deuteronomy 14:1-2 (along with Lev 19:27-28) democratized the prohibition in the conviction that all Israel was holy to the Lord. Razor stubble, scabs, and scars simply did not fit in with Deuteronomy's vision of the sacred rejoicing of a holy people.

Ritual Requirements for Table Fellowship, 14:3-21

The concluding command of vv. 3-21 encapsulates the thrust of the section: "You are a people holy to the LORD your God. You shall not boil a kid in its mother's milk" (14:21). The hoary prohibition is a ritual training in holiness, in living as a people who reflect God's mystery and love of life. The command sets life and death at odds. Deuteronomy abhors the contamination of life by death.

Verse 21 polarizes two opposites: life-giving mother's milk on the one hand and the deathful reality of a slaughtered kid on the other. The fusing of such opposites is anathema for Deuteronomy. To make mother's milk—a baby's lifeblood—part of how the baby becomes a meal is to upturn the world, to fuse and confuse life and death (cf. 22:6-7). Keeping life and death distinct and bounded is a fundamental value in Deuteronomy, a core conviction that the book embeds in ritual symbolism.

By observing the commands of vv. 3-21, God's people practice keeping life and death from mixing, practice keeping the kid out of its mother's milk. As an integral system, the regulations emphasize the separation of the living from the chaotic and the deathly. As they prepare, cook, and share meals, the children of Israel become a people of *life*. They take up a stance of defiance against chaos, refusing to accept darkness and decay as a natural, inevitable part of existence. Covenant life is set apart—distinct, holy.

The concern to contain death, to hold it at arm's length, lies behind most every rule of vv. 3-21. The entire discussion revolves around animals slated for death; the context of the rules is the human consumption of once living beings. When in contact with the sphere of death, Israel must consider itself on eggshells, even in a minefield.

Some dead animals are more "deathful" than others. That which "you find already dead" (v. 21, NIV) is now a corpse (idem, NET), the most impure item in Israel's ritual system. Never must God's people use rotting carrion as food (cf. Exod 22:31), especially since a carcass not drained of lifeblood is very much a mixture of death and life (cf. Deut 12:16, 23-25). Neither should they eat animals that feed on carrion, thus bearing "death" within their bodies (e.g., the vulture and the buzzard, 14:12, 17).

Most of the prohibited animals in the passage are carnivores, symbolizing the threat of mauling and death. The system thus reduces Israel's diet to a few domesticated herbivores along with some wild game, fish, birds, and locusts. The underlying message is apparent: a fundamental reverence for life is basic to God's will and God's blessing.

Misperceptions swirl around the meaning of ceremonial uncleanness in the Scriptures. Contrary to a popular belief, such rules are not pre-modern stabs at hygiene and health. Verse 21 excludes the idea, for it permits the transfer of unclean food to resident aliens, against whom Deuteronomy bears no ill will (see v. 29). Neither are the food commands superstitious assaults on segments of the animal kingdom. Ritual categories are *not* value judgments. There is nothing inherently sinful or ugly about a stork (thus Job 39:13 describes the stork as magnificent, see NJPS, NIV; on God's care of the stork, see Ps 104:17; on the raven as precious, see Ps 147:9). To mark animals as unclean does not diminish them, but prevents their consumption and honors their lives.

Contrary to all misconceptions, Deuteronomy's dietary rules are nothing more and nothing less than a symbolic construct, a ritual program for forming Israel into a holy community, distinctively hallowing the name of the God of life.

Deuteronomy is aware that dualistic, "either-or" rhetoric is vulnerable to misunderstanding and twisting. It thus insists on breaking out of polarizing language of purity and impurity long enough to remember the aliens among the people. These resident aliens are no enemies of the covenant but specifically its beneficiaries (see 5:14; 10:18; 16:11, 14; 24:19-21; 26:11-13; 29:11). They enjoy a justice identical to that of the Israelites with whom they sojourn (1:16; 24:14, 17; 27:19). Israel is commanded to "love the stranger," even the one who eats lobsters and shrimp (10:19). Material in the next section of the chapter explicitly parallels this theme (14:28-29).

Tithes and Firstlings, 14:22-29

By bringing in tribute, Israel honors the third "name" commandment. Tithes and firstlings belong to the deity, Israel's Lord, whose name lies upon the land of Canaan, whose claim extends to its entire populace and bounty. In making these offerings, Israel affirms one umbilical connection between the land and heaven—a connection to the Lord alone. But the practice does more. It marks the people as partakers of the sacred aura of God's name.

Other Scriptures view the tithe as a tax in support of the sanctuary (Lev 27:30-33; Num 18:21-29). Deuteronomy 14 places the focus instead on the people's own enjoyment of the fruits of the land, on their rejoicing before the Lord. What is central is the portion of the tax that the people themselves enjoy, feasting on firstlings, oil, wine, and strong drink (14:23, 26). Feasting and celebration mark *holiness*. Nehemiah affirmed it in no uncertain terms: "This day is holy to the LORD your God; do not mourn. . . . Eat the fat and drink sweet wine and send portions of them to those for whom nothing is prepared, for this day is holy to our LORD" (Neh 8:9-10). The prophets take the same view, envisioning sacred festivity as a mark of God's holy reign (cf. Isa 35:8-10; 51:11).

In the final two verses of chapter 14, Deuteronomy provides for those with no access to wealth through control of land. Israel should store up the tithe every third year, keeping it in reserve out in the land for those without steady farm income. Although this special third-year tithe does not go to the temple, it is still considered holy, a "sacred portion" (Deut 26:13). Here again, holiness functions not to weed people out from amid God's elect but to draw people closer in human mutuality. This system for sharing Israel's wealth encompasses even non-Israelites, the resident aliens living in the land.

A People of Sacred Interruptions

Deuteronomy 15:1–16:17

"Remember that you were a slave in the land of Egypt," the fourth commandment adjures; if you do, you will keep the Sabbath (Deut 5:15). The commandment's overt aim is to carve out a Sabbath life of *freedom* antithetical to Israel's visceral memories of slavery. The book of Deuteronomy now turns to a number of rules that it finds especially pertinent to enjoying a divine service that is perfect freedom.

At first glance, one strains to interconnect commands about the relief of debt (15:1-11), about the release of debt servants (15:12-18), about sacrificing firstlings (15:19-23), and about festivals (16:1-17). How does this diverse material cohere and serve to illuminate the fourth Sabbath commandment?

Upon reflection, all four sets of commands, each in its own way, appear to foster a discipline of "sacred interruption." Israel must have "Sabbath" breaks, a sort of sacral breathing room. With this fresh space, people may turn their focus away from self-concern and ambition. They may experience sacred freedom in God's intimate presence.

God has delivered Israel out of slavery into God's sanctuary land, a place of "rest" (Heb., *nuakh*; Deut 12:9-10; cf. Exod 33:14). The people are about to enter a land where residents have "freedom of the city," where they are primed and enabled to seek out true human liberty. With "rest" as the key, the people may form a "Thou" over against God's "I." Secure here in God's territory, they may come up against God's eerie freedom in true subjectivity and openness to the future. As they do, "freedom meets freedom," and all push ahead on the open journey of creative human transformation.

"The LORD your God redeemed you; for this reason I lay this command upon you today," states Moses at 15:15, echoing the fourth commandment (5:15). For God to have "redeemed" Israel from Egypt means for God to have repossessed what is rightfully God's. Israel is God's possession, God's patrimony (e.g., 9:26; 32:9). The identity puts real limits on ambition, on relentless straining for advantage. The people's lives are God's and not ultimately their own. Well-timed "sacred pauses" establish that.

For God to oppose Egyptian slavery is for God to side with life and dignity. Taking this stand, God puts the brakes of Sabbath on crushing debt (15:1-11), on servitude (15:12-18), on possessiveness (15:19-23), and even on any extended time away from togetherness in worship (16:1-17). Together, these "speed limits" constitute a powerfully concrete system of supporting all Israelite brothers' and sisters' dignity and membership in community. They sound a collective "no" to the slave-spirit of Egypt.

God's paranormal victory over Egyptian might shows that God has the means to forge Sabbath justice on earth. The God who defeated Egypt against all odds and carried Israel through the wilderness (1:30-31) is a God who can mount a preternatural pilgrimage out of selfishness. Modern readers of the global north strain to imagine how other-centeredness can ever be achieved in such realms as politics and economics. But Deuteronomy's vision of Israel's journey calls readers to just such an imagination.

Amid powerful imagination there is frank admission of challenges. The need for debt relief (vv. 1-3) implies a real world. In the here and now, loans put homesteads at risk. True, vv. 4-6 break with this reality, insisting that God's reign orient us: "There will, however, be no one in need among you, because the LORD is sure to bless you in the land" (v. 4). But, after this blessed moment of vision, we are back again in quotidian existence with vv. 7-11. Verse 11 admits, "There will never cease to be some in need."

Verses 4 and 7 of chapter 15 appear contradictory, but the passage knows what it is doing. Its central, utopian verses (vv. 4-6) insist on the highest of agendas. The surrounding stopgap measures (vv. 1-3, 7-11) train people to live into it.

The Relief of Debts, 15:1-11

The first "sacred interruption" insists on a relief of debts every seven years. The command aims to limit ambition, to urge remembrance that God's liberation from Egypt aimed at loftier dreams than mere free enterprise. By assigning debt relief to the "seventh year" (vv. 1, 9), the passage sounds the Sabbath theme. It reinforces the theme in its concern, echoing 5:14, to uplift and honor all members of society.

Some will always seize economic advantage, aided by lucky breaks, shrewd dealings, and focused effort. They will concentrate wealth in their silos and bring others into their debt. But putting the brakes on all this through a Sabbath interruption is an act of grace. It recognizes life's natural limits; any one individual can only use and enjoy so much wealth in a lifetime. Bunching up possessions is far less satisfying than aligning one's life with God's word, which claims God's people and draws them into covenantal interrelationship. For Deuteronomy, "One does not live by bread alone" (Deut 8:3).

Just what the text envisions by a relief of debt in the Sabbatical year is somewhat complicated to determine. The thrust of the provision is clear enough, however. It protects the covenant's physical infrastructure. The infrastructure buttressed families' and clans' well-being by assuring them permanent tenure on inherited farmlands.

As long as groups of kin had the produce of their lands available to them, they could sustain the life and dignity of all in their care, including distant relations and the landless (Levites, resident aliens, orphans, widows). Thus, family lands and their produce—the means of covenantal identity, group security, and human realization—had to remain the sacred possession of the group, not become a commodity. The Deuteronomic ideal is well expressed in the poetry of Micah 4:4, "They shall all sit under their own vines and under their own fig trees, and no one shall make them afraid."

The Sabbatical relief of debt aimed to help kin-groups keep their lands. At a minimum, it was a temporary "remission" (NRSV, NJB, NJPS), a "relaxation" (NAB), of a creditor's extraction of loan repayments, "the due that he claims from his fellow" (NJPS). Such extraction usually took the form of depriving families of the harvest from parcels of land held as collateral, that is, held as pledges that secured loans. Deuteronomy 15 instructs that during the seventh year, the harvest, produced on pledged properties need not go toward debt repayment. That year's payment would be deferred or written off. With more of their land temporarily back in their hands, families had a chance to secure their farms.

An earlier covenantal ideal had stipulated a Sabbatical "relaxation" from planting crops (Exod 23:10-11). During the seventh year, farms would lie fallow and the landless could eat what grew of itself. Deuteronomy reapplies the idea of a "relaxation." It alters the earlier law to protect the farmers on whom the landless depended. The seventh year would no longer see farmers, deprived of that year's income, falling victim to creditors. Rather, it would become a time for shoring up the core infrastructure of the entire community, the welfare of both landed and poor. Later readers, such as those behind the pledge of Nehemiah 10:31, have often not seen how Deuteromomy 15 supersedes Exodus 23 in this way. Rather, they have sought to harmonize the two laws.

While vv. 1-3 of this section establish a compulsory, regular pattern of debt relief, vv. 7-11 make a moral appeal to voluntarily adopt the spirit of the law, the spirit of generosity. They exhort readers to be neither "hard-hearted" nor "tight-fisted" (v. 8), to "give liberally" and "be ungrudging" (v. 10). This is fully in keeping with the book's desire to transform the mind, to inculcate God's ways in the heart and will.

The self-interested would immediately concoct workarounds to vv. 1-3. To ensure quick and full repayment, they would determine to make loans only when the year of remission was far enough out that the debt could be repaid before it arrived. It would be quite a burden, they would reason, to offer extended credit on the verge of a seventh, Sabbatical year when there would be no prospect of repayment beginning until harvest time at a late point in the eighth year. Verses 7-11 urge repudiating any such "mean thought" (v. 9). Powerful Hebrew grammar, with four emphatic imperative constructions in vv. 8, 10, 11, pushes readers to fully disavow the self-oriented "pharaoh" spirit.

Deuteronomy 15 vigorously implores readers, both ancient and modern, to live within God-given limits of human experience. It asks them to adopt a basic assumption: The clumping of resources by persons or groups results over time in a serious impoverishment of human mutuality. For the modern reader, such impoverishment is one of the greatest global threats that we face. Taking a cue from Deuteronomy 15, an adequate response must combine both society-wide, enforced legislation and voluntary, heartfelt commitment at the individual and small-group level.

The Release of Debt Servants, 15:12-18

The command to release indentured servants is a second sacred interruption within Israel's life. As noted above, v. 15 ties the verses about slaves directly to the Sabbath commandment through its quote of 5:15. God's liberality in freeing Israel from Egypt sets the example for Israel's freeing of held persons in the Sabbath year with generous provision. Note that the seventh year at issue here probably differs from the fixed Sabbatical year of 15:1-11. The year of servant release would vary depending on the date on which any given individual's servitude began. Although the text at hand does not envision a collective release in any one fixed year, Israel did know the possibility of such collective manumission (see Jer 34:8-11 and Lev 25:8-13, 39-43).

The emancipation from Egyptian slavery must be foundational in Israel's self-understanding, Deuteronomy avers. The liberated people of the liberating God must treat any practice of involuntary servitude as a minefield.

The *raison d'être* of the covenant is the struggle for freedom and fullness of life. Even the one sold to another Hebrew remains a covenantal brother or sister (v. 12, Hebrew *'akh*). The expected, standard terms "master" and "slave" do not even appear in the Hebrew text (contrary to the NRSV and in contrast to Exod 21:2), at least not until the topic of a willing commitment of permanent service is broached (v. 17). Any thought of harsh practices of slavery, practices with which Judeans were certainly familiar (see Jer 34:12-22), is thereby kept at arm's length.

A limited practice of temporary "bond" servitude over debts was a fact of life for ancient Israel. Deuteronomy 15 attempts to address and mitigate the reality. A few words of explanation may be helpful, since modern readers of the global north are far removed from the social norms of an advanced agrarian monarchy.

The vicissitudes of life in an agrarian monarchy—including ill health, infertility, bad luck, difficult markets, and drought—might have the harshest of repercussions. If for whatever reason crops failed to appear, borrowing for the next season would be requisite, and debts would arise. If it became persistent, hardship would preclude repayment of debts and force the selling off of land. Eventually the farming family would be forced to contemplate indentured servitude for one or more of its members—"slavery" (cf. Lev 25:39-44; Neh 5:5, 8; Job 24:9; Amos 2:6; Mic 2:9).

Forms of slavery were a hard reality in ancient Israel, but the commonplace assertion that the Scriptures never question the institution in no way fits Deuteronomy. Scholars quite unfairly cite texts such as "Slaves, obey your earthly masters" (Eph 6:5; Col 3:22) as evidence of the Bible's ambivalence about slavery. Alongside its realistic pragmatism, with accompanying stopgap strategies, Deuteronomy has a utopian vision that abhors all forms of human degradation. The book advocates a community completely free of slavery in all its guises. It voices an unambiguous demand: "There should be no poor among you" (Deut 15:4, NIV). To realize the demand is to remove the reality of slavery from Israel.

Deuteronomy goes beyond earlier covenantal tempering of slavery (Exod 21:2-11). In particular, it treats men and women equally. It extends the same liberatory protections to bondwomen as those to be enjoyed by male servants. Deuteronomy also goes beyond Exodus 21 in demanding that servants be released with generous provision.

Sacrificing Firstlings, 15:19-23

The next "sacred interruption" in the series is the requirement to relinquish possession of firstborn animals. The language of consecrating firstling males calls to mind the events and instructions of the exodus, when God instituted the firstborn laws (Deut 15:19 echoes Exod 13:2, 12 E). From the start, this section suggests that sacrificing firstlings is another way to "remember that you were a slave in the land of Egypt" (Deut 5:15), that is, another way to observe the Sabbath. Verse 19 drives home the connection to the fourth commandment with the phrase, "you shall not do work with your firstling ox," which echoes Deuteronomy 5:14.

God's emancipation of Israel from Egypt established God's power to overcome selfishness, to establish other-centeredness on earth. Pharaoh could not stand in the way. His life breath and that of every living thing in his land was God's to give and God's to take (cf. Deut 32:39). God instituted the firstborn commands so that Israel might never forget this truth (Exod 13:15-16 E).

The theme of the firstling sacrifices—and indeed of the exodus story as a whole in E—is heavily bound up with God's terrible claim on the life of all creation (see Exod 4:23; 11:5; 12:29; 13:2, 11-16 all E). God's claim on what is firstborn signals God's claim on everything that breathes.

Deuteronomy 15 effectively expands Sabbath virtue to include reverence for God's ownership of all life, all creation. Limits on human economic exploitation, the text adjures, must be interconnected with limits on human exploitation of natural life. "Forgive your debtors *and* give over your firstlings!" is Deuteronomy 15's holistic demand. The call rings as loud as ever in today's readers' ears, readers living in a world where the global press for economic profit entails a headlong rush toward ecological collapse.

Concerning Festivals, 16:1-17

Israel's requirement to go on festival pilgrimages forms the final "sacred inter-ruption" of 15:1–16:17. These feasts (Passover, Weeks, and Booths) are major breaks taken from daily life to assemble at the central sanctuary, offering tribute gifts to God, worshiping, celebrating, and sharing with those in need. At the sanctuary's pilgrimage feasts, Israel reorients itself on God's emancipating presence, a presence manifest both in God's word and in communal togetherness.

For Deuteronomy, observing such assemblies is part of the wider meaning of keeping the Sabbath holy. To embrace Sabbath virtue is to step off the daily treadmill, the grinding march of "work-and-get-ahead," and partake of sacred time, ensconced in a circle of holy rejoicing. A repeated use of the number "seven" reinforces the Sabbath theme (16:3, 4, 8, 9, 13, 15); indeed, the term "seven(th)" occurs seven times in this section! There are also repeat references to liberation from Egyptian slavery, the Deuteronomic basis for Sabbath observance (16:1, 3, 6, 12), and a very Sabbatarian-sounding command to "do no work" on the "seventh day" of eating unleavened bread (16:8).

Fittingly, Deuteronomy 16 turns to the Festival of Passover immediately after chapter 15's treatment of the firstborn law. The manumission from Egypt, at least in the E source, was all about firstlings. At the exodus, the blood of the Passover lambs specifically marked Israel as a firstling, God's firstborn child—a people subject to God's awful claim on all firstborn creatures (see Exod 4:22-23 E). For the Israelite, to partake of the Passover was to recognize that one's life was not one's own (see Exod 13:15 E). It was to submit utterly to God's sovereign claim on one's life breath (Exod 13:16 E), to forfeit one's life and then, paradoxically, to receive it back ennobled.

For Deuteronomy, this is the central goal of the Sabbath-oriented life. By thrusting aside selfishness and ambition, that is, one's ego-centeredness, the Sabbath observer becomes God's true vassal. As this vassal subject, one discovers "perfect freedom," that is, one finds deep contentment, human fulfillment, and relational mutuality.

Deuteronomy makes its own distinctive presentation of Israel's major festivals, with some departures from other scriptural depictions. There is a patent emphasis on feasting and celebration (16:11, 14, 15), which Deuteronomy understands to be a mark of Israel's unique holiness (see the interpretation of 14:22-29 above). There is also Deuteronomy's recurring theme of the all-encompassing hospitality of the central shrine, which includes daughters, slaves, Levites, resident aliens, orphans, and widows (16:11, 14; contrast the emphasis solely on males in Exod 23:17; 34:23). As we have seen, this inclusive welcome sounds repeatedly in Deuteronomy (12:7, 12, 18-19; 14:26-27; 15:20; 26:11). (The "male" language of 16:16-17 is vestigial; these summarizing verses recycle formulaic language from Exod 23:17 without fully updating it.)

Perhaps most striking, Deuteronomy 16 makes the revolutionary move of transferring celebration of the Passover to the central sanctuary (cf. Levinson, 95). It jarringly abandons the celebration's traditional locus in Israelite homes (Deut 16:2, 5-7, in contrast to Exod 12:46). What is more, the text combines Passover with the originally separate pilgrimage feast of Unleavened Bread, transforming the latter into a sort of reverse-pilgrimage out from the central shrine and back to the people's cities and towns (16:4, 7).

Of course, Deuteronomy reasons, the covenantal oneness of Passover should be actualized in physical togetherness at God's one shrine. The Passover blood, for Deuteronomy, marks the people's life-breath as God's and God's alone. It draws them together as co-vassals under the covenant.

The echo of 5:30 in the command to undertake a reverse pilgrimage, "go back to your tents" (v. 7), jumps out at the reader (cf. McConville, 274). It returns the reader directly to the events at Mount Horeb. It drives home how Passover is now Israel's primary recapitulation of the Horeb experience. Passover, in Deuteronomy, has become the paramount occasion for Israel to cyclically reconstitute itself as the uniquely loved, holy firstling of God.

At Passover, Israel re-members itself as a collective, holy "Thou," intent on encountering God in true freedom. Having re-experienced the encounter in awesome directness, the people disperse to their "tents," taking with them their rejoicing, their holiness, and their truly liberated spirits. The "solemn assembly" of 16:8 (NRSV) should be seen as an infusion of the Sabbatical spirit throughout the land. It is a Sabbath celebration up and down the country with no work allowed, a "holy day in honor of the LORD" (NLT).

Leadership and Polity for God's People

Deuteronomy 16:18–18:22

Deuteronomy's legal core now proceeds to interpretation of the fifth commandment: "Honor your father and your mother" (5:16). Strikingly, Deuteronomy understands this commandment to transcend family dynamics. There are subsections here on judges (16:18–17:13), on kings (17:14-20), on altar ministers (18:1-8), and on prophets (18:9-22). Deuteronomy offers a holistic vision of authority, a vision that tempers the use of power by all who wield it. It aims to foster restraint on the part of those in charge.

Some background to Deuteronomy's perspective may be helpful. Traditional Israel was a tribe, a huge family (see Cook 2004, 160–61). The core building block of the people's "family tree" was the extended family, the "house of the father." To honor elders and parents meant to uphold the basic unit structuring Israel's life, to empower local family networks and community at large. For Deuteronomy, the fifth commandment aims to build up an entire society interlocked by caring, nurturing *family* ties.

In traditional Israel, clans and families ideally held their lands in perpetuity. Thus, for Deuteronomy, to speak of honoring the father and the mother is to use language about preserving lineages on their lands. It is to uphold and protect the material and economic supports that allowed the covenant to do its work. Upholding Israel's "umbilical" lines of support was crucial. As with chapter 15's program of debt relief, Deuteronomy is bent on protecting extended families from the greed and callousness that came with monarchic society (cf. Mic 2:2, 9; 3:2-3).

In an era when Assyrian imperialism and despotism were pervasive realities, Deuteronomy's insistence on distributing authority and empowering the periphery must have stood out. Against the drive to concentrate power, which was manifest in both Assyria and monarchic Israel, Deuteronomy defends a counter vision of dignity and authority spread *across* human community. Similarly, the book's countercultural boldness reveals itself as the fifth commandment spreads power by including the mother along with the father in the demand to honor the lineage.

Deuteronomy looks to a transformation of the human spirit rooted in community—in empowered and intentional community. It wants society as a whole to reassert its collective responsibility. Moses had earlier demanded collective responsibility, insisting that Israel approve his justice system *as a body of the whole.* "The plan you have proposed is a good one," the people had declared (1:14). Now, he addresses the people as a collective "you" in his command to implement the system locally (16:18). Once settled, Israel will periodically renew its responsibility (31:10-13).

Judges, 16:18–17:13

Offering an alternative vision to the concentration of judicial power in a royal center, Deuteronomy decentralizes and disperses the judiciary. Judges and civil servants must base themselves throughout Israel's tribes, in all its settlements (16:18). Their work must accord with the idiom of local, tribal wisdom (16:19b; cf. Prov 17:23; 18:5). The motivation is the singular pursuit of covenantal justice up and down God's land (Deut 16:20; 17:2, 7). God, not the king, guarantees covenantal justice (Deut 16:20). The reader has already encountered the focus on traditional, localized justice back in Deuteronomy 1, where phrases such as "throughout your tribes" have already appeared (Deut 1:15).

Deuteronomy wants traditional judicial figures, the local elders of each settlement, empowered to enforce justice. It references them in the phrase "judges and officials" used at the start of the section (16:18). Deuteronomy 1:15-16 had already honed in on tribal lineage heads as the best judges (the text is an inner-biblical rehearsal of Num 11:16 and Exod 18:21, 25, both E). Deuteronomy 21:1-9, 19; 22:15; 25:7 will also emphasize elders' judicial authority.

Deuteronomy also wants the Levites, Israel's age-old *priestly* line, included in Israel's "judges and magistrates" (Deut 16:18). The people's traditional priests should return to their posts at the "gates," the public precincts at town entrances that formed localized settings of court proceedings (Deut 21:19; Ruth 4:1, 11; Job 29:7; Lam 5:14). A deliberate cross-referencing between Deuteronomy 21:5 and 17:8 confirms how the book wants Levites exercising their legal skills in the gates. By citing the latter text, Deuteronomy 21:5 shows it understands the Levitical adjudication of "all cases of dispute and assault" to take place specifically in local gate settings (the Hebrew word "gates" lies behind the NRSV's "towns" in 17:8; cf. NLT: "a local court").

Some ritual prohibitions in 16:21–17:1 appear to interrupt the focus on an ideal judicial system. Far from being out of place, however, these prohibitions embody and summarize the aim of all judicial enforcement: fostering an intensive, holistic adherence to the Lord. Deuteronomy's demand for just authority in the land coheres with its requirement to reverence the land's sovereign Lord.

Israel should understand God's sovereign presence as both daunting and magnetic. Sacred poles and stone pillars must go. Such objects imply that divine presence can be hosted, managed ("real *absence*" is crucial to Israel's intense experience of God, see above on 12:3). So too, sacrifices with blemishes are intolerable. Symbols of wholeness within Israel's worship proclaim the demanding nearness of God (cf. 15:21).

A set of verses follows in 17:2-7, referencing the treason of serving "other gods" (cf. 13:6-11). The verses appear to continue the topic of forbidden worship, but actually provide an example of sound judicial process. Especially in capital crimes, like this case, Israel must assure the rights of the accused through due process, particularly through reliance on responsible witnesses (also see 19:15-21).

The next section in 17:8-13 elaborates Moses' instructions about difficult legal cases back in Deuteronomy 1:17. A high court should be available to hear cases that cannot be solved locally, "in your gates" (17:8, literal translation). Even within the high court, however, final authority still rests with tribal leaders, with Levites and elders ("the judge," vv. 9, 12; "the judges," 19:17-18). The crown has no role here. Rather, figures from outside the royal capital represent the values and interests of all Israel's kin-groups. The concern is to keep "all the people" (v. 13), the whole of "Israel" (v. 12), a holy community purged of evil (v. 7). In a world where the elite of Assyria arrogated imperial authority to themselves, Deuteronomy's political vision of a checked monarch and integrated society is downright astonishing.

The justices of the high court remain resident out in the land of Judah, among the people whose interests they represent. Verse 9 with its reference to being "on duty at that time" (NLT) assumes a rotation system that brings Levites and elders from peripheral locales into the center for fixed periods. Their presence at the center exerts covenantal leverage against all temptations of the monarchy to pursue domination and tyranny.

Kings, 17:14-20

The covenant of Mount Horeb recognized only one true suzerain over Israel. For the Lord's vassals to elevate one of their number to kingship flies in the face of Horeb's spirit (see Judg 8:23). Beyond creating a human stand-in for God, it allows for an extraction of goods and services from local communities at potentially destructive levels.

A suspicion of monarchy is evident across the source-texts of Deuteronomy. Hosea 13:10, for example, sarcastically queries an Israel under attack for its sins, "Where now is your king, that he may save you? Where in all your cities are your rulers, of whom you said, 'Give me a king and rulers'?" The same skepticism about kingship appears in Micah 5:1 and in the B source of Samuel (1 Sam 8:7, cf. 10:19; 12:12). Such texts understand that the people literally wrested kingship out of a resistant God. At one point in Hosea, God furiously reminds Israel, "I gave you a king in my anger" (Hos 13:11; cf. 8:4). God can imagine no reason for Israel to want a king other than a desire to be "like all the nations" (Deut 17:14; cf. 1 Sam 8:5, 20).

Assuming the negative posture of its sources toward kingship, Deuteronomy 17 agrees that God's people would be none the worse if they had never established a monarchy. Since they appear stuck with one, however, their torah must now come to grips with the extant reality. It must apply stringent regulation tempering the monarchy's role.

Israel's king must never presume sacral status, must never boast of being God's son (cf. Pss 2:7; 89:26-27, 36; Isa 9:6-7). He must ever remain a co-vassal, a covenantal "brother" ('akh, Deut 17:15). By diligently observing the covenant, he is to learn "to fear the LORD his God," never "exalting himself above other members of the community ['ekhayw, 'his brothers']" (vv. 19-20). He should forgo hopes for a dynasty. God, not automatic privilege, decides who is king (vv. 15, 20; cf. Hos 8:4).

The king must have no standing army (v. 16). Instead, he must rely on old Israel's practice of mustering troops from tribes and clans in times of crisis. The king must not "acquire many wives," building up a harem (v. 17a). Taking foreign wives sealed foreign treaties, allegiances in conflict with the Horeb covenant. More seriously, such wives introduced foreign worship. Finally, the king must not stockpile wealth (v. 17b). Royal extraction of wealth threatened the covenant's land-vested networks for nurturing God's people. Families and clans must enjoy security on their farms.

The king's basic task according to Deuteronomy 17:18-20 is continuously to study his copy of the torah, carefully certified by the Levites as true and correct (cf. Deut 31:9). As Levinson (141) remarks, this hamstrung monarch is consigned "to 'read each day of his life' from the very Torah that delimits his powers." His study of law appears to have no practical judicial purpose. The Levites and the elders, not the monarch and his state bureaucrats, are those qualified to render final judgment based on their vocational expertise in covenantal instruction and interpretation (vv. 10, 18; cf. 31:9, 25-26; 33:10; 2 Kgs 17:27-28). This is in pointed contrast to the assumptions of other biblical traditions (such as those of Ps 72:1-4; 1 Sam 8:5-6; 1 Kgs 3:9; Isa 9:7; 11:2-5).

Although King Josiah (reigned 640–609 BCE) first brought Deuteronomy's torah to prominence in Israel, it appears that he resisted its vision of a stymied monarchy. His aggressive exercise of kingship runs roughshod over Deuteronomy 17:14-20. Especially his entanglement in worship, including his heavy-handed supervision of the Passover (cf. 2 Kgs 23:21), is strikingly non-Deuteronomic. Adopting a brazen revisionism, he appears to have harmonized Deuteronomic law and the interests of the crown (for discussion, see Launderville, 322; Cook 2011, 166). The historians of 2 Kings, sympathetic to Josiah, would scarcely have invented his authoritarian handling of Deuteronomy.

Altar Ministers, 18:1-8

"The LORD your God has chosen Levi out of all your tribes, to stand and minister in the name of the LORD, him and his sons for all time" (v. 5). Any Levite passionate about altar service may minister at the central shrine, "like all his fellow-Levites who stand to minister there" (v. 7). Breaking with current practice, 18:1-8 makes sacrificing at God's altar the prerogative of the entire tribe of Levi, not just of the monarchy's priests.

From its start, this subsection breathes the air of old Israel, embracing its ideal of inalienable tribal land. Verses 1-2 understand all tribes to have an inheritance within Israel's territory. The Levites, however, have the Lord rather than territory as an inheritance. Their means of sustenance is not crops but worshipers' offerings and parts of sacrifices (see Deut 33:10b; Josh 13:14). Now, after many disruptions of this income in the course of history (see 1 Sam 2:36; 1 Kgs 2:27; 12:31; 13:33; 2 Chr 13:9; Ps 78:60-61), the Levites would finally experience full re-enfranchisement, even in Jerusalem.

Scholars commonly claim that Deuteronomy 18's vision for re-enfranchising the Levites, restoring their full priesthood, was an ideal essentially dead on arrival. Based on 2 Kings 23:9, a text about King Josiah's implementation of Deuteronomy, they argue that the powers-that-be in Jerusalem thwarted the hopes of "the priests of the shrines" (NJPS), that is, the country Levites who had presided over worship in the towns. Despite Deuteronomy's hopes, these priests "did not ascend the altar of the LORD in Jerusalem" (2 Kgs 23:9, NJPS). Modern English translations, however, seem to misunderstand the Hebrew of 2 Kings 23. The scholarly consensus, it would appear, is completely wrong.

Second Kings 23:9 uses a specialized "unless and until" Hebrew syntax that gives it a meaning almost opposite to that sounded in common English translations (see Cook 2011, 164). What the text actually says is the following: "The priests of the town shrines did not go up to the altar of the LORD in Jerusalem *until* they ate unleavened bread among their brethren [= fellow Israelites]." That is, it conveys that King Josiah *did* allow country Levites to minister at Jerusalem's altar, but *only after* they affirmed their loyalty by properly celebrating the Festival of Unleavened Bread (see Deut 16:1-8).

In Josiah's interpretation of Deuteronomy 16:1-8, everyone was to remain in the capital for both Passover and the subsequent Unleavened Bread feast (see 2 Chr 35:17). This would have cut against traditional Levitical practice. The Levites were accustomed to presiding over local celebrations of the festival (Exod 13:6). By eating "unleavened bread" in Jerusalem, they were buying into Josiah's program. Josiah apparently demanded that all Levites wishing for his patronage observe things his way. They had to prove their loyalty by staying in Jerusalem and eating "unleavened bread among their brethren," that is, amid the assembly still gathered at Jerusalem for Passover ("brothers" means members of the covenant community; cf. Deut 1:16; 3:20; 10:9; 15:7; 17:15).

Jerusalem would not accommodate a permanent presence of Levites in the numbers assumed in 2 Kings 23:8-9, so a system of rotating Levites is likely in view. We have seen a similar rota system embraced in Deuteronomy 17:9. In such a system, a Levite would ordinarily be resident "anywhere in Israel," but might "visit" the Jerusalem temple periodically to perform altar service (Deut 18:6, NAB).

Prophets, 18:9-22

Deuteronomy considers prophets to be leaders in Israel alongside judges, kings, and altar priests. Prophets differ from other leaders, however, in several notable respects. Factors such as gender, age, and lineage have little bearing on eligibility for the prophetic office. Like the divine word that they bear, prophets are free of such delimitations. Partaking of the pure freedom of God, they play a truly creative role in history. As channels of revelation and as covenantal mediators, they inject God's personal sovereignty into Israel's collective life. They make God a tangible factor in the leadership of Israel.

Verses 9-14 begin the subsection on prophets by describing forms of intermediation forbidden to the covenantal community. The voice and power of God do not come through such means as witchery, séances, or channeling the dead. It is not that Deuteronomy would dishonor the ancestral dead or claim they are forever gone. It is rather that the book understands the alluring power of the underworld to threaten to corrupt Israel. All attempts to domesticate the supernatural—connected with Sheol or not—represent offenses against God's otherness. One cannot tame divinity. The Lord has a name that is "unknowable" (Judg 13:17-18, NJPS), "a name of wonder" (idem, NJB).

Verses 15-19 turn to discuss a unique type of prophet whom Moses refers to as the "prophet like me." To stand in the footsteps of Moses is to be God's unique channel of revelation—a singular mediator of God's covenant. Unlike the case with ordinary prophets, God communicated with Moses "face to face" (Deut 34:10). Such a prophet meets directly with the Lord, sees and hears the divine word, takes it all in, and then proclaims it and lives it out (see Jer 23:18).

The tradition of Moses' uniqueness predates Deuteronomy, appearing already in the E strand at Numbers 12 (cited by Deut 24:9). There, God declares that Moses differs from ordinary prophets who receive revelation only in the form of visions and dreams (Num 12:6; cf. Deut 13:1; Jer 23:28). "Not so with my servant Moses," God asserts. "He is entrusted with all my house" (12:7). Indeed, God continues, "With him I speak face to face—clearly, not in riddles; and he beholds the form of the LORD" (12:8).

Moses risked his life at Horeb, ablaze with fire, to stand between Israel and the Lord, to declare to the people the words of the Lord (Deut 18:16-17; cf. 5:5, 22-31; 9:15; Exod 20:19 E). The divine presence had passed before Moses and the divine name had rung out in verbal revelation (Exod 33:19 E). Hence, Moses came to know the Lord, to latch on to God. In turn, God empowered him as a unique intermediary. Through Moses, God's "irrepressible whisper" (1 Kgs 19:12) unleashed itself amid Israel.

What is most amazing about Moses is not the physical person (cf. Deut 1:9, 12) but the phenomenon of embodying God's irrepressible revelation. "Is not my word like fire, says the LORD, and like a hammer that breaks a rock in pieces?" (Jer 23:29). God's creative word must continue its work in the world, tearing down idolatry, renewing community, ushering in God's reign. To ensure that this work continues, God's promise is to repeatedly raise up prophets in Moses' line to direct Israel's journey to Kingdom Come.

Moses' role continues in Joshua (e.g., Josh 5:15), Samuel (e.g., 1 Sam 12:23), Elijah (e.g., 1 Kgs 19:8), and Elisha (e.g., 2 Kgs 2:8, 14). Jeremiah, the greatest prophetic proponent of Deuteronomy's theology, was perhaps the ultimate bearer of the Mosaic mantle. According to Jeremiah 1, the Lord stretched out the divine hand, touched Jeremiah's mouth, and inserted the divine word (v. 9). Mirroring Moses' precedent, Jeremiah directly receives God's revelation—*hand delivered* (see Deut 18:18).

Deuteronomy's provision for Moses to have successors means that Moses must die. The book has stressed the significance of Moses's death before (see Deut 1:37; 3:23-29: 4:21; 9:18, 25). It has impressed upon the reader that all who expose themselves to God's fiery presence, as Moses does, forfeit their lives (Deut 5:26-27).

Moses' death in Deuteronomy has richly suggestive meanings. His death launches a new spirit of selflessness and sacrifice in Israel. In symbolizing the people's movement through death to new life, his demise becomes foundational for the people's rebirth. Moses' death becomes a portal to God's presence.

The death of Moses conveys the radical mystery of God's paradoxical presence with God's people. That a prophet of "signs and wonders" (Deut 34:11) *must* die, never entering the land, signals that God must remain *inaccessible*. "Signs and wonders" mark *God's* presence (see Deut 4:34; 6:22; 7:18-19; 26:8; 29:2-3; Ps 78:43). With Moses alive, God is much too accessible—an immense obstacle, for God's "real absence" is crucial. Without *absence*, how is the encounter with God to be an experience of impenetrable otherness? How is it to be the meeting of freedom with utter freedom?

Verses 20-22 round off the present section, briefly treating the problem of false prophecy. To betray one's compatriots by falsely representing God's voice was heinous, bringing on death (one fulfillment of v. 20 appears in Jer 28:16-17). Some, nevertheless, presumed to speak prophetically with no true word from God (e.g., see 1 Kgs 22:6; Jer 28:2). Are there guidelines for negotiating this problem? True prophets, of course, speak exclusively on behalf of the Lord. But how can one spot the false prophet who speaks in the Lord's name but utters "a word that the LORD has not spoken"?

Critics have long found fault with the criterion offered here, that of the failure (Deut 18:22) or success (Jer 28:9) of oracles. They note that a "fulfillment" criterion is of little value if the fulfillment in mind lies in the future. Most prophets press for decisions here and now! Moreover, the criterion appears naïve. In reality, God sometimes reverses oracles granted to authentic prophets (Isa 38:5; Jonah 3:10) and sometimes allows oracles of false prophets to come true (Deut 13:2).

Rather than nitpicking the text, respectful readers perceive Deuteronomy's concern to be the long-term triumph of God's word. That word is active and invincible. It is at work getting people out of their ruts, directing the world on the right track. The divine word confronts the world with God's otherness and progressively moves it to the embrace of the *other*. One recognizes the true prophet by his or her fit with that progress.

Striking anomalies (see Deut 13:2) and temporary perplexities (see Jer 28:5-11) are part of life. The real, true word of God, however, will push forward irrepressibly. By aligning themselves with the inevitable progress of that word, true prophets establish a "track record" of success. They situate themselves in the large-screen pattern of God's work on earth. One can discern the truthfulness of their work based on their neat fit in the grand trajectory of God's program. Prophets such as Jeremiah have their own books of Scripture because of such a fit.

Protecting Innocent Life: The Public Order

Deuteronomy 19:1-21

Deuteronomy 19:1–26:15 forms a new division of the book's legal core. Centering on human relationships and societal justice, this part of the book covers the second half of the Decalogue, the sixth to tenth commandments. It concentrates on fostering human dignity and mutuality within the promised land. It also grapples with the brokenness and ambiguity of communal life in the here and now, reminding readers that openness and flexibility will be required in interpreting the torah and applying it to life in community.

In 19:1–22:8, Moses turns to six individual sections on the sixth commandment, forbidding murder. These texts take a positive, constructive tack in explicating a negatively phrased command, "You shall not murder" (5:17). For Deuteronomy, the torah is not about clamping people down with restrictions. It is about catechism for growth together.

Chapter 19 gives us the first three sections: one about cities of refuge (19:1-13), another about boundary markers (19:14), and a third about witnesses (19:15-21). The common theme is protecting life, and the rules are representative only. They treat gray areas and difficult cases, modeling how to apply the torah with deftness and agility.

Cities of Refuge, 19:1-13

The Hebrew word for "murder" in the sixth commandment (*ratsakh*, 5:17) was originally about blood vengeance, about both killing and retaliation for killing (see Childs, 420–21). In tribal Israel, a near relative might avenge a family member's death by evening the score through *ratsakh* (see Num 35:27). The word appears here three times (vv. 3, 4, 6), matching the topic of protecting life from a hotheaded "avenger of blood" (v. 6). Over time, the term came to embrace all violent acts committed in burning anger.

In 4:41-43, Moses had given instructions for creating cities of refuge on the far side of the Jordan to protect those responsible for accidental deaths from *ratsakh.* Cities of refuge were places of asylum where one could flee for one's life if one committed involuntary homicide. Now, Moses provides cities of refuge in the heartland.

Israel's cities of refuge must be easily accessible. If God enlarges Israel's territory, additional cities must be added (vv. 8-9). An avenger in hot-blooded pursuit must not be able to overtake someone straining to reach a distant city. A commitment to a fair trial must triumph over a spirit of vengeance. The wrongful death of a refugee could spread malice like a conta-gion in the land, polluting it with innocent blood (v. 10).

Deuteronomy shows significant wisdom in grappling upfront with the menace of vengeance. The spirit of revenge is a devastating and interminable problem for humanity. Acts of reprisal provoke new reprisals, setting vicious circles of violence in motion, eventually drawing in the entire social body. As anthropologist René Girard (15) puts it, "There is the risk that the act of vengeance will initiate a chain reaction whose consequences will quickly prove fatal to any society of modest size."

The Boundary Mark, 19:14

Deuteronomy wants to keep families on their farmland. It understands units of kin-plus-land to be the building blocks of covenantal society (cf. Deut 15:1-11). Those core units sustain the life and dignity of both primary and secondary groups. People without land—Levites, resident aliens, orphans, widows, and servants—require the generosity of those able to harvest crops (see, e.g., 12:12, 18; 14:29; 16:11, 14; 18:1-8). To move property bound-aries or commit other like treacheries not only puts property owners' families at risk but also jeopardizes the covenant and its provisions for supporting all persons.

To keep boundary markers in place is Deuteronomy's code language for protecting and building up community. Hosea too used an image of disre-specting boundaries to describe anti-communal treachery: "The princes of Judah have become like those who remove the landmark" (Hos 5:10). Here, moving markers is a national or systemic abuse, not merely an individual crime. Society as a whole has become corrupt. Deuteronomy shares Hosea's antipathy toward monarchy and its tendency to run roughshod over the covenantal value of land tenure (see, e.g., 1 Sam 8:14; 1 Kgs 21:2-4).

Witnesses, 19:15-21

Deuteronomy is well aware of the ingenious ways in which human craftiness may manifest itself. As with the underhanded moving of landmarks, false accusations and perjury are all too common ways of perverting justice. By tackling the duplicitous crime of false witness, Deuteronomy continues to push people to internalize and embody the torah's spirit, to wield its principles with acumen in defense of life.

The section shows readers how defending life may require intense discernment. The faithful must sometimes walk a tightrope between erring on the side of protecting the innocent (v. 15) and vigilant, objective enforcement of justice (v. 21). Negotiating this strait remains as much a challenge today as in ancient times. A fair and peaceful society requires both flexible hearts of compassion and firm, fixed standards.

Deuteronomy 17:6-7 already insisted that only the testimony of multiple witnesses can decide a capital case. Here, Deuteronomy applies the demand for judicial integrity universally, in connection with *any* offense (19:15). Hearsay and spurious accusation must have no place whatsoever in enforcing the covenant. Yet the question remains: What does one do in cases of a single accuser? Such a person may be a legitimate witness, coming forward alone in the hope of inspiring others to testify.

Cases of individual hostile witnesses, like all difficult cases, must come before the high court at the single sanctuary (1:17; 17:8-13). The court must conduct a thorough inquiry in the hope of bringing other witnesses or evidence to light, allowing for a conviction. If no additional evidence is forthcoming, the investigation will prove inconclusive and the case be thrown out. If the accuser is exposed as a malicious person with a false witness, then there is to be poetic justice. The scoundrel must get the very punishment intended for the victim (v. 19). People will hear and get the message (v. 20).

A word is necessary about v. 21, the *lex talionis*, which is now widely disparaged. Against its modern despisers, the principle here of measure for measure represents neither primitive barbarism nor sub-Christian morality. First, the formula "eye for eye" need not be taken literally. Notably, Exodus 21:26-27 follows Exodus 21:24-25 immediately! Second, far from a warrant for revenge, the principle of strict proportionality aims to halt cycles of reprisal. It prevents a chain reaction of vengeance spawning vengeance by stipulating exact justice irrespective of person. Third, the principle offers a foundational statement about the irreducible value of human life. A fine should simply not suffice as compensation for bodily injury or human death. Contrary to much modern thinking, not everything in life has a monetary equivalent.

Protecting Innocent Life: Warfare

Deuteronomy 20:1-20

At first blush, it appears passing strange that rules for warfare (ch. 20) come next in Deuteronomy's exposition of the sixth commandment (19:1–22:8). Teachings about *avoiding* war, pursuing care of the neighbor instead (see 10:19; 15:2, 7; 22:1, etc.), would seem more apt. Upon reflection, however, Deuteronomy is ingenious; its presentation is eminently tactical. The preceding chapter has used exceptional cases to argue the lengths to which one must stretch to defend life. God's people must put aside the drive to even the score (19:6); they must return hard-won land, such as territory captured in battle (19:14); they must even allow certain devious criminals to go free (19:15). To extend the same line of argument, chapter 20 now lands on war, a sphere of extremes to be sure.

Deuteronomy confronts a world where states of war were a license to drop restraints, to unleash chaos. Assyrian propaganda aimed to convince all potential adversaries of a near psychotic response to even minor offenses. As cities were sacked, husbands, wives, children, and grandparents might be beheaded or stuck alive on stakes. Although the reality of Assyrian warfare was likely often less harsh than its propaganda insisted, Assyrian court records document the brutal treatment of captured foreign cities (Barrett, 183). To this inhuman world of the eighth and seventh centuries BCE, Deuteronomy utters an emphatic "No."

Chapter 20 also uses the topic of war to extend covenantal values beyond Israel's inner life. At Deuteronomy's publication, war was an *international* phenomenon. Assyria, Egypt, and Babylonia were on the move, soon to clash on a world stage. King Josiah would meet his end at Megiddo in 609 BCE, facing down Egypt in the spirit of vv. 3-4. By speaking of warfare, Deuteronomy thrusts the sixth commandment into a global arena. It insists that care for life go "*viral*"—attain global impact. Here, for a moment, the book presents God as creator, willing all creation's weal, not God as suzerain, willing a vassal people's devotion. The shift is clearest in v. 19's emotional concern for *trees*.

The literary flow of chapter 20 is complex and choppy. At first, one imagines one is reading a discussion of conquering the promised land, of the divine warrior's battling against the Canaanites (vv. 2-4; cf. 1:30; 3:22; 7:21; 11:25). Verse 15, however, reverses all previous impressions. It gives the text an unexpected spin: "But these instructions apply only to distant towns" (NLT; see Deut 12:21 and 14:24 for similar language of restrictive judicial reinterpretation). Why does v. 15 suddenly distinguish foreign wars (vv. 10-14) from wars in the homeland (vv. 15-18)? What is going on?

The text's challenging canonical form appears to reflect a "dialectical" theology, that is, a theology holding two truths in tension. In the passage's final shape, one section (vv. 15-18) expresses particularism: the homeland is unique, an environment for fostering covenantal growth (see 7:1-6). Another section (vv. 10-14, 19-20) expresses universalism: the Lord is creator of all life (see 4:32), caretaker of all nations (see 4:34, 38; cf. 1 Kgs 20:28; Mic 5:5-6), one concerned even with the enemy's trees.

The perspective of vv. 10-14, 19-20 reappears later in Deuteronomy 21:10-14 and, briefly, in 24:5. These texts appear to form a set—an inherited body of wisdom about war that Deuteronomy has recycled. Modern readers stand at some distance from this world where city walls are breached and males are put to the sword (20:13). Contrary to first impressions, however, these texts do not celebrate violence but limit it. They markedly restrain war's assault on life. Here, military action is a last resort, undertaken only in order to win "deliverance" (Heb., *yasha'*, 20:4). When war is necessary, Israel must guard life. God's people must protect the humanity and dignity of non-combatants.

Specifically, Israel must exhaust all efforts at treaty negotiation (20:11), and submit signatories only to forced labor (cf. Josh 9:25-27; 2 Sam 20:24). Deuteronomy allows no room for pillaging, ravaging, blinding of eyes, and other such excesses (cf., e.g., Judg 5:30; 1 Sam 11:1-2). If war is unavoidable, it may target only male combatants (20:13): no atrocities—no rape and no cruel treatment of civilians. Indeed, Israel must allow room for considering individual circumstances and caring for captives' feelings (21:13). It must even love the natural world, something quite unheard of in the ancient milieu (20:19; contrast Josephus, *Jewish War*, 5.523, 6.5-6).

Alexander Rofé (32) describes our set of texts (20:10-14, 19-20; 21:10-14; and 24:5) as follows: "All these laws are decidedly humane, calling for compassion, restraint, and self-respect." They bespeak "a humanitarian idealism that sought to hold in check military abandon, bestiality, destructiveness and cruelty; in addition, they do not emphasize the distinctive peoplehood of the Israelites" (37).

These rules tie the hands of ancient commanders in hopelessly impracticable ways. They furtively *undermine* the practice of war. Some later rabbis saw the impracticality of these rules, according to Rofé, and allowed fruit trees to be cut for siege-works and some female captives to be violated.

The contemporary uniqueness of this miniature code for warfare becomes even clearer when we discover its distance from Israel's actual story. Samuel orders Saul, Israel's first king, to assault the Amalekites and "utterly destroy all that they have; . . . kill both man and woman, child and infant, ox and sheep" (1 Sam 15:3). Later, when Israel and Judah attack another people, Moab, Elisha orders a scorched-earth policy (2 Kgs 3:19, 25). It would seem that exceptions to Deuteronomy 20 are in fact the rule.

Deuteronomy 20 does *not* function to set the reader up to understand Israel's history as told in Joshua through Kings. Rather, the text hints at inclusive and universal claims about the covenant and its defense of earthly life. The reader has previously learned of God's gifts of homelands to foreign nations: Edom, Moab, and Ammon (Deut 2:5, 9, 19). Now, the reader has learned something more: God loves all life, including all the natural life that flourishes in the homelands of all peoples.

Verses 15-18 place a perspective of particularism alongside the universalism of the preceding verses. Canaanite cities must disappear to create a uniquely configured zone of formation for God's people. The particularism of these verses has a constructive and inclusive purpose: Israel must impress the world with a new form of communal life (Deut 4:6-8; 26:19; cf. Exod 19:6 E). Nevertheless, the language of eradication here *is* clearly offensive (cf. 2:24–3:11; 7:1-5; 9:5; 12:2-3, 30-31; Exod 23:31-33 E).

Deuteronomy recycles offensive language of utter destruction for a decidedly nonviolent purpose. The book has lifted the extreme language of an antiquated past, known from the Moabite/Mesha Stone (c. 850 BCE), and put it to symbolic use half a millennium *after* it could ever have been carried out literally. Verses 15-18 are now about what Dennis Olson (94) calls a *catechetical* battle: "The teaching of idolatry and other gods is pitted against teaching the love of Yahweh alone."

It bears repeating for the cogency of a proper literary and theological reading of Deuteronomy: There were no unassimilated Canaanites at King Josiah's time when Deuteronomy appeared. There were only their gods, and what Deuteronomy calls "the abhorrent things that they do for their gods." The Yahweh-war that Deuteronomy 20 calls for is a "war" solely against Canaanite *teaching*: "so that they may not teach you" (v. 18).

The spirit of vv. 15-18 is thus not the spirit of killing but of whole-hearted devotion to the Lord alone, a spirit that also runs through the initial verses of chapter 20. Verses 1-9 picture the Lord as the only warrior that matters in Israel's battles. The real presence of God completely relativizes the threat of overwhelming enemy strength (vv. 1-4; cf. 1:30; 3:22; 7:17-19; 9:2-3; 11:25). Pragmatic military considerations are sidelined, as the reader is reminded that the divine warrior accomplishes salvation.

Deuteronomy's ideal vision sees Israel at war only when accompanied by the Lord's real presence. This vision all but rules out commonly fought wars, wars of aggression over greed, control, insecurity, and revenge. One might have expected such an anti-war stance from Deuteronomy. The reader of the book by this point has already observed its resistance to obsession with massive military might (Deut 7).

Chapter 20 aligns itself especially well with Deuteronomy 17:14-20, the passage constraining monarchy. It addresses itself to the people, not to their king (vv. 1-2). It understands Israel's fighting troops to be simply *ha'am*, "the people" (v. 2, Hebrew). It has the people's local Levites and elders address them before battle. The "officials" of v. 5 are the same figures described in 16:18, local elders (see 1:15) who have been federalized. In addition, the same local officials, chosen from each community's elders, appoint the unit commanders who lead the troops (v. 9 see NIV, NET, NLT).

The situations in vv. 5-8 that exempt troops from service make clear that the recruits are farmers and shepherds, not professional fighters or merce-naries of the king. A professional soldier is not released from battle because he is a newlywed, or has just planted a vineyard, or has lost his courage. Rofé (38) is surely correct: "It would be unthinkable to exempt from duty a professional fighter—salaried all his life for the express purpose of preparing for war—because of family needs or because of sudden faintheartedness. . . . Here is no professional mercenary force, Israelite or foreign, but a citizen army rallying to the battle at the hour of need."

The Confrontation of Life and Death

Deuteronomy 21:1-23

Deuteronomy 21 adds six additional laws to the book's lengthy exposition of the sixth commandment forbidding murder. The rules at first seem a hodge-podge. Upon a closer look, however, the chapter's coherence comes into focus. Its laws confront the reader in balanced, parallel pairs, giving the chapter an outer frame (vv. 1-9 and 22-23), an inner frame (vv. 10-13 and 18-21), and a two-part center (v. 14 and vv. 15-17). Throughout, the chapter wrestles with and interprets cases where life comes up directly against death.

The outer, framing pair of laws in vv. 1-9 and vv. 22-23 revolve around the theme of avoiding death's defilement. Bluntly put, dead bodies exposed on the ground or hanging from trees in God's land are a problem (cf. 19:10). They radically offend and insult God, symbolically desecrating a land meant to nourish *life* (30:15, 19, 20; 32:47).

The reader has already learned from 14:21 that holy life in God's land involves setting life and death at odds, never boiling a kid in its mother's milk (see the interpretation of 14:21 above). Israel must practice symbolically an identity as a people living in defiance of chaos and death. Their God has planted them in a land constructed as an arena of life, intended to infuse life. Israel should honor and keep the "sacrament."

In the case of unsolved murders, the people must ritually counteract the bloody violence. It has set at risk the sacramental power of God's land. They must visually enact the land's cleansing by breaking a pristine heifer's neck down in a ravine with a flowing stream (vv. 3-4). They must pray, in their innocence, for absolution (vv. 6-8). The prayer, not the ritual, is emphasized as what is truly effective (v. 8).

The meaning of the heifer's slaughter continues to provoke debate. It is not a sacrifice per se, but it *is* considered an atoning ritual ("accept this atonement," v. 8a, NIV; "atonement will be made," v. 8b, NET). Through the ritual, Israel accepts responsibility and addresses the shed blood. Perhaps the heifer's death reenacts the human death, allowing the elders to wash their hands of it (v. 6). Perhaps it enacts a flushing away of bloodguilt in flowing water (cf. Mic 7:19b). Alternatively, perhaps the heifer's killing vicariously substitutes for punishing the perpetrator of the manslaughter.

Like the slain body found in the countryside, an exposed corpse of an executed criminal (vv. 22-23) represents a dangerous display of death in a land dedicated to life. Public exposure of dead bodies was common in the ancient world (e.g., see Gen 40:19; Josh 8:29; 1 Sam 31:8-13; 2 Sam 2:4-7; 4:12; 21:9-10; Esth 2:23). It was a means of shaming and deterrence (cf. Josh 10:26-27). Deuteronomy permits such deterrence, but limits the spectacle's duration. Exposed corpses suggest a land under curse (see Deut 28:26; Jer 9:22; 16:4; 19:7), not a land blessed with life. In a land brimming with life, not even criminals should be food for wild beasts (cf. how 25:3 similarly limits degradation).

Another parallel set of laws appears in vv. 10-13 and vv. 18-21. Their subject matter immediately repels the modern reader. How disturbing to modern sensibilities are thoughts of capturing brides from enemy nations (vv. 10-13) and parents giving up sons to stoning (vv. 18-21)! Commentators must readily admit the offense of these laws, yet remind readers that their scenarios were anomalous, perhaps unknown in monarchic Israel. One searches the Bible in vain for examples of these laws in use. What is more, the present literary context of the laws has nothing to do with compelling submission of brides and sons. If Deuteronomy's concern were to keep sons in line, would not the law threatening to stone them appear earlier, under the rubric of the fifth commandment?

Why does Deuteronomy present these odd laws here? They hardly appear relevant to its era, even if they had some use in an earlier age. It seems reasonable to judge that Deuteronomy has taken them up and placed them here for reasons that have little to do with recommending a literal use of them. Readers may breathe a sigh of relief. They are not being required literally to give up their sons for stoning!

Deuteronomy's present form invites the reader to push beyond bare readings. The book has never been content merely to preserve quirky old case laws. It *has* shown itself willing, however, to recycle powerful language to advance readers' formation. Accepted as catechism, the laws before us exhibit an artistry rich with symbolic import.

The two old laws appear here in a canonical context elaborating the sixth, pro-life commandment. Their present purpose must be illuminating the struggle to protect and enhance life. Most likely, the extreme trials that they treat are supposed to symbolize a journey of God's people through death to renewed life. Such a journey, Deuteronomy has determined, is necessary for Israel to discover life in its full, God-willed richness.

The road of discipleship, Deuteronomy knows, has been a broken one for Israel, including pivotal moments when death confronts life head on. Such times, when Israel passes through the darkest of ravines, however, may become "resurrection" moments, portals to renewed, abundant life. Paradoxically, the God of Deuteronomy is the deity who boldly declares, "I kill and I make alive" (Deut 32:39).

Verses 10-13 present a scenario in which a new bride stands in a dark, liminal ravine, neither at home in her old life nor secure in the world of her new husband. She confronts the death of an old existence and the birth of a new life. Deuteronomy is interested in exploring this wilderness point of transition. It is a juncture not unlike Moses's confrontation with death in the plains of Moab. Like the new bride and like Moses, Israel must die to old loves and embrace God—her true good (see 3:23-29).

As noted above, instances of brides taken from enemy nations are rare in the Scriptures (Judg 5:30; 21:12-14, 21 do not really seem analogous to our text). Israel itself constitutes an exception to this generalization, however. God's people are the Bible's prime example of a bride won through battle. In this case, God desires Israel and wins "her" for God's self in a battle with Pharaoh and the armies of Egypt.

Verse 11 of our text uses the rare Hebrew verb *khashaq*, "to set one's heart on someone," to speak of the warrior's desire for a woman. The verb resounds with suggestiveness. It appears only two other times in Deuteronomy, both times specifically of God's desire *for Israel* (Deut 7:7; 10:15). Because the Lord, like the warrior, "set his heart" on Israel, God brought the people out from under Pharaoh (7:7-8).

The new husband must respect his new bride's transitioning. Passage through the portal from death to life renders her extremely vulnerable. She needs to mourn her parents (presumably casualties of war), and indeed the loss of her entire past. Rites of passage help her (vv. 12-13). So serious is Deuteronomy about a sure, helpful passage that v. 12 rescinds the principle of 14:1 that forbids mourners to shave their heads. The transitioning process assures the bride's freedom to enter a new relationship. The Lord understands and respects people's human agency.

The language of the new bride's "humbling" (v. 14 NASB; NRSV, "dishonored") is again highly suggestive of Israel's experience with God. Deuteronomy 8:3 uses the very Hebrew verb at issue, *'anah*. Read in conversation with Deuteronomy 8, the language of humbling in 21:14 takes on positive new meaning. For God to "humble" God's people is a constructive measure according to 8:3. Trials of faith help push God's people to live solely by the "word that comes from the mouth of the LORD."

The old law of the incorrigible son in vv. 18-21 parallels the law of the bride won through battle. This law similarly helps readers explore Israel's transition through death to new life. Neither the Bible itself nor the history of biblical interpretation presents any examples of this law enforced literally. To the contrary, the Mishnah says the rabbis so restricted its application that one would be hard pressed ever to employ it.

Contrary to some people's impression, the law has nothing whatever to do with punishing children who do no chores and spill their milk. Even taken literally, it is not about hurting children at all. Rather, it deals with the case of an adult heir egregiously unfit to take over the landed patrimony of the family line. The heir has shown himself a complete rebel, fully unresponsive to discipline. He is a glutton and drunk, living a life that threatens the economic viability of his kith and kin. Parents would do everything possible to avoid the death of a beloved son, but this individual represents the death of the family's line on its ancestral lands. His insolent, disastrous character will soon kill the family tree unless radical action is taken.

Deuteronomy is interested in the phenomenon of unresponsive, ingrained recalcitrance. As anomalous and bizarre as it at first appears, such a state of being appears to characterize God's chosen people. Israel, it turns out, is the sort of child that is every parent's nightmare.

From as early as 1:2-3, the book has conveyed a dim view of humanity's moral ability (see 1:31-32; 4:27-28; 8:20; 9:6-17, 22-24; 28:36-37, 63-68; 31:27). Deuteronomy has accepted the view of Psalm 78:8—a Psalm of Asaph, a source of the book—that Israel has long struggled with being "stubborn and rebellious," just as the son of Deuteronomy 21:18, 20 (the phrase shared by Deuteronomy and the psalm is extremely rare).

History will confirm the view. The prophet Jeremiah will describe Israel as having a "stubborn and rebellious" heart, exactly like the son of Deuteronomy 21 (Jer 5:23). He will lament that King Josiah's reforms promoting Deuteronomy have turned out to be transitory (Jer 3:10; 22:15-17). Jeremiah believed that, like the parents of the impossible son, the people will confront an experience of utter tragedy. The tragedy, however, represents their only portal forward to renew their life.

Although Deuteronomy understood the actual stoning of an heir to be fully anomalous and unattested, it was aware of a fascinating *metaphorical* instance of the law of 21:18-21 in action. The book's sources laid an infamous instance of its symbolic actualization before its authors. That instance occurs in the prophecies of Hosea.

Back in Hosea 11:1-11, Israel—God's own beloved "son" (v. 1)—stood accused by the Lord, his own parent, of unremitting recalcitrance (v. 2). Dragged into court, Israel faced charges of determination to turn away from relationship with God (v. 7). The sentence under consideration is death, God turning to destroy the northern kingdom (v. 9). Ibn Ezra (1089–1164 CE), the celebrated medieval Jewish commentator, saw the link between Deuteronomy and Hosea. He compared the insubordinate son of Deuteronomy 21 to the "headstrong cow" of Hosea 4:16.

While human parents might bring themselves to turn in an impossibly reprobate heir for stoning, the God of Hosea, in mysterious divine otherness and freedom, recoils at the thought (Hos 11:8-9). Although Israel eventually succumbs to catastrophe in 722 BCE, even this, in God's will, is not the end. The people of God are graced to find a way through destruction. According to Hosea 11:10-11, God's people, though "stoned" to death, can look forward to a future "resurrection" experience.

Deuteronomy, like Hosea 11:1-11, understands Israel as God's son (Deut 1:31; 8:5; 32:6; cf. Jer 2:14; 3:19, 22; 31:9, 20). The son's obstinate defiance of his parent borders on the irrational; it cries out for the death penalty (Deut 32:5-6,15-22, 35). Indeed, the rebelliousness and stubbornness at issue are so completely ingrained that they will inevitably pull Israel down. Certain editorial layers of Deuteronomy stem from the exile, actually originating in the ravine of death to which God's people are fated. In one such layer, Moses declares, "I know that after my death you will surely act corruptly, turning aside from the way that I have commanded you. In time to come trouble will befall you, because you will do what is evil in the sight of the LORD" (Deut 31:29).

Deuteronomy informs Israel that exile will surely come, and that it will mark a liminal experience. Deuteronomy tells the people that, once exile comes, "Your life shall hang in doubt before you; night and day you shall be in dread, with no assurance of your life" (Deut 28:66). As in Hosea 11:10-11, however, even the eventual doom of the son does not spell the end. Israel will pass through God's destruction to a divine redemption that outshines even its original experience of exodus from Egypt (see, e.g., Deut 4:25-31; 30:6).

A pair of rules in v. 14 and vv. 15-17 occupies the center of chapter 21, two parallel instructions that reinforce the surety of promised commitments. Verse 14 rounds off the law concerning the bride won in battle (vv. 10-13), but contemplates a disposition on the part of the husband that really does not fit God's feeling for Israel. Verses 15-17 address a similar unfair happenstance arising from a fickle human disposition.

Verse 14 insists that a captured bride has a permanently free status. She has become a full member of the covenant community. Verses 15-17 insist that a firstborn son *must* receive his birthright, allowing him to inherit the standard double share of the family estate. (Attesting to this custom are the Middle Assyrian Laws, Tablet B, no. 1, and the Nuzi-Akkadian Laws, no. 3. For Babylonia, see ANET 173, nos. 165, 170.)

Israel can rely on God's promises of freedom and inheritance. They are guaranteed, not to be trifled with. God's people should take hope that this bedrock of security lies at the center of a chapter in which death and life have repeatedly come up against each other. Like a bride taken in battle or a cursed son, Israel will encounter death. At their time of extreme vulnerability and jeopardy, when every shadow terrifies and the unknown lurks around the next corner, they can fully trust God's commitments.

Just at the point when Israel has experienced everything, both covenantal blessing and curse, God will give them new life. As 30:4 puts it, "Even if you are exiled to the ends of the world, from there the LORD your God will gather you" (cf. 10:1-4, 10).

The Obligation to Protect Life

Deuteronomy 22:1-8

Deuteronomy concludes its exposition of the anti-murder commandment with eight additional verses insisting on everyone's obligation to support human and natural life. The Hebrew word for "neighbor" used in the section means *sibling* (*'akh*). All members of the covenant community, from servant to king (e.g., 1:16; 15:12; 17:15), are "siblings." Israel is a single family "tree," each leaf dependent on the selfsame sap.

Verses 1-4 call for active attentiveness to all siblings' well-being, attentiveness based on an *inner* appropriation of the torah's spirit (cf. 15:9; 22:7; 24:15). Care for siblings means intervening when their possessions are in jeopardy, resisting all temptation to look the other way or to grab them for oneself. One must go out of one's way to return a lost personal item or a stray animal. If the owner's identity is unclear or the person lives too far away, one must hold on to the possession until it is claimed. If a neighbor's animal is injured on the road, one must stop and help it back to its feet.

Deuteronomy builds on earlier biblical law here, significantly modifying it. It transforms the Covenant Code (Exod 21–23), specifically the requirements of Exodus 23:4-5. First, it warns against the natural inclination to look the other way. Second, it broadens the scope to include "anything" a neighbor loses, not merely that which wanders off. Third, it insists that one must act even "if the owner does not reside near you or you do not know who the owner is." Finally, whereas Exodus 23 spoke of the "enemy," Deuteronomy 22 uses language of the "sibling" (NRSV: "neighbor"). The intention is to generalize the earlier law, so there is no mistaking that it applies universally to all in need.

Verse 5 jumps to a law against cross-dressing, the wearing of clothes and personal items designed for the opposite sex. A verse like this involving gender and sexuality makes many modern people anxious, but those on edge can relax. The law is unlikely to relate to transvestism (cross-dressing for sexual gratification). If restricting sexual expression were the concern,

Deuteronomy would have placed the law later under the rubric of the seventh commandment. By associating the law instead with the sixth commandment, the book signals that the concern here is protecting and enhancing *life*.

The modern phenomenon of male ("fetishistic") transvestism was rare or absent in ancient Israel. Israelite culture did not eroticize female clothing the way that ours does. Israel had nothing like modern bras or lingerie, only (1) social constructions of sexual vigor related to dress and (2) knowledge of rituals that challenged gender roles. We know what this law is *not* about, but given our great distance from Israel's world, we can make only educated guesses about v. 5's specific symbolic functions.

We know from texts such as 21:17 and 23:1 that Deuteronomy uplifts procreative vigor—the generative energy of new life. In Israel, the firstborn son was an embodiment of this energy (cf. Gen 49:3; Ps 78:51). Reproductive power, for the book, is God's mysterious gift infusing the Israelite family tree with life, pumping sap up into every new sprout. The book may want this honored and reinforced through dress.

In this view, v. 5 would be constructing a symbol system in which female clothing marks maternal power and the "virile male" (Heb., *geber*; contrast NRSV: "man") bears the "weapon" (Heb., *keli*; contrast NRSV: "apparel"). The Hebrew term "weapon" (*keli*) had sexual associations in the ancient world (e.g., in Ugaritic stories). Naturally, such a symbol system does not apply to modern readers of faith, who have a different culture. We no longer cling to the family tree; we are uncoupling the link between fixed gender roles and fecundity. Readers must find new ways to celebrate God's generative energy at work creating new life and nourishing human mutuality.

In a second possible interpretation, v. 5 pits itself against certain ancient worship rituals. This approach gains steam when one realizes that the examples of actual cross-dressing from ancient Mesopotamia and Canaan are almost all from worship settings. Most at issue are the rites of the goddesses Inanna/Ishtar and Ashtarte.

Inanna/Ishtar, a goddess with power over death, had the ability to change a person's gender. Some of her processions included individuals dressed in both male and female clothing as well as men and women carrying symbols of the opposite sex. Such parading of gender ambiguity surely offended Deuteronomy, which celebrated God's gift of procreative power through a separation and contrast of the sexes.

The cross-dressing servants of Ishtar possibly played a role interconnecting the world of the living and that of the dead. Their embodied polarity signaled an ability to transcend the paradox of order and disorder, of cosmos and underworld. They were liminal figures, ranging across the divide between earth and the beyond. Deuteronomy would abhor any such mixing of life and death. The book wants Israel—God's people of *life*—to hold the realm of death at arm's length (see Vedeler, 467; Maul).

Verses 6-7 introduce a different symbolic expression of life's sacred value. They stipulate that people may take eggs from a bird's nest, but must not take the mother with the young. If these birds represent all wildlife, this law aims to uphold the integrity of nature. It leaves mature animals free to breed again, upholding life's balance.

More may be going on in vv. 6-7, however, than merely wildlife management. Back at 14:21, Deuteronomy appeared to be insisting on contrasting death and life. One must keep a kid out of its mother's milk. Similarly, chapter 22 may be offering potent symbolism about holding death at bay: Kill animals for food if you must, but do not mix their death with an act that destroys life-giving, procreative powers. Killing mothers with their children simply reeks of death (cf. Hos 10:14).

The section concludes in v. 8 with a rule about having guardrails or barrier walls on roofs to protect people from falling. This sort of safety device was necessary, since Israelite houses had flat roofs used as domestic space for everything from processing agricultural products (Josh 2:6), to bathing (2 Sam 11:2), to napping and sleeping in warm weather (1 Sam 9:25-26). It would be criminal negligence not to think ahead and put adequate safeguards in place to protect the lives of everyone on one's roof. The basic principle should apply broadly. The commandment not to kill really entails the proactive safeguarding of all human life, the proscription of all apathy that endangers life.

Exposition of the Commandment against Adultery

Deuteronomy 22:9–23:18

Now begins Deuteronomy's exposition of the seventh commandment against adultery. *Adultery* is very broadly defined here as confusion over proper boundaries, over what should mix and not mix within Israel's covenantal existence. The section highlights adultery proper—the "mixing" of marital and extramarital intercourse—since it threatens the basic kinship building blocks of covenant society. But more generally, it identifies all sorts of other improper admixtures, "adulterations." They may occur in many realms of Israel's collective life, including the spheres of agriculture, clothing, membership in the covenant assembly, conduct in the war camp, prostitution, and worship offerings.

Deuteronomy outlines a symbol system of purity and holiness. Israel is to observe specific separations, distinctions, and boundaries to bear witness to and celebrate God's ordering of the cosmos. God has pushed chaos beyond fixed boundaries, creating intentional space for an array of classifiable life forms. For Israel to celebrate life through symbolic practices is for God's people to bask in life's bounded, ordered substance. It is for all persons to side with God and God's love of life. It is for God's vassals to be *holy*.

To practice notable separations, to embrace a symbol system of purity, is to become set apart from other peoples. It is to wear a "badge" of collective distinctiveness, of "oneness" (cf. 6:4-5; 7:6; 12:5; 28:10). Wearing such a badge day in and day out, Israel presents itself to the world as uniquely unadulterated, as especially holy. Israelites show themselves as children of the living God. This is the lofty vision of Deuteronomy.

The distinctive tassels that 22:12 wants on every Israelite's hem mark Israel's uniqueness and its holy status. They signify the nobility of the covenant community, the people's identity as God's holy people (Deut 4:20; 7:6; 14:2; 26:18-19). One may compare how specially fringed garments distinguished royalty in the Assyrian palace reliefs of Deuteronomy's time. The "royal" blue dye in the chords of Israel's tassels (see Num 15:38) was an expensive extract from the murex snail, about forty times more expensive than other dyes. Such dyed chords distinguished Israel as special indeed.

Many modern readers object, however, that chapters 22–23 do not stop at fancy tassels. There are laws that appear overbearing and disturbing. A farmer who mixes his seeds must forfeit his total production (22:9). People of Ammonite and Moabite descent are forever barred from public worship (23:3-6). The penalty for adultery is execution (22:22). Perhaps most shockingly, at first blush it appears that 22:20-21 orders the death penalty for an unmarried woman caught losing her virginity.

To read our text fairly, one must keep in mind Deuteronomy's radical vision of the covenantal community as a *genealogical* tree, rooted in God's rich soil, highly dependent on stable, tightknit families and kin groups. Adultery involving married persons is a heinous crime in this vision. There was little that could undo the evil of adultery: "Jealousy detonates rage in a cheated husband; wild for revenge, he won't make allowances. Nothing you say or pay will make it all right" (Prov 6:34-35, *The Message*).

Deuteronomy's harsh sanctions *are* frightful. The book is loath to soften death penalties already present in law (e.g., Exod 21:15, 17; 22:19), and is well aware that in ancient Near Eastern politics, undermining a covenant is a capital offense. Deuteronomy, however, is *not* out for blood. Its sanctions aim to nurture a radically new imagination, to create a numinous new world (cf. Deut 13:11; 17:13; 19:20; 21:21). To ensure only rare enactment of dire penalties, it locks in escape clauses. Knowing the rule of 22:15, all parents of brides will save their "evidence" (wedding-night bed cloths, stained with the hymen's blood). In cases where good evidence is absent, parents can easily concoct it!

But still—the modern reader will object—are not these purity rules intrusive into private affairs? To make matters worse, are they not downright sexist?

Such objections lose a good deal of their force when one considers the text and its thinking carefully. True, Deuteronomy bucks our contemporary assumptions about the autonomy of private life. But its laws are *not* for implementation by modern secular culture. Rather, they constitute the internal catechesis of an ancient community discovering wells of life within an intricately bounded and ordered creation, supple and sensitive at all points. Here, a notion of "private sin" with no real ripple effects is absent.

Objections about intrusiveness and sexism most often arise in connection with 22:13-21. The true sense of this text, however, eludes most readers. The issue at stake is not the virginity of new brides. That is, there is no tension here with Exodus 22:16-17 and with Deuteronomy 22:28-29.

Rather, as with the perverse men of Gibeah (Judg 19:2-24), the woman here has committed an "infamy in Israel" (NJB), a "crime against Israel" (NAB). The expression "infamy" (Deut 22:21) signals that which is utterly destructive of covenantal mutuality. The new husband takes action only upon discovering the woman to be the female counterpart of the twisted heir of Deuteronomy 21:18-21. Her flagrant, unrepentant promiscuity is an insane assault on the extended family, the "father's house" (22:21).

This is not to deny the phenomenon of patriarchy in Deuteronomy. The book comes from a culture of patrilineal organization and authority, where male heads of household wield public power, where chastity is a woman's attribute. Fathers control daughters' sexuality (22:29). Marriages involve monetary contracts with grooms (22:15).

Again, 22:13-21 raises particular concern. A man's vicious lie does not get him the death sentence when faced by the accused, a blatant injustice (19:19). Such a sentence is excluded in this symbol system; it would leave the bride in limbo—an unmarriageable single woman. Nevertheless, the man's fine is harsher than first appears. He is "arrested and flogged" (22:19, NJB), allowed no divorce, and heavily fined (twice the fine of 22:29).

The law of 22:13-21 upholds the honor of the bride and protects her and her family, as does the legal provision of 22:29. Going beyond the earlier form of the same law in Exodus 22:17, Deuteronomy 22:29 guarantees the security of marriage to the woman who has lost her virginity. Her father may not keep her a permanent *de facto* widow.

By the same token, 22:23-27 honors all women's humanity. A woman's consent to sex is a key factor in whether or not she is guilty of adultery. If a woman commits adultery, she receives the same penalty as her male counterpart (22:22, 24). She is a moral agent, not an object—not her husband's "property." In extra-biblical Near Eastern laws, by contrast, the husband of an adulterous wife decides her fate.

Earlier Israelite law in Exodus 22:16-17 seemed to treat daughters as property by placing the rule we find in Deuteronomy 22:28-29 after a series of property laws. Deuteronomy, eschewing the thought of women as property, moves the law to its section on adultery. Women in this book are far from "womb commodities," as was obvious as of 21:13's insight that marriages entail deep human interrelationship (cf. 24:5, NJB and NJPS).

After an in-depth study of all the sexual laws of chapter 22, Adele Berlin (112) characterizes them positively as follows:

> A man who has sex with another man's wife or fiancée is put to death for adultery. A man who has sex with an unbetrothed woman must pay the

full bride-[wealth], marry her, and may never divorce her. Although chastity is a women's attribute, a man's extramarital sexual activity is also constrained by it; for him, too, the outcome is death or marriage. In this sense, Deuteronomy treats men and women equally.

Alongside rules that seem (to modern eyes) patriarchal and parochial, Deuteronomy exhibits sure signs of creativity and flexibility. The reader is by now well aware of the torah's adaptability and openness in this book. Here, God's people, propelled by God's word, are on a journey in which growth in understanding is constant.

Just four verses into its adultery section, the text punches a large hole in all airtight views of purity boundaries. Immediately after a prohibition of adulterated clothing (v. 11), v. 12 jarringly appears. This instruction about tassels feels out of place among legal details of purity. To be sure, as noted, the tassels provide Israel with a badge of distinctiveness. Apparently, however, v. 12 is here to do more than mark Israel holy. In addition, it reminds Israel to be agile, to keep out of mires that trap and dull the spirit.

A bit of cross-referencing shows the tassels of Deuteronomy 22:12 had a unique makeup. Each tassel had a striking blue cord attached amid the other threads that dangled down from the cloak (Num 15:38, another manifestation of the same law). Most Israelite cloaks were made of white linen, but the blue cord within the tassels would have been of dyed *wool* (linen did not dye well in the ancient world). Here, linen and wool are mixed!

The early paraphrase of Deuteronomy 22:12 in Targum Pseudo-Jonathan attests that wool and linen were combined on people's garments: "On a linen covering you are permitted to put woolen fringe threads." Furthermore, tassels found in the Qumran caves have blue cords of wool amid white cords of linen. Clearly, a taboo mixture has muscled its way inside Israel's world of purity. This world is malleable, not fixed and stifling.

The book's system of purity boundaries again proves adaptable in 23:15-16. People in the ancient Near East knew that freedom and slavery do not mix. A slave is a slave, and must be returned. Bounty hunters deserve rewards. Not to return a slave risks a penalty of death (*ANET* 200; Hammurabi secs. 15-20; Hittite Laws secs. 22-24).

Israel, however, must offer refuge to slaves fleeing from foreign masters. No group anywhere within the community can refuse to harbor them. The Hebrew phrase "in any one of your gates [NRSV: 'towns']" (23:16) instructs that any locality must offer welcome; any kin-group must give support (for the latter sense of the term "gate," cf. Ruth 3:11 and one connotation of the Akkadian term *bābtu[m]*).

Modern readers' distance from the cultural constructs of ancient Israel makes it a challenge to decipher all the original meanings behind the various boundaries of chapters 22–23. Why does the text make some admixtures taboo—for example, yoking an ox and a donkey (22:10)—and not others? The various "adulterations" listed probably constitute representative examples, intended to jog original readers' minds about other related rules.

The initial rules in 22:9-12 address boundaries in the use of God's natural gifts. In the original context, the symbolism functioned to express the community's love of life and balance. Maintaining distinctions kept the community oriented on this affection. Verse 11's prohibition of wool-linen mixtures, however, likely had an additional signification. It probably marked the distinction between laypersons and Levites (the wool-linen blend was approved for specifically sacral uses; e.g., Exod 26:1).

A large subsection then delves into the area of sexual "adulterations" proper (22:13-30). Two taboos stand out: there must be no adultery (v. 22) and not even the hint of incest (marrying a widowed stepmother, v. 30; cf. Amos 2:7b). Notably, an unmarried, non-virgin woman raises serious concerns (vv. 20-21, 23-29). Such a woman gravely destabilizes Israel's supple, branching genealogical life. She, together with the male involved with her, must immediately be secured within a marriage or, in irredeemable cases, be extirpated. As noted, one would need to work hard to land in the latter situation.

The discussion next turns in 23:1-8 to maintaining boundaries around Israel's worship assembly. Many modern readers find this sort of concern offensive, jumping to apply terms such as "particularistic," "intolerant," and "chauvinist." Modern communities of faith should not, and do not, adopt the symbol system here (there are no more Ammonites and Moabites)! It is imprudent, however, simply to dismiss the section as primitive or prejudiced. There is a creditable theological stance here against deathly decay and purposeful defiance of God.

Take, for example, the rule of 23:1, which bans males with damaged sex organs from the Lord's assembly. The ban pushes back against Ishtar's flaunting of androgyny, which impeded the progress of breathing, embodied life on earth. Naturally, the law has no literal force today; no longer does Ishtar worship purposively transgress the categories that buttress procreation. Now, 23:1 simply highlights God's gift of sacred, generative energy to the promised land (see Deut 11:9, 11). It echoes Deuteronomy 14:21; 21:17; 22:5-7, which uphold the same reverence for this numinous, "sacramental" power.

Deuteronomy keeps life and death separate, celebrates life's assured victory over chaos. A very rare term based on a Hebrew root meaning "decay," "rot" describes those associated with an "illicit union" (23:2). Whatever the exact nature in antiquity of these unions and their outcomes, in the canonical context they now symbolize violations of God's boundaries against the forces of rotting decay in the world.

Next, the ban in vv. 3-6 on the Moabites and Ammonites is not xenophobia; there is neither fear of Moabite culture here nor belief that Moabites are ethically inferior persons. No, this is a symbol system built around concepts of structure, order, and purity. Motivations such as enmity or ethnic prejudice are not at issue. If enmity were at issue, why the surprising openness to welcoming traditional enemies such as Egyptians and Edomites as God's worshipers (vv. 7-8)? If the concern is with ethnicity, why are certain Israelite bodies considered just as taboo as a Moabite body?

Damaged genitals symbolize a taboo "mixture," chaos mixed with life. Just so, the Moabite body symbolizes a volatile mixture of curse and blessing. Moab hired an expert at cursing to stop Israel's settlement in God's land. Moab represents *curse*, the curse that the Moabites demanded of Balaam (23:4-5; cf. Num 22:6 E). God's sanctuary land, burgeoning with life and blessing, must not be associated with curse (21:22-23).

"But why the rigidity and hopelessness?" modern readers may object. Why an inflexible, *permanent* ban on all future descendants of an "illicit union" (NAB: "incestuous union," 23:2), on all persons of Ammonite and Moabite descent (23:3-6)? Here, first impressions may be deceiving. To be sure, Deuteronomy is absolutely firm about ideal boundaries; it sets life and death in antithesis. *Never* shall the twain meet. At the same time, the book is realistic, theologically flexible, and strikingly creative. It stresses the torah's adaptability and openness to the future. It stands out as humane.

On first reading, the ban on mixing wool and linen (22:11) appeared absolute. A close look, however, unearthed a waiver. It turns out the blend was actually encouraged for sacral cloths and garments. Moreover, every Israelite was required to wear tassels of the selfsame blend on their garments. As discussed below, Deuteronomy 23:15-16 functions similarly to set aside a recognized ban.

Texts such as 22:11 and 23:15-16 invite the sophisticated reader to work creatively with 23:1-8. Notably, Ruth's storyteller worked in just such an imaginative manner to show a viable way through the prohibitions of Deuteronomy 23 into an *inclusive* future. In Ruth, striking literary parallels with the story of Abraham make Ruth a symbolic new ancestress for Israel, a jump-starter of new creation for God's people. As Ruth rebirths Israel, old rules excluding Moabites vanish.

Miracles of new life like that in Ruth 4:13 *can* annul a permanent ban; in Ruth, Israel comes to welcome both a Moabitess and her great descendent, King David (Ruth 4:22). Given the messianic hope that becomes attached to David, the miracle birthed by Ruth represents a new start for existence on earth. (An echo of Ruth's being accepted into Israel's worship assembly is found in the book of Judith. In Judith 14:10, an Ammonite named Achior is circumcised and joins the house of Israel.)

Notably, Isaiah 56:3-8 neither contradicts nor relaxes Deuteronomy 23; *it fulfills it.* In this apocalyptic text, all restrictions on foreigners, eunuchs, and other excluded individuals vanish in God's new creation. The New Testament understands this inbreaking of God's reign to be underway. It assumes the eschatological "smashdown" of purity symbolism described in Isaiah to be in effect right now (e.g., see Acts 8:38).

With vv. 9-14, Deuteronomy 23 moves to rules for maintaining purity in the military camp. The assembly of Israel was an institution of worship, but could also go forth to battle. The purity of the assembly was crucial when it functioned militarily, since the Lord would be traveling "along with your camp" (v. 14; cf. 1:30; 3:22; 20:1, 4).

God's presence with the camp elicits careful attention to ritual purity. Nocturnal emissions of semen (23:10-11) are a ceremonial and symbolic concern, although they raise no issues of morality whatsoever. They render a warrior ceremonially "unclean" in that they symbolize the loss or "waste" of life force. Latrine procedures (23:12-14) are completely neutral in moral terms as well, but have great symbolic value in honoring the holiness of God, the Lord's separation from all that is vulgar.

Verses 15-18, which focus on slaves and prostitutes, conclude Deuteronomy's treatment of the seventh commandment. Given the scant evidence for officially sanctioned temple prostitution in the ancient Near East, the term "temple prostitute" (NRSV) has no foundation (see further below).

In a section that has worked hard at erecting symbolic boundaries, these verses stand out for their effort to fully *dissolve* two categories. Ideally, Israel should know neither prostitutes nor runaway slaves. These stigmatized and ostracized individuals should be pulled from their liminal situations outside the social order and "reside with you, in your midst" (v. 16). With their status of "other" removed, they will no longer bear power to adulterate Israel.

Deuteronomy appears to push back against firmly entrenched ideas of the "otherness" of prostitutes and foreign slaves. International norms of the ancient Near East demanded that runaway slaves be judged untouchable, and be extradited. Another people must neither harbor nor absorb them. Deuteronomy disagreed (23:15-16). After all, at the exodus God had liberated Israel from its then "permanent" status as slave in Egypt.

Prostitutes constituted another sort of "other." The Hebrew term here for prostitute (*qedeshah*) essentially means "one set aside." Why this connotation? Other less cryptic euphemisms were surely available. The answer is that many in Israel considered illicit sex as "set aside" by its preternatural power, including power over agricultural fecundity (Exod 32:6; Num 25:1-5; 31:13-20; Hos 4:13). Deuteronomy begs to differ.

The character Tamar in Genesis 38 famously plays the role of a *qedeshah*, and her story is rife with connotations of sacral mystique. Mark Leuchter (7) insightfully observes, "The backdrop to the tale is that of the spring sheepshearing and agricultural festival, a time of sensual celebration bound to the concepts of agrarian and human fertility; as such, the understanding of Tamar's behavior as pseudo-priestly and mytho-sacral in nature seems appropriate." Deuteronomy denies that illicit sex has any such mystique. There is no validity to imbuing prostitution with fertility-related sanctity. People should cease its practice and focus instead on solidifying webs of mutuality in community.

One reason that ancient Israelites engaged in prostitution was to obtain money to fulfill vows (i.e., promises to make gifts to a sanctuary, see Prov 7:14). This was likely true of women especially, who often had no independent wealth to use in making good on votive promises. Verse 18 outlaws paying vows using the wages of prostitution. Such fees are tainted with vulgarity and unacceptable in God's pure sanctuary.

Interestingly, Deuteronomy includes the rule of v. 18, despite the total ban on prostitution just announced in v. 17. Verse 17 should actually render v. 18 unnecessary. Here again we see the realism and pragmatism of Deuteronomy (cf. 15:11). It puts stopgap measures such as 23:18 in place until that time when God's reign comes in fullness and the book's ideal agenda is conclusively realized.

Exposition of the Commandment against Theft

Deuteronomy 23:19–24:7

Deuteronomy now moves to the eighth commandment against stealing (5:19). Here again, the section gives its commandment a broad interpretation. Many forms of exploiting other people, including highly subtle ones, may constitute theft. They are stealing in so far as they rob others of their due as human persons. In the final analysis, theft for Deuteronomy is any diminishing of another's life and joy.

Any *using* of people and their circumstances for one's own advantage, even charging interest on loans ("usury"), is fundamentally wrong. One should uplift the neighbor, not use an occasion of need to make a profit. Self-oriented motives impoverish life in community, especially when they reduce relationships to a "bottom line." Valuing life together above self-interest is paramount. It may even mean relaxing claims to one's rights. Diligence is necessary, for opportunities to exploit others arise frequently.

The section begins in 23:19-20 by prohibiting interest. The rule builds on earlier law in Exodus 22:25, which defined loans as acts of kindness. Deuteronomy expands the idea, aiming to constrain all manner of commercial drives. Loans to sibling Israelites must be non-commercial, solely for communal welfare. That is not to say that business has no place in life; international trade may remain a commercial undertaking. Israel may extend interest-bearing credit to foreigners (cf. 15:6; 28:12).

Deuteronomy's vision is one of covenant community holding itself together through sturdy bonds of mutuality and the support of God's good land. God's vassals take care of each other even at personal cost (cf. 15:1-18). The text is not hopelessly naïve. Its spirit appears, for example, in modern cooperative associations whose members covenant to cover each other's medical needs and thus avoid the bureaucratic tangles and prohibitive costs of commercial health insurance.

Verses 21-23 address acts of theft from God. These may take the form of breaking a vow (a promissory oath to God, cf. 1 Sam 1:11) or even being slow to fulfill one. "You promised God an offering if your request was granted, so make good on it" (cf. Asaph Ps 50:14b; 76:11, sources of Deuteronomy). The theme that "promises are promises," of course, applies broadly. Justice delayed is justice denied (cf. Deut 24:15).

Verses 24-25 concern hospitality toward hungry wayfarers passing through one's fields. Remarkably, the subsection's thrust is that refusing hospitality is theft! In the spirit of 14:28-29; 24:19-22; 25:4, the passage elevates covenantal mutuality over self-interest and profit. While in one sense one's grapes and one's grain are truly one's own (cf. 19:14; 27:17), in a greater, irreducible sense, the produce of the land is a tool for blessing the community as a whole.

Interpreters have long puzzled over the regulation prohibiting a couple from remarrying in 24:1-4. Why should it "bring guilt on the land" to remarry a former (now twice-divorced) wife? Upon a first reading, the language of a tainted land suggests that the issue is ceremonial uncleanness. In this case, the actions outlawed transgress Deuteronomy's symbol system of distinctions and boundaries (22:9–23:18). Since at least the time of the medieval Jewish commentator Nachmanides, interpreters have suspected that "adultery after the fact" is the specific transgression in mind. By "adultery after the fact" is meant that Deuteronomy judges that if a remarriage to an ex-spouse occurs, it makes the woman's second marriage look like an "adulterous" spree.

In this interpretation, the taint of illicit sex renders a woman "defiled" after a second marriage (24:4)—symbolically ineligible for any renewed relationship with her initial spouse. Such an interpretation fits with Jeremiah's understanding of Deuteronomy. The prophet declares that Israel's flings with alien gods have rendered it defiled for any renewed relationship with the Lord (Jer 3:1-3). Adultery is Jeremiah's key point: "You have played the whore with many lovers; and would you return to me? says the LORD."

As strong as this interpretation of Deuteronomy 24:1-4 appears to be, it is incomplete. It is hard to see how the aversion to *adultery* in the text constitutes a transgression against the eighth commandment, the commandment against *stealing*. To make sense of the passage in its canonical shape, one must explore the financial issues at stake in the case. Such issues might loom large, as they do in 22:13-19 where a groom slanders his bride out of greed. That groom aims to get and keep his bride's dowry, divorce her free of alimony, and have his bride-wealth refunded (Exod 22:16; cf. Deut 22:29).

Given the level of a husband's greed in 22:13-19, it is far from a stretch to interpret 24:1-4 as taking a stand against mercenary calculations. Such calculations especially mock the eighth commandment in this case, since they pervert something as sacred and intimate as marriage. In this reading, our passage provides an extreme example of how piling greed upon greed robs a person and her family of assets, honor, and basic human dignity. The slandering groom of chapter 22 looked to get his hands on a dowry. The "first husband" of the present text (ch. 24) goes farther. He acquires a dowry or penalty payment through his charge of finding "something indecent" (NAB, NIV) in his wife. Then, marrying the ex-wife anew, he appropriates a second dowry—the one her father gave her upon her second marriage. Beyond that, he also gets any divorce settlement that the second husband has rendered the woman.

Deuteronomy concludes its section on stealing with vv. 5-7, which present examples of stealing people's free enjoyment of life. Verse 5 insists that a newly married man must have a year at home to soak in the joy of marriage. For this period, he is exempt from military service and all other public obligations. The spirit of this rule is close to that of 20:7, which grants an engaged solider a deferral from military service so he may go get married. Both texts uphold life's deep blessings brought by covenant, God's promise of "rest" for the covenant people (see 12:9-10; Exod 33:14 E).

The form of the Hebrew verb of happiness in v. 5 gives the verse a sense of genuine concern for the *woman's* joy in marriage (see NAB, CEB, NJB, NJPS, NIV). The NRSV's translation, "be happy with the wife," is not based on the Masoretic Hebrew text but on the Syriac version and other textual witnesses, such as the Vulgate.

Verse 6 addresses the "stealing" of a neighbor's means of subsistence. One is allowed to take pledges (collateral) as securities on loans (see 15:1-3; 24:11), but the practice must never cross the line into extortion (cf. 24:12-13, 17). "It is wrong to take a set of millstones, or even just the upper millstone, as security for a loan" (NLT). One used the mill, a two-part tool, to grind one's grain and feed one's family (cf. Jer 25:10). The protection of self-interest must have nothing to do with grabbing such an implement.

More egregious than stealing peoples' means of subsistence is stealing people themselves. Verse 7 concludes the book's section on stealing with a prohibition of this ultimate type of theft. In the Hebrew, the verse actually speaks of "stealing life." As in Exodus 21:16, kidnapping is a capital offense, the only such capital crime in this section.

At its worst, "stealing life" would entail slave trading, turning a person into a commodity for sale to foreigners (the Hebrew verb "enslave" here is from the language of commerce). Sale of persons for enslavement abroad was a known practice (see Gen 37:28; Deut 28:32, 68; Ezek 27:13; Joel 3:3, 6; Amos 1:6), horrific for its threat of ripping a life out by the roots from community and land. The law, however, may also aim to stop a more common Israelite practice, the practice of creditors violently seizing family members as debt-servants (cf. Deut 15:12-18). The wresting of children from debtors could feel a lot like kidnapping to its victims, as attested by texts such as Job 24:9, "The orphan child is torn from the breast, the child of the poor is exacted as security" (NJB; cf. 2 Kgs 4:1; Amos 2:6; Mic 2:9; 3:2-3; Neh 5:5).

Exposition of the Commandment against False Witness

Deuteronomy 24:8–25:4

In characteristic fashion, Deuteronomy defines the ninth commandment against false testimony (5:20) broadly, highlighting a series of laws about honoring the dignity and reputation of every community member. The ninth commandment's technical sense holds firm; earlier passages of the book have made that clear. Perjury is a grave injustice that can get an innocent person killed (17:6; 22:21; cf. 1 Kgs 21:13). No pity can be shown to a lying scoundrel of a witness (Deut 19:21). But although wrongful testimony in court has no place among God's people, neither does any treatment of one's neighbors that defames them or fails to value them as holy, treasured possessions of God (Deut 7:6; 14:2). The passage moves logically through representative levels of the social order. It begins with the proper respect of leaders and ends with the humane treatment of the lowly ox.

Verses 8-9 begin the section with an instruction about any "leprous skin disease" (the Hebrew seems to refer to a range of dermatological maladies). Since skin disease is a ritual and symbolic matter (a mixing of life with decay and death), one might have expected the topic earlier under the rubric of adulteration (22:9–23:18). Why does Deuteronomy treat it here? Getting skin disease is not defaming anyone; it is not a moral offense at all (clothes and walls can contract the condition; see Lev 13:47-48; 14:34-35).

A rule on skin disease begins this section because an outbreak of this dread condition demanded immediate deference to leaders. The culture understood the malady to be complicated to diagnose and gravely threatening. An outbreak called for speedy priestly intervention and meticulous honoring of priestly judgment. Everyone must rally around the Levites' instruction in such a matter or else put the community at dire risk.

In Deuteronomy's source texts, being struck with skin disease is a horrific misfortune. In the E source, the malady turns one's skin "white as snow" (Exod 4:6; Num 12:10). When it strikes his sister, Moses fears that she will soon become like "one stillborn, whose flesh is half consumed"

(Num 12:12 E). With such disease, rotting decay has indeed infiltrated God's people. At such a time one defers to the Levites! Three times v. 8 uses the Hebrew verb *shamar,* meaning "watch," "guard." Israel is to be on "guard," to be "very careful," to "carefully observe" the Levites' teaching. The rhetoric drives home the gravity of the Levites' role and the peril of attaching any false witness to it.

Verse 9 directly connects the topics of care in bearing witness and skin disease. At an infamous instance in the wilderness, Miriam bore false witness against Moses, and was immediately stricken with the trauma of snow-white skin (Num 12 E). Hammering away at Moses' reputation and dignity, she defamed him, according to the E story. She engaged in insults or gossip about his marriage to a Cushite woman (Num 12:1). (Was Miriam playing on community prejudice against foreigners?) Her core gripe, however, involved Moses' claims to authority. Her jealousy contrasts sharply with the humble leadership of Moses, "the humblest man on earth" (Num 12:3, NJB).

Moses was himself a Levite (cf. Exod 4:14 E; Ps 99:6) and upon his death wants Levites to assume his leading role (Deut 31). Thus, Deuteronomy uses the figure of Moses in Number 12 to represent the Levitical leadership of the Israel of its day. The circle of Levites, not the king, wields final judgment in Deuteronomy's ideal covenantal society. They occupy the book's highest tier of leadership and come first in this section. They are the ones with expertise in interpreting the covenant (see Deut 17:10, 18; cf. 31:9, 25-26; 33:10; 2 Kgs 17:27-28). For this reason, v. 8 of our passage emphasizes their ability and divine authorization to "instruct."

Next, vv. 10-13 cover two more gradations of society, turning the reader's attention first to the community's debtors (vv. 10-11) and then to the poorest of those owing money (vv. 12-13). As an example of honoring such persons' reputation and dignity, the text places restrictions on demanding collateral from them. One cannot barge into a neighbor's house to demand a pledge, even if repayment is long overdue.

One must take even more care if the debtor is destitute (cf. 24:6). If one takes such a person's cloak as a pledge, it must be returned each evening at sunset (as stipulated by Exod 22:26-27). It is surely a false witness to treat people as less valuable than their clothing, letting them suffer through a cold night (the garment doubled as a blanket). Why would anyone bother taking a cloak with this restriction in effect? Probably only to prevent a destitute borrower from getting entangled in multiple loan arrangements. Multiple indebtedness of a poor person would be to no one's advantage.

Snatching garments off the backs of the poor was proverbial in Israel for cruel excess (cf. Prov 20:16; 27:13; Amos 2:8). The wicked were said to have "exacted pledges . . . for no reason," to have "stripped the naked of their clothing" (Job 22:6). The seizing of garments was not just a saying, however, but an actual practice. The Yavneh Yam inscription from the late seventh century BCE attests it. In this text, a field worker asks the district governor to make a lower official return a confiscated garment.

Verses 14-15 move another rung lower on the social ladder to treat day laborers, both natives and resident aliens. Such persons were on the edge of survival. Without land to farm or a trade to practice, they hired themselves out as seasonal help. Such a laborer must not be denied his daily pay, since "he . . . urgently depends on it" (v. 15, NJPS). It might often have been all that stood between him and starvation.

One can imagine that day laborers might be maligned as deserving their lowly station, their dirt-poor life. You can just hear the slander: "These people are as lazy and stupid as their parents who lost their ancestral farms through sloth." "Like father, like son—they are all lazybones and louts, slated for a premature demise" (see Prov 24:30-31). Deuteronomy has positioned v. 16 here to stand against this false witness and any other assumption of "guilt by association." Never mind that there were many ways to lose a farm other than stupidity and vice. Even if parents are blameworthy, children should not inherit their guilt (cf. 2 Kgs 14:6; Jer 31:29-30). The principle must certainly obtain in the law courts: "Only for their own crimes may persons be put to death."

Verse 16 does not deny that stupidity and vice have long-term ramifications, that parents pass on the consequences of sin (Exod 20:5; 34:7; Num 14:18; Deut 5:9). Even the exilic prophet Ezekiel, who strongly stressed the moral independence of generations (Ezek 18:1-32), affirmed that sin's aftereffects are long lived (see Ezek 16:44; 20:4, 30). Ezekiel just insisted that despite this, God always honors the integrity of each separate human life (see Ezek 18:4; cf. his source material in Num 16:22-24). Deuteronomy 7:10 similarly emphasizes God's concern with personal responsibility.

Verses 17-22 continue to address the status of the most vulnerable in society, those without land of their own to farm. In addition to resident aliens, the subsection also mentions the orphan and the widow. Despite their dependence and low social status, the vulnerable have both dignity and a good name. They must receive justice (cf. 16:18-20). One must not bear them false witness, treat them as subhuman. There must be no snatching of garments off the backs of widows (v. 17; cf. vv. 12-13; Job 24:3).

So that the poor not be reduced to begging, landowners must allow them to glean harvest leftovers from fields, orchards, and vineyards. Owners must not hoard the land's blessings (a similar spirit imbues 23:24-25). They must not go back over their lands, milking them of every bit of produce. Substantive portions must be left for the needy to pick up after the harvesters' work is done, thereby finding sustenance and preserving a sense of self-reliance. The book of Ruth illustrates well how this worked.

The two parts of this subsection share a concluding refrain urging Israel to remember that "you were a slave in the land of Egypt" (vv. 18, 22). Having lived through a brutish existence themselves, community members should be in a place to empathize with those still in dire straits. The reader has repeatedly observed Deuteronomy's penchant for such moral appeals, its constant exhortation that God's people incarnate God's own spirit of other-centeredness (e.g., see the commentary on Deut 10:12).

Next, in 25:1-3 the section moves down near the bottom of the social ladder to the criminal. In a world where beating was an accepted punishment (cf. Prov 10:13; 26:3; Exod 21:20; 1 Kgs 12:14), these verses demand proportionality, limitation, and a judge's direct supervision. Forty strikes is the uppermost limit, lest the guilty person be degraded to something less than human. Despite his or her sentence, the convicted criminal remains a covenantal sibling (NRSV: "neighbor," v. 3). All should expect the person to return to full communal restoration with some sense of dignity intact.

A definitive restriction on beatings like Deuteronomy's is unknown among ancient Near Eastern laws. Middle Assyrian Laws speak of people receiving up to one hundred lashes! In this context, Deuteronomy's rule stands out as unique, and is also notable for maintaining a single standard that applies across the board in society.

Lest readers imagine that the book has now exhausted its coverage of those for whom reverent respect is required, 25:4 concludes the section by demanding humane treatment of animals. Apparently, there are *no limits* on who should be considered one's neighbor! Even the lowly ox must be allowed its dignity and honor. It is wrong to muzzle one's ox while it is threshing, treading out grain. The owner's own humanity is diminished by depriving the animal of its share in the fruits of its labor (cf. Prov 12:10).

The ox is part of the great matrix of life associated with the promised land. All is interconnected because Deuteronomy's God is *one,* its covenant *holistic* (6:4). One must respect this vibrant, supple system as a zone of spiritual formation, an arena for practicing reverence for life. God planted Israel in the land to be formed as a holy, life-loving people nurturing such reverence (see the commentary on 5:14; 14:3-21; 22:6-7).

Do Not Covet Your Neighbor's Wife

Deuteronomy 25:5-12

Deuteronomy now arrives at the final, tenth commandment, the prohibition against coveting (5:21). As with the grammar of 5:21, it sets the sin of coveting a wife off from other types of wrongful desire. Intentionally supportive of women's humanity, it gives the sin of craving another's wife its own initial section (25:5-12) before moving on to the coveting of material property (25:13–26:15).

As just happened at the start of the last section (24:8-9), the text immediately throws a curveball. For six verses, there is a discussion of *levirate marriage*. Just as in chapter 24 where skin disease at first seemed unrelated to bearing a false witness, the connection here of levirate practices with coveting is not immediately apparent.

Levirate marriage is the practice of a dead husband's brother (Latin *levir*) marrying the deceased man's widow in order to father a child and continue the sibling's descent line. Through a legal fiction, the marriage allowed the posthumous birthing of an heir. The custom is known from elsewhere in the Bible (Gen 38:8; Ruth 4:5-6), and it fits ancient Israel's culture where the continuation of family lines was so valued. If anything, however, the *levir* appears to be handed a huge loophole to the command against coveting. Is not the man licensed both to covet a wife and to land her in his arms?

Things are not as they first appear. As one reads and rereads the passage, it increasingly emerges as no license for coveting but a rebuke against any such vice. The element of rebuke is strongest in vv. 7-10, where the widow pulls the sandal off the *levir*'s foot, spits in his face, and publically denounces him. The description of these acts of censure takes up two-thirds of the passage, and seems to represent its main thrust.

To understand the passage in its present context, one should probably assume that it aims to rebuke the flawed character of a *levir* who is *grasping* and *covetous*. The two most relevant cross-references shed light on the issue. Tamar, who had several *levirs*, was so desirable that Judah paid the price of a goat to have sex with her (Gen 38:15-19). Ruth was also sexually desirable enough to have her pick of any of the young men (Ruth 3:10). As many commentators note, Ruth's next-of-kin is technically not a *levir*, a literal brother-in-law (see Ruth 1:11-13). Apparently, as in traditional African cultures today, the so-called levirate duty is a responsibility of the whole kin-group, not of the immediate family alone. There was a definite order in the clan's line of obligation to the childless widow and her dead husband (see Ruth 1:11; 2:20; 3:12).

Deuteronomy likely assumes its readers have the stories of Tamar and Ruth in mind (Ruth 4:12 assumes this sort of memory). What is more, the book presupposes readers' familiarity with the sexual connotations of the sandal ceremony of vv. 9-10. In Hebrew culture, the foot was a phallic symbol, the word "foot" a euphemism for the penis (see Exod 4:25; Ruth 3:4, 7-8; 2 Sam 11:8; Isa 6:2). The sandal, which slips over the "foot," likely called to mind the vagina and the womb. A customary Arab announcement at a divorce refers to the wife as the husband's "slipper." Her soon-to-be ex proclaims, "She was my slipper, I have cast her off" (cited in Biddle, 372). If the parallel is apt, the widow of Deuteronomy 25:9 proclaims, "I reject this man; keep his overeager 'foot' away from me!"

There is yet more to suggest covetousness at play. The levirate duty was applicable to a range of circumstances, but our passage focuses in on one in particular, when "two brothers are living together on the same property" (v. 5, NLT). Why this particular focus on an individual family compound, when the custom at issue was a duty of the entire clan (as seen in Ruth)? Deuteronomy has zeroed in on this scenario for all its suggestiveness. Humans tend to covet what they see every day (cf. Gen 39:7).

As v. 5 spells out, the *levir* at issue in Deuteronomy 25 is an eldest brother within a family compound, a figure with special rights and powers. Especially when the family's patriarch grew old or died, this particular figure exercised authority over brothers and sisters, nephews and nieces (1 Sam 10:14-15). He convened the family for ceremonies, commanding family members' presence (1 Sam 20:29). He directed family burials, and was in charge of venerating the ancestors (Lev 10:4; Amos 6:10). Given his role, he might assume automatic access to his dead brother's widow—no questions asked.

The eldest brother might presume that convention handed him this woman, opened a loophole for gratifying his coveting. He covets her and assumes she is his for the taking, with no assurance from him of performing the levirate duty. But Deuteronomy insists that this is complete presumption and an instance of the coveting of women at its worst. It is treating women as objects for the taking, not persons with rights and feelings.

Deuteronomy likely chose to present this particular text at this juncture for its strikingly rich images of opprobrium and contempt. A spouse-coveter of any ilk really deserves to feel the community's scorn. He should have the sandal pulled off his foot, his face spat upon, and his lineage be named "Family-No-Sandal." His sexual desire reflects an internal imbalance absent of any true care for the other person and for those she loves.

Verses 11-12 present a ruling on another scenario, which appears equally challenging to fathom. Here a woman intervenes in a fight, trying to rescue her husband, and attacks the genitals of the man hitting him. Such an act is deemed horrific enough to require one to "cut off her hand; show no pity" (v. 12). The modern reader is repelled.

Severe punishments were part of Deuteronomy's world; the Middle Assyrian Laws order the physical maiming of lawbreakers. The mutilation of v. 12 is unique in Deuteronomy, however, and it strikes the reader as a disproportionate punishment, alien to the reciprocal justice ("talion") of 19:21. Driven to additional reflection, the reader begins wondering what rationale could possibly be at play in this rule's inclusion. How often could the situation of vv. 11-12 arise? Must there not be a richer, more relevant, sense about this law than at first appears?

While the NRSV speaks generically of two men engaged in a fight, the Hebrew of v. 11 speaks of something much more specific and germane. Echoing v. 5, it speaks of a man and his "brother," "together." Is this fight, then, not between v. 5's "brothers" who reside "together"? Are they not fighting over one brother's coveted wife?

Such an understanding would both fit the details of vv. 11-12 and answer several of the questions raised by the odd verses. A scenario of two brothers sharing a family compound makes it natural for the wife of one combatant to intervene in their fight. More significantly, a connection with vv. 5-10 means our text is less out of place and esoteric than at first appeared. It means Deuteronomy is simply giving us another look at two brothers desiring the same woman. She is at the center of their altercation. Her husband—unlike in vv. 5-10, very much alive—has discovered his sibling's craving for his wife, an argument has ensued, and it has turned violent.

If this is the likely background of vv. 11-12, as Deuteronomy under-stands it and presents it to us, an interpretation of the present meaning and teaching of these verses suggests itself. The reader can begin to see what the book is trying to do at this juncture. It is likely portraying what complex and painful consequences might flow from coveting a neighbor's wife. It is suggesting that the wife, as well as the coveter, might incur guilt.

If a person allows an illicit craving to nest in the heart and mind, passions can easily intensify and lead to immoral action. The object of one's desire may respond in a number of possible ways. If the other person toys with unfaithfulness, some sort of love triangle may begin to form and a variety of highly tangled and confused emotions come into play. Some of these may be dark and dangerous. Lust when gratified may turn to hate (cf. 2 Sam 13:15). The coveted woman may end up violently defending her husband.

Given the text's paucity of detail, the reader can only guess at the woman's thoughts and motives as she seized the coveter's genitals. Completely fed up with the man's arousal, perhaps she is after his body to "fix things" definitively. Alternatively, she had perhaps been receptive to the man's lust, and was now lashing out in shame and regret at the "instrument" jeopardizing her marriage. Deuteronomy surely envisages some such aggressive meaning in her action. The wife's handling of the "foot" in v. 9 was rich with nuance. Her seizing of the "foot" in v. 11 must have an equal significance.

Whether she acts in tortured regret or in rash entitlement, she has let her passions overcome her, presumed a control and an intimacy that are not hers, and transgressed a sacred boundary. In fascinating ways, her actions and attitudes mirror those of the covetous *levir*. Like him, her desires are out of balance. Like him, she presumes a right of access to another's body. Both he and she have no regard for the importance in Israel of seed, progeny, and family line. He withheld the promise of seed when it was sorely needed; she strikes at the source of seed, threatening to annihilate it.

The command "cut off her hand" sends a strong message. People must not allow their desires to corrupt them, must not arrogate to themselves the prerogative to seize another's sex. As in vv. 5-10, the emphasis in vv. 11-12 is on extreme rebuke of sexual exploitation. The force of the language lies in deterrence, in sober warning—that is the reason for the idiom "show no pity." There may be no intention that a hand ever actually be severed, just an exhortation about the rigor of living with purity of heart. No one should pretend this is easy. No one should pretend that internal desires are harmless.

The New Testament parallel in Matthew 5:27-29 does not commend a literal severing of body parts. Rather, it drives home how damaging passions and lusts may become. If nursed, they may dump a person on the moral trash heap, ostracized from communal fellowship. Is the female "hand" of v. 12 a euphemism for her genitals, just as the male "foot" of v. 9 was a phallic symbol? If so, the verse is code language for public shaming over sexual aggression. Both male and female disregard of the tenth commandment should get a perpetrator labeled an exploiter, his or her sexual reputation permanently sullied. That is a punishment more fitting than physical mutilation.

Do Not Long for Anything that Belongs to Your Neighbor

Deuteronomy 25:13–26:15

Deuteronomy now moves to treat wrongful desires that threaten others' belongings and security. The book warns especially about desires and ambitions that impoverish the humanity of others. When drives and passions take over, ends come to justify means. The vulnerable become prey, subject to exploitation. An appetite-driven spirit directly opposes that which Deuteronomy strives to inculcate: a spirit of mutuality and outreach.

The character Haman in the book of Esther exemplifies the predatory spirit that so concerns Deuteronomy. A glutton for honor, Haman has an ambition and a lust for prestige that know no bounds. Offended by one Jew, the honorable Mordecai, he determines to vent his fury on all Jews throughout the whole kingdom of Persia. He gains his king's permission to destroy an entire people, simply because they are odd, an "affront," and because their property is worth an enormous sum, 333 tons of silver (Esth 3:8-11).

Verses 13-16 begin this section of Deuteronomy by condemning a predatory spirit in buying and selling. A fraudulent trader could cheat a grain supplier by using larger than standard measuring containers. The merchant could then turn around and cheat buyers by using an inaccurately small measure. Similarly, one could make a killing using two sets of rigged counterweights. Too light a counterweight allowed one to purchase grain dirt cheap, while an alternate, heavy counterweight tipped the scales in one's favor when determining how much silver one's customers had to pay.

The use of crooked standards in the ancient world was hard to detect and even harder to prosecute, allowing covetous merchants to give little and take much (see Prov 11:1; 16:11; 20:23; Hos 12:7; Mic 6:10-12; Ezek 45:10-12). According to the prophet Amos, there were plenty of rapacious traders around, "eager to sell less for a higher price, and to cheat the buyer with rigged scales" (Amos 8:5, NET). For Deuteronomy, to even possess dishonest weights and measures is a vice, signaling a willingness to prey on the vulnerable, to trample on the needy and bring the poor of the land to ruin.

Verses 17-19 on "Amalek" continue to illuminate the tenth commandment, but they also begin to prepare the reader for a new turn in the book. Having been immersed for fifteen chapters in the book's central legal code, the reader must get ready to emerge. This text's reminder of an event on the journey out of Egypt begins to return to a narrative storyline that is moving out of the wilderness and into Canaan.

Another subsection about offering God "first fruits" once safe in the land (26:1-15) further prepares readers to shift gears. The book's in-depth study of God's commandments draws to a close. It will soon be time to ratify the covenant and push forward on the trek of discipleship oriented on the promised land and the reign of God.

How is what the Amalekites did to Israel on the way from Egypt relevant to the present discussion of coveting? Quite simply, for Deuteronomy, the actions of Amalek epitomize coveting at its worse. As they encountered Israel, these fierce desert raiders showed themselves for the wanton predators that they were. They proved that good and evil had no meaning for them, that they "did not fear God" (Deut 25:18). The intelligence of their evil lay not in brutality alone, but in brutality that lacked discernable meaning. According to Deuteronomy's source (the E strand), Amalek's enmity was fully without provocation—horrifyingly *helter-skelter* (Exod 17:8-16; see Chapman 2013b).

Chapman (2013b, 15) reviews the many textual details pushing the reader to understand "Amalek" as now symbolic of "primordial, spiritual resistance to God" (a move well attested in Jewish and Christian tradition, cf. Barnabas 12:9). Terence Fretheim (194) aptly summarizes Amalek's emblematic representation of evil: "At a point of supreme vulnerability for the people of God, when their future was hanging in the balance, Amalek had sought to exterminate them. The Amalekites thus become an embodiment of evil, Pharaoh revisited, a veritable Hitlerian specter, threatening God's creational purposes."

By the time of Deuteronomy's appearance in the seventh century BCE, the Amalekites had ceased to exist as a people (1 Chr 4:43; cf. 1 Sam 15:8). There is no xenophobia or ethnic hatred here. Rather, Deuteronomy is voicing an unrelenting opposition to a spirit—the spirit of terrorism. For *terrorism* is perhaps the most apt term for Amalek's mode of operation. The raiders attacked non-combatant stragglers at the rear of Israel's procession. They "struck down all who lagged behind" (Deut 25:18).

Amalek's spectacle was destined to live on in infamy. "Do not forget!" Moses commands in 25:19. The raiders' assault had particular symbolic potency over against Deuteronomy's opposite value system, where life and wholeness were prized. To kill the innocent, the stragglers, was anathema. It flew in the face of the book's core aspiration for "rest" (v. 19), for safe space to realize existential freedom. "Rest" on every hand, for Deuteronomy, would mean opportunity to encounter God's otherness in intimacy. This divine otherness could make the human soul "other," could utterly ennoble it.

Despite Amalek's disappearance as a people, the Bible records the survival of at least one Amalekite descendent. In the book of Esther, Haman—the vile enemy of the Jews—is an "Agagite," that is, a descendent of King Agag of the Amalekites (Esth 3:1; cf. 1 Sam 15:8). The Targum of Esther specifically makes the connection. The pedigree is significant, for the book continually refers to it (Esth 3:1, 10; 8:3, 5; 9:24). It wants to emphasize that this arch villain incarnates archetypal covetousness.

Deuteronomy 26:1-15 turns to the topic of offerings of "first fruits," emphasizing especially the ceremonies and confessions of faith surrounding their presentation. The central law corpus (12:1–26:15) began with God's chosen worship site and the offerings to be brought there (ch. 12). As the code now comes to a close, things come full circle and the book rounds off its presentation of the core torah with a return to the central shrine. But we are still in the context of illuminating the tenth commandment. The book believes that worshipers' ritual statements of belief at presenting offerings at the shrine illuminate the essence of living in opposition to covetousness.

The text stipulates that every Israelite farmer must attend the three annual pilgrimage festivals (see 16:16-17) and bring some of the land's first (or "choicest") ripe produce (cf. Exod 23:19; 34:26). The farmer must present these "first fruits" from each crop that is harvested across the year at the central sanctuary as an offering. At the Festival of Weeks (16:9-12), for example, one must make a token offering of grain to the Lord (cf. Num 28:26). Such offerings serve as pledges on full payment of tithes and provide ceremonial occasions for responding to God's gift of the promised land.

Israel does not roam the promised land as a covetous predator but carefully forges a symbiotic relationship with a holy environment. To confess one's responsibility as a steward of the holy land, and one's gratitude for God's good gifts that spring from it, is to embrace a spirit opposite to the self-oriented drives of Haman and the Amalekites. It is to deflate the ego and make oneself attentive, receptive, and responsive in relationship to God, to God's supple land, and to one's co-vassals under the covenant. The spirit of this text was already clear in Deuteronomy 6:10-15 and in Deuteronomy 8. These passages nurture a humble spirit of interdependence that should spread everywhere and foster true mutuality.

In vv. 1-3, the festival pilgrim arrives at the central shrine and hands the Levite on duty a basket of first fruits (cf. 18:4). The ritual act abounds with significance. So does the emotion-packed statement that accompanies the presentation: "I have come into the land that the LORD swore to our ancestors to give us." The unique territory of Canaan is a land sworn to the ancestors (Gen 15:16 E; Exod 13:5, 11 E; 32:13 E; Num 11:12 E). Israel's presence there is no accident, but part of an arching trajectory of the word of God. This theme of Deuteronomy occurs repeatedly (see Deut 1:8, 35; 4:31; 6:10, 18, 23; 7:13; 8:1; 10:11; 11:9, 21; 19:8). Now each vassal confesses its fulfillment in his or her own personal experience.

In vv. 4-11, the worshiper makes a second confession as the Levite receives the basket and sets it down before the Lord's altar. The declaration is short but sweeping (cf. Hos 12:12-13). It sketches the entire history of salvation leading to the enjoyment of God's land. The worshiper identifies with Israel's experience at each stage of the history. Each "leaf" on the "tree" of Israel, planted by God in God's sacred, sanctuary land, interconnects with all other members of the organism across the generations. The tree of Israel is a transplant, unaffiliated with the land's previous inhabitants (cf. Deut 4:25-26; 8:19-20; 9:4-5). Unlike the Canaanites who never took root, Israel must accept the land's orientation on nurturing a true vassal community (see Deut 12:29-32; 18:9-14).

It was not by chance that a hapless mass of homeless aliens now inhabit a land "flowing with milk and honey" (vv. 9, 15). God took what started as a handful of siblings, abused in a cruel Egyptian slavery, and through terrible wonders gave them a land to be thankful for, a land of world-affirming, festive life. God intends this new homeland to make Israel holy—a rejoicing community, celebrating life before the Lord. In Deuteronomy, feasting and celebration mark holiness (see on 14:22-29).

The rehearsal of salvation history has not included the encounter with God at Sinai/Horeb. That encounter is instead made dynamic in the present, as the pilgrims encounter their Lord and the torah in bringing their offerings to the central sanctuary. The Lord meets Israel in the here and now, knitting all souls closely together as a unified "Thou" encountering the divine "I." As the people feel their fragility before God and tighten their bonds with each other, every predatory spirit of covetousness vanishes.

The first fruits mark a pledge on tithes and freewill offerings to be brought to the sanctuary (12:6-7, 11-12; 14:22-29; 26:12). The tithe is not for the shrine to keep, but for the pilgrims themselves to eat, and to share with the landless—with the Levites and with the resident aliens of the country. As this happens, desiring (coveting) gives way to communion in the presence of Israel's numinous God. In place of longing for private belongings, one instead celebrates *collectively* "all the bounty that the LORD your God has given" (v. 11). This is the positive, constructive force of the tenth commandment.

Verses 12-15 conclude the section by turning to the special third-year tithe that does not go to the temple but stays in the towns to support the landless (see 14:28-29). The practice of this tithe again embodies the spirit of collective sharing. Since the people receive the bounty of God's land as a gift, they should distribute it graciously in the spirit in which it was given. They must particularly remember those without lands to harvest, namely "the Levites, the aliens, the orphans, and the widows." All these people must not merely subsist but find themselves *satisfied*. Perhaps a joyous public feast in the towns, where all ate "their fill" (v. 12), accompanied the offering of the triennial tithe.

The person offering the tithe again makes a declaration, the third confession of this section. Its content reinforces how collective sharing of God's bounty is a distinct mark of Israel's *holiness*, of its commitment to reject private hoarding and to feast on life in togetherness (notably, v. 13 calls the tithe "sacred," "holy"). To be a holy people, sending roots down deep in God's sanctuary land, is to see *everyone*, particularly the vulnerable, rejoicing and feasting to their heart's content. The defining point for any claim to be practicing holiness, thus disavowing covetousness, is the well-being and joy of the landless, "the Levites, the resident aliens, the orphans, and the widows" (v. 13).

Since uplifting the landless constitutes an act of holiness *par excellence*, farmers must confess that the tithe was set aside without any taint by association with death and decay (on how the holy abhors death, see the commentary on 14:1-21; 22:5, 6-7; 23:1, 2). They must state they have not eaten from it, or even handled it, while ritually impure—for example, while mourning near a corpse. None of it has been left as food at burial sites (cf. Tob 4:17). Mourning is acceptable, of course, as is leaving food at graves (a way of keeping the dead and the living connected). Feasting and mourning are symbolic opposites, however, not to be mixed; the tithe is for merry-makers, not grim spirits.

Verse 15 concludes the section by enjoining God to "look down" from "heaven" and bless both covenant people and sacred ground in all their symbiotic ties. The language placing God up in heaven at first feels odd, especially since the worshiper has just made confessions in God's immediate presence, speaking directly "to the LORD" (v. 3) and "before the LORD" (vv. 5, 13). What is going on with this talk of heaven?

Deuteronomy characteristically holds two truths about God's presence in tension (cf. Deut 4:35-37). God's presence is scandalously imminent (4:37); yet God surely rules earth from heaven (4:35). At 26:15, as the core torah of Deuteronomy concludes, the emphasis falls on the latter truth. The torah, although directed at Israel, has its place within God's *universal* rule of all creation from heaven. The torah of God, just examined through fifteen chapters of in-depth treatment, has universally inclusive, global implications (cf. 2:5, 9, 19-22; 10:14; 20:19-20; 26:19). The work of God in Deuteronomy will someday change the world as a whole.

Conclusion to the Legal Corpus: A Mutual Covenant

Deuteronomy 26:16-19

The phrase "statutes and ordinances" has not been heard since the law code's very start (12:1). It occurs again here in v. 16 as a concluding bookend to the entire torah. Indubitably, the frame is intentional: the terms "observe" and "diligently" are also repeated from 12:1. The law corpus has been put in a literary "envelope"; it stands delivered.

Now, Moses draws his audience into the here and now and presses them to affirm the covenant. "This very day" they must commit with everything in them. They must ratify for themselves the agreement first concluded at Horeb and now rebirthed in their hearing on the plains of Moab. Deuteronomy's later readers too, no matter what their "here and now," are drawn in to recommit themselves. Certainly, King Josiah understood v. 16's "this very day" to apply to his generation (2 Kgs 23:1-3).

Moses's language rings with *mutuality*. The covenant is a *two-way* affair, for acceptance and ratification by two parties. Israel today, here on the plains of Moab, confirms the Lord's "agreement" (v. 17) to be the people's God, an agreement repeatedly emphasized by Moses (see 4:20; 7:6; 14:2; 29:13). So too, the Lord today confirms the people's decision to be God's treasured people (vv. 18-19), a decision publically established at Horeb (Exod 19:8; 24:3, both E; Deut 5:27).

Verse 17 and vv. 18-19 reflect one another rhetorically. Taken together, they affirm the *bilateral* nature of the ancient covenant formula: "I will be your God, and you shall be my people" (see Hos 1:9, a source of Deuteronomy). Our text leaves no doubt: the covenant entails God and Israel's *reciprocal commitment*. This core tenet of Deuteronomy means the love between God and people is free, authentic, and risky—a relationship of two lives knit together, an existentially valid "I-Thou" encounter.

Verse 19's language of Israel's global elevation as God's holy people really stands out. Israel's trek to the promised land has an enormously lofty goal: "for him to set you high above all nations that he has made, in praise and in fame and in honor; and for you to be a people holy." The covenant presses forward with momentum toward its divinely established end, aiming to become a center of orientation for all earth's peoples.

The reader is by now familiar with Israel being God's treasure (see 7:6; 14:2; cf. Exod 19:5-6 E). This passage, however, insists that Israel is not only special to God but also to the nations, who are drawn to revere and honor God through God's elect people (cf. Deut 4:6-8; 28:1; Jer 13:11; Zeph 3:19-20). What Israel becomes through God's power will bring shudders of awe across the globe (cf. Jer 33:9).

The postexilic prophet Malachi, propelled by Deuteronomy's theology, elaborates this theme. Malachi foresees earth's nations pressing for inclusion in God's worship once God restores and enforces Israel's covenant through a new Moses, a new "messenger of the covenant." Everywhere on earth, because of what God will do in Israel, people are about to offer God incense and pure offerings (Mal 1:11; cf. 1:5, 14).

Ceremonies at Shechem

Deuteronomy 27:1-26

Just as the preceding section in 26:16-19 reached back to chapter 12 to form a literary "envelope" around the law code, the present section in 27:1-26 reaches back to the text immediately before chapter 12, that is, to 11:26-32. There, before delving into the torah's details, Moses made clear that Israel's covenant had both blessings and curses attached to it, just like comparable Near Eastern suzerainty treaties. Once Israel entered the land, the people must ritually enact this truth through reciting blessings and curses at Mounts Ebal and Gerizim, near Shechem. This ceremony would properly begin their settlement of Canaan.

Deuteronomy 27 elaborates on the procedure for implementing the instruction of 11:26-32. Together with chapter 11, it sets a pair of outer "bookends" around the law code, and witnesses to the high stakes involved in a binding covenantal relationship. Blessings and curses are of the utmost seriousness, matters of life and death. To make the oath of covenantal allegiance to the Lord is to receive the hope of abundant life, of monumental blessing. Simultaneously, however, it is to bind oneself so deeply to a preternatural "other" as to expose oneself to ghastly trauma should breaches in the relationship occur.

From the start of the passage, the theme of the necessary death of Moses reemerges. Moses has the elders stand with him as he addresses the people (v. 1). Then, the elders step back and the Levites join Moses in announcing the sealing of the covenantal relationship (v. 9). Moses has not shared the stage before. Not in Deuteronomy. Now begins the process of the entire community, represented by its traditional leaders, taking up for itself the enterprise of living out the covenant (cf. 31:9-13). Israel must rebirth itself in a new spirit of maturity, freedom, and mutuality.

The book has prepared us for this death and rebirth, this shifting of power and responsibility out from the center to local communities. Texts such as 1:6-18; 16:18-20; 21:2, 19; 22:15; 25:7 have targeted Israel's elders for re-empowerment (note their key role in E texts behind Deuteronomy, such as Exod 3:16; 17:5-6; 19:7; 24:1, 9-11; Num 11:16). Similarly, texts such as 17:9, 18; 18:1-8; 21:5 have re-enfranchised the Levites (again, key traditional leaders in E; see Exod 32:26-29). Now, all these instructions and preparations are set to go live. Israel is on the verge of a new existence.

According to the address of Moses and the elders in vv. 1-8, the first order of business in the promised land is to erect large stones and coat them with a stucco writing surface. God's revelation is to go up on permanent display on Mount Ebal, sharply incised in plaster. Israel is to have a standing, public exhibition of the torah.

The display of law codes and other key texts in monumental fashion was a familiar practice in the ancient Near East, and the specific idea of a plaster imprinting is realistic. The same thing appears both in the case of the Deir 'Alla Inscription, in red and black ink on a plaster wall (eighth century BCE), and in the case of three plaster inscriptions at Kuntillet 'Ajrud (end of the ninth or beginning of the eighth century).

The inscription on Mount Ebal is nothing other than the first written edition of Deuteronomy (this is a *literary*, not a historical claim). *Sacred writing* should now become the guiding beacon of God's people. God's word is established, fixed in stone; however, it calls for constant rereading in an ongoing search for current meaning and relevance. After the death of Moses, Israel should move to a mode of discipleship centered on the inscribed word of God—on its ongoing centrality and continual reinterpretation.

After inscribing huge stones with God's revelation, the people are to erect beside them an altar of uncut fieldstones, "stones on which you have not used an iron tool" (v. 5). On the altar, they can roast sacrifices. "Rejoicing," they can celebrate the immediate presence of God. They can stand directly "before the LORD" (vv. 6-7). (For bibliography on probable archaeological remains of an Ebal altar, see Arnold 2010, 64; Cook 2013, 125.)

The altar's construction fulfills a command of God at Mount Horeb, one reported by the E source (Exod 20:24-25). At Horeb, God had instructed the people that upon entering the promised land they should build an altar of either clumps of earth or unhewn stones. It was to mark a place of God's name. There, Israel would encounter God directly: "Where I cause my name to be remembered I will come to you." The parallelism between Deuteronomy 27:5-7 and Exodus 20:24-25 is striking. Both speak of an altar of fieldstones. Both speak of burnt offerings and offerings of well-being. In both, Israel experiences an immediate encounter with God. Deuteronomy's God is present to Israel!

Scholars have long puzzled over the rationale behind the requirement of unfinished, unhewn stones in Exodus 20:25 and Deuteronomy 27:5-6. Are these undressed stones intended to contrast with Canaan's elaborate sculpted worship objects, its graven images of silver and sculpted gods of gold? Both E and Deuteronomy would surely affirm such a contrast, but unique Hebrew language about "whole stones" in Deuteronomy 27:6 (see NET) suggests something more. This requirement likely manifests the reappearance here of Deuteronomy's embrace of purity and wholeness.

In Deuteronomy's purity system, the emphasis falls on symbols of order, wholeness, and completeness, which stand against chaos and impotence. Holy things, in God's service, must not appear incomplete or denuded. People with damaged genitals are banned from the Lord's assembly (23:1). Animals with physical defects are unsuitable as sacrifices (15:21; 17:1). In some cases, such as that of the heifer in 21:1-9, a ritual animal must even be free of bruises, such as might come from wearing a yoke (21:3).

To this way of thinking, an altar must be made of "whole" stones. Just as a yoke would bruise a ritual heifer, a chisel would symbolically bruise and degrade an altar stone: "If you use a chisel upon it you profane it" (Exod 20:25).

As Saul Olyan (1996, 171) aptly puts it, Deuteronomy's insistence on unfinished stones links up with a concern "to separate the deity and his space, conceived as holy, from forms of physical alteration understood to produce defilement of that space. Just as 'full' and 'complete' sacrifices and altar personnel are required . . . , so 'full' and 'complete' stones are required for Yhwh's altar."

The stone altar on Mount Ebal might raise eyebrows for some given Deuteronomy's insistence on a single sanctuary (ch. 12). Thus, judging chapter 27 inconsistent with the book's "centralization requirement," some readers may see independent traditions here, fossils out of place. If so, they are mistaken.

Deuteronomy never ties the divine presence permanently to one site, never grants Jerusalem an eternal covenant (see on ch. 12 above). No, God's people are on the move, on a discipleship trek. They pause only periodically to worship at sites where God places God's invocation name, the name that Israel uses to encounter God. At such places, God becomes directly present and *freedom meets freedom* (Steiner, 154, 174).

Moses commands Israel to pause on its trek and worship on Mount Ebal (cf. 11:26-32). In Joshua 8:30-35 God's people will do exactly that. It will be one among a number of such pauses. They pause at Mount Horeb (Exod 24:3-8 E; Deut 5:27), on the plains of Moab (Deut 26:16-19; 27:9b), and at

Gilgal, immediately after crossing the Jordan (notably, the events at Gilgal narrated in Josh 4:19-20 parallel Deut 27:2; furthermore, Deut 11:30 also mentions the site).

The pause for covenantal rites in Exodus 24:3-8 (E) is of special interest. During that pause, the vision of Exodus 20:24 is realized. On that occasion, there at Horeb, Moses acts just as he does in Deuteronomy 27. Moses writes down God's torah, sets up standing-stones as monuments, and builds an altar for worship. He makes ready for the promised encounter with God: "I will come to you" (Exod 20:24 E).

In every one of the places of pause along Israel's trek—Horeb, Moab, Gilgal, and Ebal/Shechem—God fulfills the divine promise, "I will come to you" (Exod 20:24 E). Just so, the promise of presence will be fulfilled anew when the assembly reforms periodically in the promised land at (an) unspecified place(s) that "God will choose as a dwelling for his name" (Deut 12:11; 31:10-13; cf. Exod 20:24; both Jerusalem and Shiloh spring to mind as locales of fulfillment, see Jer 7:11-12; see also McConville, 116.)

The second half of chapter 27 adds two additional covenant rituals to the ceremonies at Shechem already described (e.g., in vv. 6-7). The text is murky, however, about exactly how all these ritual prescriptions fit together.

In vv. 11-13, Moses organizes Israel into two groups of six tribes. One, including Levi, stands on Mount Gerizim to pronounce blessings; one stands on Mount Ebal to proclaim curses. As noted above, this parallels and fulfills Deuteronomy 11:26-32. Verse 13, however, leaves the reader hanging. The verses immediately following it do not follow through as expected.

Puzzlingly, no actual blessings or curses occur at this juncture. They seem to appear later on in the following chapter, in 28:1-14 and in 28:15-68. Instead of describing blessings and curses, vv. 14-26 turn to a new ceremony. The Levites catalog twelve prohibitions, each of which Israel affirms in unison, not by groups of tribes. There are no curse-descriptions here, only the phrase "cursed be." The phrase merely introduces prohibited actions, delineates evils. One finds no actual consequences of evil listed here, no real *curses* (contrast 28:15-68, which lists actual curses, real consequences of sin).

Clearly, vv. 14-26 surprise us with their lack of curses and by not depicting *alternating* proclamations. More dissonance soon reveals itself. Mount Ebal is a site of rejoicing in v. 7, whereas in v. 13 it suddenly becomes a site of curse. Perhaps most jolting, the Levites who have just stood beside sibling tribes on Mount Gerizim in v. 12 now quickly move apart to address all Israel in vv. 14-26.

All this literary unevenness likely results from chapter 27's combining a number of distinct rites—ceremonies with a history of celebration extending back before Deuteronomy (back before the seventh century BCE). These rituals were likely repeated cyclically at Shechem (although some of ch. 27's content may stem from Gilgal). On the basis of substantial biblical evidence, we can identify Shechem as a base of Levites up through the eighth century BCE. It surely harbored many precursor traditions of Deuteronomy (see Gen 33:18-20 E; Hos 6:9; Josh 8:30-35; 24). Joshua 24:26 specifically speaks of a sanctuary at Shechem preserving a copy of the covenant.

Despite the choppiness of chapter 27, due to its mixing and combining of various archaic rites, sense can still be made of the passage. The reader need not stop short, refusing to proceed! In the logic of the present text, Moses commands the people to proceed as follows. First, Mount Ebal must be their destination immediately upon entering the land ("on the day," v. 2, signals urgency, not a twenty-four-hour time limit; cf. NJPS, "as soon as"). As soon as Israel arrives in Canaan, it enters the covenant afresh. Second, the people must set up stones and an altar on the mountain, and celebrate the covenant. The choice of Ebal, the mountain of curse, for these rites is in line with the emphasis on taking responsibility in this part of Deuteronomy. At this point, Israel's role is accepting culpability ("curse"). That is what makes the covenant binding.

Next, third, the tribes are to divide themselves into two groups of six, with one of the groups going over to Mount Gerizim (or do both groups move to the valley and stand facing their respective mountains as in Josh 8:33?). The specific division of the tribes in vv. 12-13 is unique, but there is actually a startling mathematical sense to the division. It is the one grouping (out of 462 possibilities!) that splits the population of Israel evenly between the two mountains. For a truly even split, however, some of the Levites must break off from the bulk of their kinfolk. Thus, fourth, those Levites on active priestly duty should move apart and lead the people as a whole, now evenly divided, in pronouncing "Amens," that is, oaths of commitment (27:15-26).

Fifth, and finally, with the covenant now attested and in place circumscribing the people, and with the population now evenly divided, Israel should finally get to the business of blessings and curses. They should fulfill the command of 11:26-32. Thus, they now proceed to further bind their covenantal commitment with alternative proclamations of well-being (28:1-14) and disaster (28:15-68).

The catalog of prohibited actions affirmed as "cursed" in 27:15-26 is fascinating from several angles. The number of offenses cataloged, *twelve*, corresponds to the number of Israel's tribes—here, two groups of six tribes.

Twelve, like the number ten, represents completeness (think of the twelve months in a year, the twelve hours in a day or in a night). With its full twelve-count, the list of "cursed" offenses appears to symbolically encapsulate the torah, just as the Decalogue does.

One can rightly term this list the "Shechemite Dodecalogue," that is, the twelve words/rules of Shechem. The first offense—that of making an idol— echoes the beginning of the Decalogue of Mount Horeb in Deuteronomy 5:6-8. So too, the second offense (27:16) echoes Horeb's fifth commandment (5:16), simultaneously reinforcing Deuteronomy's constant reference to the covenant's kinship infrastructure. Verse 24 resonates with the sixth commandment (5:17). The final verse (27:26) specifically encompasses the entire torah, again suggesting that to affirm this list is to circumscribe life within core boundaries that are summarized in a verbal and liturgical "capsule."

By giving their "Amen" to each item in this formal Dodecalogue, Israel solemnly reinforces its declaration to be God's people at 26:18-19. The people swear a loyalty oath to the covenantal relationship, bringing down curses upon themselves if they depart from their promise (cf. the typical oath-form at 1 Sam 14:44; 20:13; 1 Kgs 2:23; 19:2). The promise, of course, is still ringing in readers' ears—a promise to be God's "treasured people," to "keep his commandments" (26:18). Officiating Levites administer Israel's curse-secured oaths to a perfectly arrayed twelve-tribe nation.

Deuteronomy has compacted ("collapsed") events at some temporal distance. Declarations of covenant ratification in Moab (26:17-19) here lead directly into oath taking at Shechem (27:14-26). By jumping to Shechem, the narrative insists on immediacy and decision. Shechem has zoomed front and center; Israel starts its formation in the land *now*. It *must* say its Amens, *must* cement its covenantal identity.

The Shechemite Dodecalogue has a distinctive emphasis on *clandestine* offenses. Many offenses here are by nature furtive and hard to prosecute, such as moving a boundary mark (v. 17), taking advantage of the blind (v. 18), and engaging in illicit sexual rendezvouses (vv. 20-23). With this theme, the book again stresses an inner transformation that deeply alters people's personal lives. Individuals must support this ethos even in private matters, since individual immorality has huge ripple effects. It unsettles the entire sanctuary-land, a supple and sensitive matrix (cf. 19:10, 13; 21:1-9). Modern readers of Deuteronomy may really struggle to sympathize with this spirituality.

Covenant Blessings and Curses

Deuteronomy 28:1–29:1

Chapter 28 ends the second and longest of Moses' discourses in Deuteronomy (4:44-29:1). The ideal community of human mutuality envisioned by the book has now been set before the reader. We have experienced this vision in the form of the Decalogue, the Shema, a series of sermons, and the core legal corpus of the book. The vision's worth is incalculable. Resisting apostasy will be crucial for Israel, no matter how challenging the task. Deuteronomy 28's vivid presentation of blessings and curses drives that home.

For ancient readers, our text's ferocious demand for faithfulness would have seemed natural—a familiar way to end a national covenant. Liberal democratic readers of today's world, however, will doubtless find Deuteronomy 28 highly challenging. They will balk at God's *religious* concerns with civic affairs and real politics. Many will push back hard against a covenantal program offered in specific defiance of alternative political visions.

Blessings and curses featured in the Near Eastern treaties that informed Deuteronomy. Chapter 28 bears a particularly close similarity to the Vassal Treaties of Esarhaddon of Assyria (dated 672 BCE, about three decades before King Josiah's reign). In adopting covenantal curses and other key features of vassal treaties, Deuteronomy definitively presents itself as a political arrangement in competition with what it finds in its surrounding world. With great intentionality, the book adjures God's people to pursue a form of society alternative to the despotic and imperialistic will of the Assyrian state.

Most loyalty commitments today are "movable," that is, dissolvable without fear of sanctions. Children grow up and separate from their parents; spouses often divorce. Deuteronomy's covenant, by contrast, speaks of *immovable* bonds, of a *permanent, societal-level* relationship that challenges all other claims. Few modern relationships are comparable, but Rob Barrett has recently pointed out at least one. It is incumbent from birth upon citizens in most nations to obey laws, pay taxes, and fight in wars. If one refuses, one is compelled to comply by sanctions such as police actions, imprisonment, and even execution. Barrett (20) states, "The modern nation-state demands ultimate loyalty from its citizens. Furthermore, the modern nation-state wields its monopoly on coercive force most potently against disloyal citizens."

A modern state's use of force helps the reader appreciate what is going on in Deuteronomy 28, but, although helped with the logic of the chapter, many may remain unsettled. People today understand compulsion by force, especially violent force, as suspect and regrettable even when wielded by their own nation. Is the God of Deuteronomy right to resort to violent covenant curses in order to define and stabilize the covenant?

Deuteronomy's treaty sanctions bear a necessary theological witness. The book's vassal treaty format—including the violent aspects—serves to highlight the parallel and competing claims of two opposed systems: mutuality-based society and despotic society. Israel had an either-or choice to make, in which religion and politics were inseparable and with life-and-death consequences at stake. The way of mutuality, the way of the Lord, demanded a political allegiance at least as intense as that demanded by despotism. It is not simply that the Lord arbitrarily chose to dictate this state of affairs. Rather, it appears to be a consequence of the very nature of God's being as conceived by Deuteronomy. One cannot draw near in relationship to a numinous God without immediately sensing the intense claims attendant to this God's presence.

Deuteronomy's God, who speaks from the midst of the fire, cannot help but evoke human awe. Encountering the presence of this God necessarily draws in God's followers like moths to the flame, even as it threatens their lives. That is why Deuteronomy uses language of God's people fervently "clinging" to their Lord (Deut 10:20; 11:22; 13:4). But to revere and cling to God in this manner, which is the natural result of standing in God's presence, is essentially to embrace the role of a treaty vassal. It is to willingly endorse the *immovable* loyalty of a suzerain's subject, to want to conclude a suzerainty treaty with all of its blessings and curses that signify immovability.

There is more. Unlike the pragmatic curses of a political treaty, those of Deuteronomy do not aim primarily at societal stability. Deuteronomy wants a pilgrimage out of the contemporary social world, which it views as calculated, self-interested, and unfree. It sets its sights on a reign of God rid of all "accessible," enslaving idols. In such a world, the radical freedom and intense intimacy associated with the divine name may come into its own. Such an exclusive reign of God, granting true human liberty and transformation to

God's people, is of unrestricted value to Deuteronomy. Thus, it views as appropriate God's demand of undivided and immovable commitment.

Should Israel veer off course in its covenantal commitment, an initial taste of chapter 28's hardships should set it back on track. Thus, the curses of Deuteronomy have disciplinary purpose, at least up through v. 44 or v. 46. This is to be expected, since even in international relations destruction of a treaty partner is a course of last resort. It was undertaken only when diplomacy and shots across the bow failed (cf. 2 Kgs 18:31-35).

A variety of chapter 28's curses (e.g., vv. 27, 35, 38-40) entail a tempered, gradual severing of the people's ties to God's land. Jeremiah too, operating in Deuteronomy's wake, assumes that covenantal threats are graded and corrective. "At one moment I [God] may declare concerning a nation or a kingdom, that I will pluck up and break down and destroy it, but if that nation, concerning which I have spoken, turns from its evil, I will change my mind" (Jer 18:7-8). Insofar as the experience of sanctions averts utter disaster, hopelessness, and dread, God's implementation of curses is divine *grace*. (A different grace is at work in 28:47-68. On this passage, see the discussion below.)

In Deuteronomy's thinking, God's people's experience of hardships and "humbling" trials pushes them to live solely by God's word. In Deuteronomy 21:10-14, God's "bride," captured in battle, experiences the recent trauma as a liminal state leading to new life. There, as in 8:2-6, God is committed to Israel's constructive discipline and growth (both 8:3 and 21:14 use the same Hebrew verb, "humble"). In light of the theology of chapter 21, the covenant curses of chapter 28 are not bursts of divine vengeance but empathetic divine care along a painful path of reinvention.

Promises of blessing begin chapter 28, marked off as an independent section by framing verses (vv. 1-2, 13b-14). The frame surrounds the blessings with descriptions of Israel's elevation above earth's nations if the people will only persevere. A coherent little poem in vv. 3-6 promises Israel a complete and total blessing, encompassing all comings and goings. Promises in vv. 7-13a assure Israel that if it stays true to the covenant it will emerge victorious from all attacks, experience true prosperity, and become the holy nation amid earth's peoples that God created it to be (Exod 19:6; Deut 7:6; 14:2; 26:19).

The passive language leaves it unclear whether the covenant's blessings are mostly "self-generative," flowing automatically out of the torah's lifestyle. Not all the blessings appear to be natural outcomes of covenantal life. Certainly, blessings such as sanctification and the scattering of enemies sound like *direct* interventions of God. Elsewhere in the book, however,

Deuteronomy presupposes the innate "good" of the covenant (4:40; 5:16, 29; 6:3, 18; 12:25, 28; 22:7; cf. Jer 7:23). It assumes an interconnection between virtuous human life and nature's health and ability to bless.

In Deuteronomy's vision, inhabitants of the promised land prosper as they live into the lifestyle of God's sacred territory, "the good land," "that good hill country" (3:25). They flourish as they put aside their control needs, become interdependent with one another, and align with the ebb and flow of the environment (e.g., 6:10-12; 8:7-10; 11:10-12; 20:19). The "sacred interruptions" outlined in Deuteronomy 15:1–16:17 help train Israel in this way of thinking and living. The postexilic prophet Malachi, heavily influenced by Deuteronomy, assumes that life under the covenant is innately advantageous. In Malachi 1:1-5 he describes Edom—and thus all the "Esaus" of the world—as handicapped by profanity and lack of covenantal tutelage.

Nowhere does Deuteronomy envision a tit-for-tat system of rewards (see, e.g., 8:16-18; 9:4-6, 24). Entirely lacking is any notion of a "prosperity gospel," assuring each adherent of the covenant that he or she will get ahead. Texts such as Deuteronomy 8:3 definitively exclude such an idea. Malachi, from his first chapter, depicts an Israel elected and loved by God yet complaining of a dearth of obvious blessing (Mal 1:2; cf. 3:14-15; Deut 29:19). To live by "obvious blessing," by "bread alone" (Deut 8:3), is to live a constricted life. Moses died *outside* of the promised land to demonstrate a deeper meaning of prosperity (see the commentary on 3:23-29). The real blessing in life is the joy of aligning with the divine word, which then inevitably brings other goods in its wake, the kind of faithful living that survives trials and proves victorious (Mal 3:10-12, 17-18).

Verse 15 of Deuteronomy 28 begins a long section of curses, far outweighing the section of blessings (by a ratio of three to one). There are so many curses, several of which are mutually exclusive, that even a massive default on the covenant could not evoke them all. Since the covenant is holistic and integral, the ripple effects of discarding it are pluriform and unpredictable. The shape of the book buttresses the theme of curse, bookending the legal core with two parallel passages of curse in 11:26-28 and chapters 27–28. The emphasis is deliberate. To accept culpability is to accept the gravity of the relationship. Israel is committing itself for both good times and times of pain and disaster.

A rhetorical "envelope" (vv. 15, 45-46) frames a first set of curses in vv. 15-46. At the start of the section, vv. 16-19 present a curse poem that reverses the blessing poem in vv. 3-6. Verses 20-46 then move to emulate the form and language of Assyrian treaties. At points, the sequence of curses reflects the Assyrian practice of listing together specific misfortunes associated with individual deities (rape, dispossession, and pillage, for example, cluster as Venus's ills). "Futility curses" appear in vv. 30-34 and vv. 38-44. This type of curse, in which human efforts or labors prove fruitless, is well known from Aramaic and Assyrian treaties and was adopted by the prophets Hosea and Micah ahead of Deuteronomy (see Hos 4:10; 8:7; 9:12, 16; Mic 6:14, 15).

Certain verses (e.g., vv. 36-37, 41) refer to the specific curse of Israel's exile off God's land. Some of these verses may have been included here as part of Deuteronomy's exilic edition (sixth-fifth centuries BCE). The editors of this edition vehemently insist that the suffering of the exiles is due neither to the power of foreign gods nor to the blind forces of an amoral universe. Israel does not suffer meaninglessly.

Verses 47-68 take a shocking new turn. Now, in this dramatic section, the curses of the covenant are no longer constructive, disciplinary warnings. Rather, they are veritable prophecies of Israel's national downfall (cf. 31:29). Here, Deuteronomy resigns itself to Israel's inevitable failure, to the whole of Israel's struggle to pattern its life after the torah breaking and crumbling in its hands. Fortunately, the verses do not leave us completely bewildered. The language of siege warfare, lifted from ancient vassal treaties, helps us unpack the theological dynamic at stake in the nation's experience of death.

In Deuteronomy, Moses must die (see the commentary on 1:37-38; 3:23-29; 4:21-22; 5:27; 9:18, 25; 18:15-19). The book understands this dreadful requirement as programmatic. Israel as an entire community must emulate Moses' relinquishing of self-orientation. Notably, self-will is a phenomenon squarely at the center of *siege dynamics*. It can be no coincidence that 28:47-68 immerses readers so thoroughly in siege imagery. The text explores such imagery as a metaphor of Israel's necessary spiritual transformation.

Siege warfare is a horrific reality, an all-or-nothing affair, a "total war" that directly engages all of society and puts everything at risk. It is an ultimate test of wills, spiraling in intensity as defenders grapple with starvation and as attackers' vengefulness grows. Just as a besieged city's defenders dig in and hunker down, God's people have nursed rebelliousness and self-determination. Stubbornness has only escalated over time. Moses opines, "I know well how rebellious and stubborn you are. If you already have been so rebellious . . . how much more after my death!" (31:27).

Perhaps the fundamental spiritual conflict of human experience is the contest between self-willed life and God-willed life, between undisciplined self-orientation and dogged God dependence. Just as Assyria would eventually besiege a vassal kingdom in response to its stubborn rebellion, the God of Israel eventually engages this fundamental spiritual contest. God "besieges" a people bent on egoistic self-determination. Using the imagery of siege warfare, chapter 28 sees this contest between Israel and its suzerain, between humanity and God, play itself out to a definitive, eschatological resolution. The chapter sees the spirit of spiraling self-willed life checked and overturned, so that true human freedom and ennoblement emerge from the ashes.

A conflict of wills lies at the heart of 28:47-68. As Barrett (194) writes, in chapter 28 "the contest of wills between YHWH and Israel is readied: Israel's stubborn will and natural drive to create its own prosperity in its own settled homeland and YHWH's stubborn will to be in relationship with his people in his special land." The more God's people trust in their national resolve, the more they intensify and lock in this ultimate clash of wills.

Verse 63 uses highly anthropomorphic rhetoric reflecting the *polarized* dynamics at issue. This chilling verse pins God with the raw emotions of a vengeful Assyrian commander. One should not take it literally. The meaning is simply that all false confidences in the status quo, *even confidences in divine mercy*, are inappropriate until the "all-or-nothing" engagement between God and people ends in Israel's death and new birth. God cannot and will not compromise when Israel's complete metamorphosis is at hand. After the resurrection, God's "delight" in Israel will return in full (30:9).

Before leaving this passage, one must acknowledge the horrific, indiscriminate suffering that it presents. Such a passage truly raises tough questions about divine goodness and justice. Here, God uses third-party instruments in a judgment so blunt and uncontrolled as to inevitably result in unfair tragedy. How can this be right?

The difficulties of theodicy come into play here because of the *scale* of Israel's irrational obduracy. The dynamics of obstinacy at stake raise the situation to the level of a national and absolute crisis, a societal-level conflict. This is a "total war" encompassing combatants and non-combatants alike. Images of cannibalism akin to what is described in the Vassal Treaties of Esarhaddon drive home the sweeping inclusivity and total reinvention entailed in Israel's coming journey through death to new life.

THE THIRD DISCOURSE OF MOSES

29:2–30:20

Ratification, Part 1: Review of Israel's History

Deuteronomy 29:2-9

Moses's third major "discourse" (29:2–30:20) reflects a covenant ratification ceremony on the plains of Moab. Today, in Moab, Israel confirms God's declaration to be its God. God, in turn, confirms Israel's declaration to be God's people (see 26:16-29; 29:13).

What Israel does now, in Moab, is in addition to the Horeb experience. It is not additional in the *sense* of agreeing to anything new, but in the sense of realizing Horeb in the here and now, commending it to the present and coming generations. The *one* Horeb covenant (29:25) is binding throughout the generations (4:9, 10; 5:3; 6:7, 24; 11:19), but Moses' impending death is now opening a portal to transformed existence. Now, the covenantal relationship, a *prophetic* promise, is beginning to find fulfillment.

The book has been, and continues to be, deadly serious about Israel's struggle at faithfulness. No reader can deny that Moses has powerfully stressed the consequences of curse and death attendant on Israel's persistent stubbornness. He is not yet done with this dark task (see 31:17-21, 27, 29). Yet Deuteronomy now becomes clearer than ever about how sure God's promised future is. Though a dark threat looms at present, God promises to bring the covenantal lifestyle to earth regardless of all human failings.

In a prophetic mode, the Lord promises to "circumcise your heart and the heart of your descendants, so that you will love the LORD your God with all your heart and with all your soul, in order that you may live" (30:6). The reader is assured that despite all human self-orientation and intransigence, God's gift of life will triumph at the last. God's future salvation will overcome the problematic *contingency* of the covenant, a contingency that ends Israel's national existence at the Babylonian assault of 586 BCE.

The sermon about covenant making begins with a recital of God's past actions on Israel's behalf (29:2-9). Moses reviews God's saving deeds at the exodus, during the forty years of wandering in the wilderness, and in the preliminary battles to take the promised land. He reiterates the miracle-wonders of Egypt, the divine care in the wilderness, where clothes and sandals did not wear out, and the defeat of the forces of kings Heshbon and Og, who met Israel primed for war but never stood a chance.

Such retrospective summaries have appeared before (cf. 1:6-4:43; 6:21-23; 8:2-6, 14-16; 26:5-10). Recital of all that they have been through with God reinforces the people's unique relationship and motivates their pledge of faithfulness. The people must seize the day. Until this moment, they have not properly responded to God's mighty deeds (v. 4; cf. 9:7-24). Now is the chance to show perceptive eyes and attentive ears, opened to God through Moses' speeches. The language of God's "giving" in v. 4, however, is notable. It suggests the need for a miracle of transformation. God will have to *give* humans what the covenant demands: the requisite mind, eyes, and ears (see 30:6).

As in chapters 4–11, Deuteronomy continues to use powerful rhetoric to express the covenant's vitality for present and future generations. The generation now in Moab had not been with Moses at the exodus and at Horeb. Their parents, who are now deceased, had been present. Yet Moses uses well-chosen language to bring salvation history alive for those immediately engaged in covenant ratification: "you have seen" (v. 2); it was "before your eyes" (v. 2); "your eyes saw" (v. 3).

This form of language is intensely personal and contemporizing. Readers feel the power of God's word, binding Israel into a collective whole that stretches across time (cf. 5:2-5). With this word, the old Horeb covenant becomes something constantly new—something living and packed with power for the here and now.

Ratification, Part 2: A Reciprocal, Immutable Commitment

Deuteronomy 29:10-29

Israel is about to "pass into the covenant" (v. 12, NJB), accepting the agreement's "sanction of a curse" (v. 12, NAB). A signatory to an ancient treaty might signal the permanence of the commitment by walking between split carcasses. To break the treaty oath was to call down upon oneself the fate of the dissevered animals. Israel now accepts such consequences by making an immutable, indefeasible pledge (cf. 27:14-26).

Verses 10-15 highlight the *mutuality* of the covenant. At the core of Deuteronomy's covenant lay the reciprocal relationship of God and God's people. Just so, at the center of this group of verses stands the emphatic language of a bilateral, two-way bond. God here establishes Israel to be "his people"; the people, for their part, hear Moses declare that the Lord is to be "your God" (v. 13).

The *covenant formula* occurs elsewhere in Scripture, in texts such as Deuteronomy 26:17-18; Jeremiah 7:23; 11:4; 24:7; 31:33; 32:38. This language derives from Deuteronomy's sources, such as Hosea 1:9. It speaks both to God's sure grace and to Israel's committed obligation. Without God's unmerited election of "his people" and promise to stand with them, the torah becomes legalism and works-righteousness. Without Israel's sense of gratitude and obligation to "your God," the covenantal promise becomes "cheap grace" with no true appreciation of the cost of discipleship.

The Hebrew leaves no doubt that in Moab Israel commits to *the Lord's* covenant (v. 12). The Lord's purposes are at work, purposes aiming to establish Israel as God's people (v. 13a). The Lord is fulfilling ancient promises, sworn to the people's first ancestors (v. 13b; cf. 1:8, 35; 4:31; 6:10, 18, 23; 7:8, 12, 13; 8:1, 18; 9:5; 10:11; 11:9, 21; 26:3, 15; Gen 15:16 E; Exod 13:5, 11 E; 32:13 E; Num 11:12 E). What is being realized in Deuteronomy is an arching, sweeping plan of God, with origins and goals far outstripping the concerns and perspectives of any one generation.

God's bilateral covenant with Israel is radically *inclusive*. Verses 10-11 enumerate with some detail the entire spectrum of society encompassed by the covenant: leaders, elders, officials, men, children, and women, even "the aliens who are in your camp" (cf. 31:12). The spirit of inclusion here seems to go beyond even that in texts such as 23:7-8. If the reference to those who cut wood and draw water alludes to Joshua 9:27 and the story of the Gibeonites, Deuteronomy's carpet of inclusion is now rolled out even to the Canaanites. As evident at several points, assembly in the presence of Israel's numinous Lord (v. 10) evaporates society's hierarchies and promotes humble mutuality as sibling co-vassals. The Horeb encounter is surely a profoundly *leveling* experience.

Inclusivity extends not only horizontally but also vertically, across future generations. In v. 15 Moses declares, "I am making this covenant both with you who stand here today in the presence of the LORD our God, and also with the future generations who are not standing here today" (NLT). Just as with the Vassal Treaties of Esarhaddon, the covenant of Deuteronomy binds future generations, those as yet unborn.

Verses 16-21 now turn explicitly to the topic of the covenant's immutability. That is, the text again impresses upon the reader the permanence of the covenantal oath, which is secured by curse. A dramatic new emphasis on individual liability to the covenantal curses suddenly appears.

A sensitive web of interrelationship interconnects the covenantal community, so that a problem in even a small part of the system can soon radically affect everyone. The secret treason of even a single individual or group jeopardizes the entire covenantal community. Such a person or group represents nothing other than "a root sprouting poisonous and bitter growth" (v. 18).

The notion that God's anger can express itself on an individual level (vv. 20-21) has appeared in Deuteronomy before (see Deut 13; 17:1-7; 22:21), but the present text takes a new turn. Instead of delegating small-scale enforcement of the covenant to human representatives of the Lord, it warns of transcendent retribution aimed directly at individuals. It suggests that the curses of the covenant may sometimes operate not only at the national level, as Deuteronomy elsewhere affirms, but also in an individual fashion.

The reader should not jump to conclusions. Despite first impressions, there is no naïve thought here of a mechanical justice enforced across creation, applying to everyone at all times. Rather, the text's concern remains resolutely *communal and national*. God moves against individuals when small-scale infractions threaten *the entirety* of God's people, "moist and dry alike" (v. 19). What is more, the divine means and timetable in ferreting out localized sedition are mysterious and variable.

A supple, *non-mechanical* moral order is specifically why treasonous individuals may think they have won out. It is why they assume they can slip through the cracks: "We are safe even though we go our own stubborn ways" (v. 19). God's limber workings mean that one must trust divine justice to work itself out *in God's time* (see 27:15-26; Mal 3:18). "The secret things belong to the LORD" (29:29a). While secrets will be exposed only in time, Israel knows *now* how to observe God's words (29:29b).

That God's concerns are primarily holistic and national is reinforced in vv. 22-28. Now the scene jumps to Israel's collective destruction witnessed by a coming generation. The people's children, along with foreigners from far countries, will be appalled to see God's devastation. Verses 16-21 have indeed taken up the problem of individual disloyalty, but only because it can so easily grow into a national crisis.

According to vv. 22-28, the covenant's curses will eventually become inescapable. They will come down upon the people inexorably, uprooting them from God's land and dumping them in foreign exile. Scholars agree that this horrific description of God's overthrow of the nation comes from the second, exilic edition of Deuteronomy. From the perspective of this edition, God's destruction of the nation at the hands of the Babylonians in 586 BCE is "now the case" (v. 28).

Certainly, the exilic insertion in chapter 29 does not intend to rub salt in the exiles' wounds. What then is the constructive purpose of the added text? There is no escaping the fact that wrath is of prime concern. The passage speaks of a "fierce anger" (v. 23), a "great display of anger" (v. 24), the Lord's anger "kindled" (v. 27), and God's "anger, fury, and great wrath" (v. 28). Paradoxically, the emphasis on wrath here must intend to comfort the exiles. The presence of wrath signals how deeply God cares about the covenant. The hottest anger only burns between those most deeply connected.

God's passion could be construed as abusive, of course, if this angry deity were anthropomorphic and spiteful. But the numinous Lord of Deuteronomy is "God and no mortal" (Hos 11:9; cf. Ps 50:21; Deut 4:24). This Lord is not merely "playing god," having no true authority over life, no power to undo death. Rather, the God at issue has sole prerogative to declare, "I, even I, am he . . . I kill and I make alive" (32:39).

For a God such as this, Israel's death as a nation, like the death of Moses, may constitute a radically creative moment. The state of exile may be a moment in God's providence where divine wrath and mercy meet, where death becomes a portal to new life. This is not to say that Israel should actively seek a momentous deathful punishment. No, God has revealed to Israel its necessary path of observance (v. 29b). It is to say, however, that God can mysteriously use even Israel's horrific disaster, turning it on its head as something startling. "The secret things belong to the LORD our God" (v. 29a).

Later Deuteronomistic texts did not view the exile as a completely irredeemable event. God knows that all human beings are entangled in sin according to 1 Kings 8:46. Thus, God must be ready and willing to forgive even a justly exiled people (1 Kgs 8:50). Readers of Deuteronomy 29 in exile can take heart. God has always assumed that Israel will betray the covenant and fall on its face. Therefore, God surely has a mysterious plan in mind to take this evil and turn it around for good.

Ratification, Part 3: Assurance of the Future

Deuteronomy 30:1-10

Deuteronomy 30:1-10 constitutes another addition from the time of the exile, but one with a radically different mood from 29:22-28. Here, God promises not only to pick up the pieces of Israel's shattered life but also to transform Israel's very being. According to this deeply weighty and paradoxical passage, God purposes surgically to alter the heart of God's people, freeing them to love God unreservedly. The covenant will finally stick.

In Hittite and Assyrian treaties, covenant curses inevitably spelled a nation's absolute end. Here in Deuteronomy, by contrast, curse and death become passageways to new life. As in the case of the bride captured in battle (21:10-14), a dark ravine becomes a passage to "resurrection." Imminently, Moses's own death will blaze the trail.

The central metaphor of the present text, the "circumcision" of Israel's heart (30:6), appeared earlier in 10:16. There, however, it functioned primarily to show the depth of commitment required by God from Israel. Now Deuteronomy redirects the metaphor in a new context where the covenantal curses have hit with full force, ending Israel's national existence. At this juncture, Israel's "heart condition" will clearly require a divine surgeon. It is beyond the capacity of Israel, the frail patient, to correct. God must give Israel the very thing that God requires (see 29:4). God must transfigure the inner self to reflect God freely and naturally. God must sculpt the heart.

Deuteronomy knows that simply repeating the conditions of covenant that applied at Horeb will not do. Even when God took the people by the hand and guided them into the covenant's lifestyle, they inevitably self-destructed. No, instead a "new covenant" is needed. Deuteronomy 9:1–10:11 foreshadows this requirement. After Israel's shocking betrayal in the making of the calf-god, God inscribes a new set of covenant tablets (10:1-4). Moses descends Horeb with a new covenant inscribed in stone in just the manner as he brought down the initial set of commandments (see 9:15; 10:5).

What, according to chapter 30, can make a difference for God's people in the fully new start that God will afford them? Nothing can help short of a veritable "hardwiring" of the inner constitution so that it permanently embodies God's teachings. The solution immediately raises problems of its own. It is an offense to the modern mind to hear that God will impose obedience. Do not love and fidelity lose their meaning if they are coerced? Does not God's surgical intervention here effectively nullify human agency?

Uniquely, our text wrestles deftly with such challenges and objections. To begin, the central metaphor of a circumcision of the heart (30:6) is well chosen. God does not injure or destroy the authentic human heart in Deuteronomy 30, but cuts away all constraining and numbing thickening about the heart. This action frees up the heart to become more agile, pliant, and available to God. By surgically removing what insulates the human will, God frees people to receive God's life (29:4). Divine grace does triumph, but precisely in enabling a genuine turning to God from the heart (30:10b).

A telling symmetrical organization of the text creates a delicate balance (a dialectic) between Israel's decision to obey and God's creation of obedience. On the one hand, the start of the passage in vv. 1-5 puts Israel's initiative and action first. If and when the exiles reflect on their experience and see their problem (v. 1), God will restore them (v. 3). On the other hand, vv. 9-10 flip the sequence. Here the emphasis falls on God's initiative. God, front and center, makes Israel "abundantly prosperous" (v. 9). When God acts, Israel comes to obey the Lord (v. 10). The double use of Hebrew *ki* in v. 10 likely has the sense of either "when" or "indeed," not "if." Taking a cue from the CEB, I would render the logic as follows: "God will help you" . . . "everything will be great, for, indeed, the LORD will return" (v. 9), . . . "for, indeed, you will obey" . . . "and "for, indeed, you will return" (v. 10).

The passage makes both Israel and God the grammatical subject of the Hebrew verb *shub*, meaning "turn," "repent," "restore." Both God and God's people appear as the agents of the great future "return" to intimate relationship. Israel is the subject of the verb four times. Verse 2, for example, speaks of Israel's "return to the LORD your God." God is the verb's subject three times, as when v. 3 promises that God "will turn and gather you" (NET). (It is easiest to count in the Hebrew text, since the English representations of the verb are varied, including the rendering "restore.")

Our passage raises another nagging question, one it does not directly answer. If God's circumcision of the human heart finally creates God's ideal people, then why has God waited so long to implement the solution? Why have the people had to endure difficult centuries of struggle? The answer can only be that the best possible world cannot be delivered on a platter. An extended journey toward God's reign remains essential. For the relationship between God and Israel to grow authentic and deep, the two parties must struggle with it in real history, travel with it through a definite moral terrain. God's circumcision of the people's heart makes sense only as a culminating act of divine love in a complex relationship that has developed over time. Along the journey, the people must develop in the capacity to shun all curses and soak in true blessings. God's passion about Israel must develop as a parent's love and knowledge of a child deepens over time.

By chapter 30, the journey has proven highly broken, including impasses and dead ends (cf. 9:17). Yet that does not mean the trek should never have been attempted, nor that some other trek should now replace it. No, the very Israel with whom God's involvement has grown ever more passionate must complete the selfsame journey that they began at Horeb. They have not been on the journey for nothing, but in order to see themselves enabled to complete it through God's setting things right.

Readers of Deuteronomy have not yet arrived at a utopia, where all is set right. God is still at work sculpting their hearts, delaying to perfect the work already begun. Therefore the journey continues, with the faithful conserving the memory and hope associated with the long, dogged march begun at Horeb. The end goal of a perfectly sculpted heart orients the journey, but, because no one has yet arrived at this target, the order of the day is still engagement, expectancy, and openness to transformation.

Ratification, Part 4: A Word Very Near

Deuteronomy 30:11-14

Verses 11-14 pull back from Deuteronomy's utopian vision and return the reader to the here and now, to the "commandment that I am commanding you today" (v. 11). The future will arrive in God's time; the relevant truth for the moment is that God's word of life is presently available to human experience (cf. Mic 6:8). It is "in your mouth and in your heart" (v. 14). The requisite response is obvious: Do it!

This is likely a layer of early text within Deuteronomy, specifically a text that originally continued the thought of 29:29. The final editors have arranged their content to show readers how a futuristic vision is relevant for workaday life. Israel's new, circumcised heart of the ideal future will observe precisely those commandments that Moses reveals now, in Moab—the ones he is "commanding you today." Not all of life is impenetrable mystery, as enigmatic as the thought of divine circumcision. No, God has made enough plain for Israel to know the way forward. Readers know the catechetical path that leads across the horizon to a circumcised heart.

Verses 11-14 emphasize the new covenant's *relevance*; at the same time, the text pushes back against some official wisdom and royal thinking. It argues that the torah does not require expert mediation. Sages and visionaries are irrelevant in following God. Mountaineers need not bring the torah down to earth. Sailors need not retrieve it from across an ocean. God's revelation is relevant *as is*; it is intelligible to the common person. The book of Deuteronomy knows nothing of elitism or asceticism. Rather, it levels society's hierarchies and promotes Israel's humble living as sibling co-vassals.

The text's insistence on the torah's accessibility shows the practical relevance of an ideal future for present life. At the same time, the text feels jarring in its present literary context. Deuteronomy's final editors have placed a claim that the torah is simple and doable immediately following a description of Israel's inability, apart from heart surgery, to internalize and uphold even the basics of God's will. Were the editors blind to the tension? Have they ineptly juxtaposed contradictory ideas from different eras?

Not at all. Verse 11 actually coheres with what precedes. The problem demanding divine surgery lies not at all with the covenant itself but with Israel. God's people, the text avers, need to wake up, refocus, and return to their senses. According to 30:1, this will finally happen when the covenant's curses fall with all their deadly force. Then, Israel will finally awaken to the seriousness of the blessing and the curse, finally "take them to heart" (NJPS, NIV). Up until this point, the people's basic senses had failed them. They lacked "eyes to see," "ears to hear," and a "mind to understand" (29:4).

In short, throughout Moses' third discourse, Deuteronomy holds that in its inattentiveness to the covenant, Israel has not been in its right mind. The covenant's curses do not fall on the people because the torah is a highly unrealistic moral program. Neither does the covenant doom to failure all who fall short of its overly exacting standard. The problem lies, rather, in a distortion of the human heart.

Out of insecurity, self-orientation, and shortsightedness, human beings consistently find themselves acting against their own best interests, their own ideal nature. Mark Biddle (445) hits the nail on the head: "The great enigma is that, despite the fact that Israel knows what is good and right, it consistently and repeatedly chooses to do wrong. In other words, Israel is *capable* of doing right, but it does not *want* to do so."

Ratification, Part 5: A Necessary Choice

Deuteronomy 30:15-20

Moses' third discourse of chapters 29–30 now concludes with a climactic exhortation to choose the way of blessing. The passage, from Deuteronomy's exilic editors, draws in themes and expressions from throughout the book to make a final, powerful appeal to "choose life so that you and your descendants may live" (v. 19). As elsewhere in Deuteronomy, "life" here is more than merely biological. Moses sets before Israel a vision of expansive communal life, of a free, shared, and integrated life. The vision is wrapped up in the *land*, the highlands of God in all their sacramental power. One recalls God's charge back in 1:8: "See, I have set the land before you; go in and take possession of the land" (cf. 1:21; 2:24, 31). Deuteronomy's ideal life consists of thriving interconnectedness with God, with one's sibling vassals, and with the promised land.

Immediately, 30:15-20 confronts the reader with a choice between life and death, requiring an "either-or" (existential) picking of sides (cf. Jer 21:8). Deuteronomy 11:26-32 sets the same two ways of curse and blessing, of death and life, before Israel as a preamble to the laws. That prior passage began in the same way: "See, I am setting before you today . . . ." There, as here, Deuteronomy brings its audience up against an immediate crucial choice, insisting on a commitment in the here and now. An intensely personal, infinitely significant decision of the heart, mind, and will is at hand.

Challenging people with an either-or choice can be highly effective in forcing a decision, pushing the human psyche off the fence. This is surely one reason prophets make effective use of paired images. One notes the efficacy with which the following bits of scriptural parenesis use binary opposites (such as pure/adulterated; cooked/raw; healthy/injured; hot/cold): "Ephraim is a cake with foreign ingredients" (Hos 7:8). "How much longer will you waver, / hobbling between two opinions? //" (1 Kgs 18:21, NLT).

"You are neither cold nor hot; / I wish that you were either cold or hot //" (Rev 3:15).

In v. 19, Moses calls upon "heaven and earth" to witness Israel's covenant ratification (cf. 31:28). His first discourse ended with the same invocation (4:26). Psalmists and prophets call in these cosmic, foundational witnesses when God puts Israel on trial for betrayal. The elements become appalled at Israel; they declare the rightness of God's judgment (see Ps 50:4; Mic 6:1-2; Jer 2:12). The Song of Moses upcoming in Deuteronomy 31:30–32:47 is a revised prophetic lawsuit that invokes cosmic witnesses (32:1).

Verse 20 ends the third discourse by reiterating the terms of true attachment to the Lord. It again highlights the prospect of "life"; it celebrates the anticipated fulfillment of God's promise to the ancestors. Moses stresses that loving the Lord "means life to you." As the NIV puts it, "The LORD is your life." The sort of love of the Lord in mind entails both "obeying him" and "holding fast to him" (cf. 11:22; 13:4).

In the idiom of ancient Near Eastern treaties, to "love" the suzerain is to maintain covenant loyalty; to "hold fast" is to endorse this loyalty's *immutability*. Deuteronomy gives the language of loving and clinging an additional connotation. It imagines a passionate interconnection. In this book, and in related Scriptures, the numinous God who speaks from "the midst of the fire" fascinates, draws in, and overwhelms. In the presence of this unseen, fiery God, one is love struck.

In Jeremiah 13:11, God uses the symbolism of a tight-fitting undergarment clinging to the loins to illustrate how passionately Israel should "hold fast" to its suzerain. A more personal and intimate image could hardly be found. "As the loincloth clings to one's loins, so I made the whole house of Israel and the whole house of Judah cling to me, says the LORD, in order that they might be for me a people, a name, a praise, and a glory."

EPILOGUE: THE DEATH OF MOSES AND THE TORAH'S FORMATION

31:1–34:12

Transferring Leadership and Depositing Witnesses

Deuteronomy 31:1-29

With chapter 31, the fourth major discourse of Deuteronomy (31:1–34:12) begins, which revolves around the death of Moses and the formation of the torah. The emphasis on Moses' death in chapter 31 is hard to miss. Moses admits that at age 120 he can no longer function as a leader (v. 2; for the idiom, see NJB, NIV). In vv. 14, 16, God tells Moses directly that he is about to die. Near the close of the chapter, Moses worries greatly that after he dies evil and ruin will befall the people (vv. 27, 29).

The theme that Moses must die so that Israel can properly pursue the journey of discipleship has run like a scarlet thread through Deuteronomy. For this book, no mortal, not even Moses, can claim magisterial authority. Instead, command and responsibility must spread out to the entire community and God's word must constantly open itself to new situations, even as it arcs forward toward God's promised future.

Moses must die and other witnesses to God's character and word succeed him. God provides Israel three successors to Moses: (1) Joshua, next in the line of covenant mediators; (2) a normative, written torah; and (3) a new catechetical song or poem. Surely, God has amply provided for revelatory witness among God's people.

At multiple points, chapter 31 specifies Joshua as God's new agent, the next "prophet like Moses" promised in 18:15-19. (That Joshua is like Moses in this way is clearest in Joshua 5:14-15, which echoes the call of Moses in Exodus 3:5-6. Notably, Joshua also renews the covenant in Joshua 24, just as Moses does in Moab.) In chapter 31's first section (vv. 1-8), Moses reminds Israel of God's direct presence as they begin the settlement and assures them that "Joshua also will cross over before you" (v. 3; cf. vv. 6, 8). Summoning Joshua, Moses appoints him the new leader (vv. 7-8). Joshua's role as Moses' attendant and successor is explicit in texts at the start of Deuteronomy (1:37-38 and 3:21, 27-28). The new focus on him brings the book full circle, returning the reader now to Deuteronomy's outer frame, in which chapters 1–4 and 31–34 balance each other.

An emphasis on the new role of Joshua resurfaces later in chapter 31, both in vv. 14-15 and again in v. 23. Editors have apparently spliced into the chapter an older E-strand account of Joshua's commissioning. The E source, which stands behind Deuteronomy, mentions Joshua about eleven times. At some of these points, it presupposes his role as Moses' understudy, e.g., at Exodus 17:14. In Deuteronomy 31's present form, references to the commissioning of Joshua function as a kind of literary glue fastening together some varied but interrelated provisions for Israel's future. At each return to mention of Joshua, he rises in stature. Joshua increasingly overshadows Moses!

At first, the spotlight shines fully on Moses, with Joshua offstage (v. 3). Joshua then appears in person for commissioning, but with Moses still in charge (vv. 7-8). By vv. 14-15, things shift markedly. Now, Moses and Joshua appear before God as a pair. God, we learn, intends to commission Joshua directly. Finally in v. 23, Moses, not Joshua, is offstage. *God* carries out the commissioning of Joshua.

Joshua keeps coming up in chapter 31, but he is but one of three successors of Moses. The two passages of vv. 9-13 and vv. 24-27 signal the reader to reflect on something novel. Moses' oral word is giving way to an authoritative scroll or "book," bearing his stamp. Written torah will now play a crucial and central role in Israel's life.

Moses commands the elders and Levites to archive a book of torah that he has written (v. 26). They are to read it periodically before all Israel (vv. 10-11). The scenario is natural. Contemporary Near Eastern treaties contained a provision for depositing a written copy of the agreement for safekeeping and periodic reading. That provision is reflected here, but something additional is also going on, something *theological.*

Before the reader's eyes, Deuteronomy is emerging as a written, *scriptural* guide on the journey of discipleship for the faithful of all generations. It is becoming a guide for a radically inclusive audience, for "all Israel" (v. 11), "men, women, and children, as well as the aliens residing in your towns" (v. 12). From now on, through the reading of an inspired text, the community will encounter God's character. By means of its power, Israel will be inculcated with holy awe before the Lord (vv. 12-13), the awe before God's numinous being at the heart of Deuteronomy's spirituality.

Amazing! Deuteronomy narrates its own future canonization (28:58, 61; 29:27; 30:10; 31:9, 11-13, 24, 26), just as its principal speaker and protagonist, Moses, narrates his own death and burial (ch. 34)! One might imagine, *too facilely*, that sloppy logic has tripped up the book's authors and editors here. It is jarring, after all, that they describe Deuteronomy as fully written down (31:9, 24) three chapters shy of its end. A sensitive reading, however, perceives simple theological truth here. God *owns* the entire contents of Deuteronomy. God easily has Moses write it down in its entirety as of chapter 31.

The testimony of Deuteronomy in its present form is that Moses does not invent God's word, but *receives* it and bears witness to it. Traditional Jewish thinking represented in the Talmud does not doubt this. Rather, the Talmud knows that Moses received both the content of Deuteronomy and Israel's future with the book *as prophetic revelation*. The book's account of his impending death Moses transcribed "in tears." The tears attest to God's widening of Moses' mind, unveiling to him the sorrows that the future hides. Such power to unveil embedded in the book makes Deuteronomy *Scripture*.

The point merits restating. Modern readers no longer share the Talmud's innocence about the actual history of Deuteronomy's composition long after Moses' day. Nonetheless, they may affirm its theological acumen. As scriptural revelation, Moses' book transcends the constrained perspective of a normal author. With a little theological imagination, one can well conceive of the entirety of Deuteronomy, right through chapter 34, down in ink at the point of 31:9 or 31:24! Moses here has his jots and tittles in place "to the very end," right through his own burial (Rabbi Shimon, Baba Bathra 15a).

Revelatory, "canonical," text has certain key advantages over finite human leadership, such as that of Moses. It represents the active will of Israel's Lord who, unlike mortals and idols, will never let the people down (see 31:6, 8, 23). Written Scripture spans generations, speaking anew to children and grandchildren "who have not [yet] known it" (v. 13a). Its witness rings out perpetually, "as long as you live in the land" (v. 13b). The faithful may continuously reinterpret written Scripture for their own circumstances. To signal this, Moses' book is placed "beside the ark of the covenant" (v. 26), not sealed up, untouchable inside it like the Ten Commandments (10:1-5; cf. 2 Sam 6:6-8). The book is *available* to Israel for continual reinterpretation and reapplication.

In his theological commentary on Deuteronomy, Dennis Olson (136) aptly comments on how textualizing and canonizing God's word are enlivening, vitalizing processes, not deadening ones. He states,

> The writing of the Mosaic *torah* did not freeze the tradition into a dead letter. Instead, the writing of the text freed it to become a dynamic witness by which God's word could tangibly transcend boundaries of time, genera-

tions, and space. Moreover, the provisions for its continued reading, studying, and interpreting by human priests, elders, and all people ensured that its words would be constantly reinterpreted and reapplied to new situations and times.

According to v. 26, the written torah is also a *witness* to the covenant. Third-party witnesses have already been assumed in 4:26 and 30:19 (cf. 31:28). In the ancient Near East, such arbiters or referees provided an external check against a vassal's selective memory and bending of commitments. As a covenantal witness, Deuteronomy will remind Israel of its binding, immutable commitment, especially at times when the people stray (v. 29). In the best-case scenario, it will lead a wayward people to repentance and reformation. It had this effect, at any rate, in King Josiah's era, when the scroll of Deuteronomy emerged amid apostasy to provoke a great national reform (2 Kgs 22–23).

In the worst-case scenario, the book will help a people already condemned to exile interpret the disastrous curse of national collapse. Such collapse is not arbitrary and meaningless, the witness will affirm, but a sign of God's intense emotional passion (v. 29). In the witness of Deuteronomy the exiles will discover their dark situation to be a liminal state, a portal out from enslavement to a "rebellious and stubborn" spirit (v. 27).

Verses 9 and 25 entrust Israel's Levites and elders with the safekeeping of the covenant and its torah. These figures were leaders of old Israel's tribal society, traditionally vested with responsibility for transmitting and enforcing the Horeb revelation. The eighth-century prophets Micah, an elder, and Hosea, a Levite, performed the role admirably. The reader has often encountered Deuteronomy's attempt to reinforce elders' and Levites' traditional covenantal roles (see 1:15-17; 10:8-9; 16:18-20; 17:9-12, 18; 18:1-8; 19:17-18; 20:2, 5; 21:1-7, 19; 22:15; 24:8; 25:7; 27:9).

In addition to Moses' leaving behind a book of the torah, the section in vv. 16-22 describes him writing down and bequeathing Israel a key poem, a "song." The text appears to be part of the second, exilic edition of Deuteronomy. The words of the Song of Moses do not appear until Deuteronomy's next chapter, but because of its significance, the book's exilic editors introduce the song here. References to Joshua's commissioning form inner "bookends" around the section, making it a sort of centerpiece of chapter 31. At least for the final, exilic editors, the witness of Moses' Song holds central importance.

The Song of Moses parallels the torah-book of Deuteronomy. Verse 19's divine commands about the song echo key facets of the torah's preservation:

"Write this song (see 31:9, 24), and teach it to the Israelites (see 31:12-13); put it in their mouths (see 30:14), in order that this song may be a witness for me (see 31:26)." Like the torah, the song must be written, taught, put on the lips, and invoked as a witness.

Suddenly, without warning, the reader is handed this God-privileged work of poetry. Is it just one more reminder to the exile generation that its fate is deserved (cf. 29:22-28; 30:17-18)? No, though seemingly harsh in tone, these verses from exilic times (vv. 16-22) signal that the Song of Moses has a constructive purpose.

Like the written torah, the song will be God's *witness* at a dark time (vv. 19, 21). Reinforcing the prophetic spirit of Deuteronomy, it will help the exiles understand their present plight in the light of their past history with God. The torah contributes its prose and its laws, but the Song of Moses brings the special inspired and prophetic power of poetry to the exiles' disorientation.

One should not underestimate the power of poetry. The ancient Greek philosopher Plato keenly perceived it. "All good poets," Plato wrote, "composed their beautiful poems . . . because they are inspired and possessed." Poetry represents the sound and tenor of authorization. In Numbers 10, for example, poetry bursts forth amid a technical description of Israel's wilderness camp. According to v. 35, when the ark set out, Moses would sing: "Arise, O LORD, let your enemies be scattered, / and your foes flee before you. //" The poetry brings a sense of Moses in touch with God— of God present.

The right brain, the same area that perceives and creates art and song, is what pushes prophecy forth through the mouth of God's messengers. The right brain is the seat of musings, of sudden and unaccountable emotions, and of assured inspirations. What emerges from this cerebral seat effectively speaks to listeners' emotions, spirits, and wills. Through the right brain, inspiration and possession grip the soul. In poetry one encounters God most directly—as an audible voice, as an active agent.

Deuteronomy 31:16-22 deals directly with God's absence as active agent. In 31:17, the exiles say, "Have not these troubles come upon us because our God is not in our midst?" In a sense, they are correct. At the center of their misery lies their separation from God's shrine, their removal from "before the LORD" (see, e.g., Deut 12:7, 12, 18; 14.23, 26; 15:20; 16:11; 18:7). Twice—in both v. 17 and v. 18—God announces the hiding of the divine face (a motif picked up from within the song; 32:20).

The Song of Moses is a healing force at this time of separation. At a time when God's face remains hidden, the song will most certainly be present.

The exiles have it written down; they have been taught it; it is on their lips (v. 19). It will "confront them as a witness, because it will not be lost from the mouths of their descendants" (v. 21). Its poetry will be there to give them inspired assurance, to remind them of their God-driven history, to evoke right-brain contact with God. Even in exile, Israel will not be left bereft.

There is a dynamic here of divine absence and presence akin to the interwoven paradox of God's real absence and real presence that runs through the book of Deuteronomy. The placement of the Song of Moses at this point in Deuteronomy asserts that the paradox holds even when the shrine at Jerusalem is destroyed. In Babylonian exile, God's real absence only signals God's passionate involvement—an involvement that has presently led to God's angry hiding of the face.

This initial section of the fourth discourse concludes in vv. 28-29 with another addition to the book from the time of the exile. Moses recites "these words" to Israel's elders and officials, probably the words of the song. Moses reiterates the premise that Israel will break the covenant after his death, as will be attested by witnesses. The inevitability of failure continues to disconcert the reader, but this final outer "bookend" to chapter 31 must be balanced against the more positive assurances at the text's beginning. The promise of v. 6 and v. 8 remains: "He will not fail you or forsake you."

The Song of Moses

Deuteronomy 31:30–32:47

The Song of Moses represents a unique poetic climax to the book of Deuteronomy. At points resembling historical review, hymnody, liturgy, and even wisdom literature, the poem resists any simple categorization. The voice of prophecy undeniably makes a strong showing. The poem bears witness to God's active word guiding Israel's past, present, and future. As with the problem of literary classification, the dating of the song is a challenge. Mythological imagery and early Hebrew language (see NAB, NRSV at vv. 8-9, 43a) suggest a core from at least as early as the ninth century BCE. The song in its present form dates later, perhaps to Josiah's era. It has evolved as Israel adapted it in worship.

The poem has distinct similarities with certain Psalms of Asaph, especially Psalms 78 and 82. Psalm 78, for instance, has God move past anger to side again with Israel, just as the Song of Moses does. It shares the song's name "Most High" for God and the metaphors of God as "Rock" (Ps 78:35; Deut 32:4, 8) and divine warrior (Ps 78:65-66; Deut 32:40-42). The resemblance is not surprising; the Asaphite psalms characteristically correlate with Deuteronomy. The Song of Moses likely played a didactic role alongside the Asaph psalms within liturgy, probably under the direction of the Asaphite Levites.

The exilic editors who composed the brief introduction to the Song of Moses in 31:16-22 may have been the ones who placed the poem in its present position in Deuteronomy. Perhaps more likely, the song was already part of the law scroll of Deuteronomy found in King Josiah's time (2 Kgs 22:8-11). Its prophetic-like indictment of Judah for infidelity would have contributed a strong impetus for Josiah's reform.

The song's form is somewhat reminiscent of a prophetic lawsuit for breach of covenant (cf. Asaphite Psalm 50; Hos 4:1-6; Mic 6:1-5; Jer 2:4-13). This character of the song had power to convict the populace of Josiah's era, even given how the poem also transcends the form of a lawsuit to describe God relenting, turning against Israel's oppressors, and saving God's people. The prophet Jeremiah appears to have drawn on the Song of Moses specifically to inspire such conviction. The prophet echoes the song more than once in his own prophetic lawsuit in Jeremiah 2:4-13 (e.g., cf. Jer 2:6 and Deut 32:10).

As argued in the commentary on 31:16-22, the poem's final editors understood it as more than a prophetic indictment of its exilic audience. They treasured it as a poetic voice of inspiration and authority that spoke to the exiles' disorientation. Joining with the witness of the torah, it brought Israel's covenantal relationship with God front and center at a time of God's hiddenness (see 32:20). The Song of Moses played an ongoing role in Israel's worship prior to the exile, so no Israelite would likely have viewed it as a time bomb awaiting a definitive betrayal of the covenant. God's people knew the song as a body of *teaching* (31:19, 22; cf. 32:2), to be handed down in the land through the generations as a sign of the covenant and an impetus to embrace it (32:46).

From the song's start, Moses describes his words as "instruction" (32:2, NAB), as persuasive insight (cf. the same term in Prov 1:5; 4:2; Job 11:4). Such insight is like sprinkling rain on new grass, refreshing and nourishing, promoting growth. Verse 47 confirms that the song can be source of wisdom and vitality: "By this word you will live a long time in the land" (NET). In its constructive intent, the Song of Moses thus resembles its poetic sibling in Asaphite Psalm 78, which describes itself as "teaching" (v. 1), intended to help each new generation depart from stubbornness and stand firm with God (v. 8). Both Psalm 78 and the Song of Moses assume that if one reflects on God's pattern of interaction with Israel, one immediately comes to one's senses. One gains discernment about where God's history with Israel is leading (Deut 32:28-29).

One response to such news is praise. Through the song, Moses determines to "ascribe greatness to our God!" (32:3). An additional response is introspection. Many times Israel's life has fit the pattern of betrayal in vv. 15-18. What generation, the reader may wonder, will bring things to a head? Nathan MacDonald (145) writes, "Whenever the Song is recited deep heart-searching is provoked. Are they the generation who have abandoned the rock?"

God's patterned dealings with Israel stretch back to the people's very beginnings. The Lord is the people's "father, who created you"; this is the deity who "made you and established you" (v. 6). The words reverberate with texts such as Exodus 4:22 (E); Hosea 1:10; 11:1; Deuteronomy 1:31. In this family of texts, Israel's relationship with the Lord is foundational, personal, and emotionally intense. God has been there for them, and always will be. The Song of Moses can be no mere lawsuit. It holds Israel not only to the covenant of Horeb but also to the more basic standards of human relational morality.

In vv. 7-9 the song shockingly draws on mythological poetry to ground the bond between God and Israel in divine plans from the dawn of time (not just from Horeb). It risks grave misunderstanding, using old mythological language in order to push Israel to live in touch with amazing roots. The old mythology raised eyebrows early on, as seen in the MT, the standardized text of the Bible produced within Judaism. The Masoretes, the Jewish scholars who transmitted the MT, altered readings both at v. 8 and at v. 43. They apparently found them simply too dangerously polytheistic.

Evidence from the Dead Sea Scrolls, supported by the Septuagint, strongly suggests that the NAB, for example, provides something close to the original sense of both verses. Verse 8 properly refers to "sons of God" (NAB), that is, divine members (NABre: "divine beings") of the "heavenly assembly" (NET; NLT: "heavenly court"). Such sons of God appear in Psalm 29:1; 89:6; Job 1:6; and Ugaritic texts. For v. 43, the Dead Sea Scrolls attest a similarly disquieting clause, "Bow down to him all you gods."

The song puts coopted mythology to good theological purpose. The recycled material sets Israel's election within a *sweeping* temporal and spatial context. Israel here becomes the Lord's personal offspring and charge, unique within the span of the ages and the expanse of the globe. From *primordial* times God singled out Israel, vv. 7-9 affirm; God made the people what they are, entered with them into an incredibly special bond, and gave them a unique place on earth. Other nations are not as blessed, apportioned for now among menials, not directly under the Most High (cf. 4:19-20; 29:26).

Although put to innovative and constructive use, the appearance of undigested mythology here, even in fragmentary form, challenges the interpreter and often creates the wrong impression about Deuteronomy's relationship to Canaanite polytheism. Several scholars have too hastily concluded that the Lord appears as just one among many deities in vv. 8-9. "Do not these verses relativize, not enhance, the uniqueness of the bond between Israel and the Lord?" they ask. "Does the text not render the Lord's people just as average as the folk assigned to the next god?"

No, the Song of Moses is far from polytheistic. It contains no thought of the Lord as a national god akin to Chemosh of Moab or Milcom of Ammon, a subordinate member of Most High's divine pantheon. Rather, for Deuteronomy, the Lord (v. 9) is none other than Most High (v. 8)—the two appellations belong to one and the same deity. The sister text of the Song of Moses, Psalm 78, says so incontestably in v. 35.

The parallel Hebrew language in Asaphite Psalm 74:16-17 makes certain that *Israel's God* alone established earth's boundaries. Deuteronomy 4:19, clarifying the Song of Moses, leaves no doubt that *Israel's God* divided the heavenly host among earth's peoples. A third parallel text, Asaphite Psalm 82:8, corroborates both witnesses, insisting that Israel's God is earth's only true judge, the one who apportions the nations.

Psalm 82 interacts intensively with the same mythic source material behind Deuteronomy 32:7-9. In a masterwork of bold polemic, it deconstructs the old poetry. The God of Israel effectively marches into the myth (Ps 82:1), indicts the mythic assembly (vv. 2-5), and sentences its gods to loss of divine status, mortality, and expulsion from heaven (vv. 6-7). With the gods stripped of all rank, the old myth collapses. As does Deuteronomy 4:19 (see the commentary above on ch. 4), Psalm 82 de-animates the gods of the nations.

Subsequent verses within the Song of Moses express solidarity with the polemic of Psalm 82. They confirm that pantheon members in the old myth no longer have any legitimate commission to oversee anything. People must no longer believe this part of the myth; its claims have collapsed. Such gods are "abhorrent things" (v. 16); no-god "demons" (v. 17); "what is no god" (v. 21); gods with little power to save (vv. 37-39). Indeed, the no-gods are "futilities" (v. 21, NJPS), vapors or vapidities (cf. Jer 10:15).

The song's sarcasm in characterizing the gods mirrors Psalm 82's declaration that the deities are ignoramuses, allowing the world to come unglued (Ps 82:5). In its present form, therefore, the Song of Moses has no more bought into polytheism than has Psalm 82. Rather, it has proven itself willing to appropriate critically mythic source material for its own purposes, purposes witnessing to how God has had Israel on the mind from time immemorial. The Lord is Israel's birth-God, who both conceived it and brought it forth.

Verses 10-14 of the song continue to describe God's bond with Israel from its very birth, recounting the history of God's faithfulness through the wilderness wandering and the settlement. At its origins Israel was God's fledgling, attended to with the care of a mother eagle and carried on the wing (v. 11; cf. Exod 19:4 E). God set Israel atop God's sanctuary highland, on whose heights the people would flourish (v. 13, cf. Exod 15:17 E/D). All this the Lord did alone, establishing sole claim to Israel's devotion (v. 12).

Inexplicably, according to vv. 15-18, Israel met God's constancy with utter fickleness. The people allowed prosperity to spoil them, to inculcate an attitude of entitlement, of having *arrived*. As in 8:17 they now proclaim, "My power and the might of my own hand have gotten me this wealth." This claim does not differ from the claim of arrogant pagans: "Our hand is triumphant; it was not the LORD who did all this" (32:27).

As in 8:19-20, Israel loses its sense of dependence on the Lord and attaches itself to new-fangled deities—"the latest in gods, fresh from the market" (32:17, *The Message*). In so doing, the people sever their intimacy with a God of sheer wonder. They scoff at a God beyond gender, their mother who "brought you forth" (v. 18, NJPS).

Verses 15-18 do not review Israel's entire history with God but present a sort of model rebellion, a compact paradigm. Unlike Psalm 78 where historical references are clearer, the song's language is "spongy." That is, vv. 15-18 fit any number of crisis moments in Israel's history, fostering true discernment in such circumstances. The poetry makes crunch times into teaching moments, moments of heart searching.

The paradigmatic rebellion of Israel in vv. 15-18 and the account of God's reaction in vv. 19-27 eerily resonate with the account of the golden calf in chapters 9–10. As at 9:18, Israel's rebellion provokes the Lord (32:16). Matching the divine response to the infamous idol, God's response is fiery, with an incinerating displeasure (9:19, NASB; 32:22). As at 9:14, God determines to blot out Israel's memory (32:26). Only dread of enemy misunderstanding moves the Lord to abate (9:28; 32:27).

Since Israel provokes the Lord with "what is no god," God will provoke them with a "no people," that is, with hostile foreigners who do not enjoy Israel's elect status (v. 21). This hollow, hot-air enemy consists of simpletons who have no more insight into God's ways than does Israel apart from the tutelage of the Song of Moses. The invaders imagine that their own strength brings them victory (vv. 28-31; cf. Israel's own self-delusion at 8:17). They cannot see what lies ahead, namely God's "recompense" (v. 35). Doom will repay their corruption and cruelty. They are a vine out of Sodom; its grapes: poison (v. 32); their wine: asp venom (v. 33).

By vv. 26-27, 28-35, the Song of Moses moves definitively beyond the scope of a mere covenantal lawsuit. God was Israel's mother and father long before Horeb, long before the covenant was ever concluded. Now, God defends the primordial bond with Israel in the face of the enemy misconstruing God's discipline of God's child.

The purview of the song has fully changed by vv. 28-43, with the focus shifting to judgment on Israel's self-assertive oppressors. In vv. 40-42 God appears as the divine warrior (cf. Ps 78:65-66), just as at the conquest of Canaan (cf. Deut 1:30; 3:22). The heavenly champion appears not merely to enforce a covenant but to defeat all who hate God (vv. 41, 43), all who drag the world down to chaos. When this warrior appears, shrinking and dread replace pride and cruelty (cf. 2:4, 25; 7:23; 9:3; 11:25).

The guise of the divine warrior strikes the modern reader as unfortunate, as distastefully vengeful and bloodied imagery for God. For the ancient Near Easterner, however, combat-myth poetry was fundamentally positive. The flashing storm was the warrior's ensign (cf. Judg 5:4; Pss 18:13-14; 29:3, 7; 68:8). As in the coming of a dreadful thunderstorm, new life blooms in the wake of nourishing rains (see Deut 33:26-28; Ps 68:9-10). The divine warrior's coming is awesome and upsetting, but God overturns the world with good intentions, purposing to flood it with new life. God's people may hope for a blessed abode, "where the heavens drop down dew" (Deut 33:28).

The Song of Moses exudes awe before God's fiery anger, which "burns to the depths of Sheol" (Deut 32:22). It knows that the divine warrior enters the fray as "a devouring fire" (cf. Deut 9:3). Truly, "before him is a devouring fire, and a mighty tempest all around him" (Ps 50:3). The wise know to ask, "Who can endure the day of his coming, and who can stand when he appears?" (Mal 2:2). Yet the sagacious also know that the coming storm bears the power of resurrection. The warrior intends to "show the salvation of God" (Ps 50:23), to rescue "the widow . . . the orphan . . . the alien" (Mal 3:5).

For the combat myth, new life is reached by passing through death-dealing fire, fire deep as Sheol. The pattern has powerfully influenced Deuteronomy at many levels. Repeatedly in this book, "holy destruction" (*kharam*) fructifies the soil to prepare for new life (e.g., 13:17). Its key central section on life and death deploys shocking images of movement through Sheol's depths: the shaved head of the bride won in battle (21:12); the stubborn son's stoning (21:20-21).

From the book's beginning to end, the necessary death of Moses looms always not too far from consciousness. Moses' death outside the promised land models Israel's need to sacrifice self-orientation to receive the land's blessing (see the commentary on 3:23-29). Assuredly, all this attests a move through death to resurrection as a powerful *deep structure* within Deuteronomy. In this book, God disrupts the "foundations of the mountains" (Deut 32:22) to establish earth on firmer footings.

Verse 39 makes explicit the fundamental truth of Deuteronomy's deep structure. God states, "See now that I, even I, am he; there is no god besides me. I kill and I make alive; I wound and I heal; and no one can deliver from my hand." Verse 39's first line might possibly mean merely that God ends the life of some and grants the blessing of birth to others. Such a reading, however, is unlikely. The verse's next line speaks of a cohesive movement through wounding to healing. The poetic artistry indicates a theme of resurrection running through the verse as a whole.

The parallel thoughts of 1 Samuel 2:6 buttress this interpretation. In that verse, part of the Song of Hannah, a message of awed thanksgiving rings out: "The LORD kills and brings to life; he brings down to Sheol and raises up." Does it not appear that the Lord here reverses the fate of the dead? True, the snares of Sheol sometimes injure without taking life (see Ps 30:3-4). Here, however, the preceding line speaks specifically of a killing. This is no deliverance from near death. The song is about God's whole-scale power, which extends to include authority over the dead (cf. Ruth 2:20; Jonah 2:2, 7).

A message of resurrection fits the overall context of the Song of Moses. In this context, Israel lies stricken, in dire need of rebirth. "Their power is gone, neither bond nor free remaining" (v. 36). A message of rebirth would have been an especially powerful reassurance to Israel in exile. In exile, Israel would also finally have ears to hear the message. At the point of death, in exile, the old, unregenerate heart of God's people has nothing more to offer them. As MacDonald (149) writes, "It is only in Israel's utter desolation (32:36) that YHWH is able to confront the people and enable them 'to see' (32:39; cf. 29:4). Only in YHWH's provision for them at that moment of hopelessness can they recognize their utter dependence on YHWH, the one who kills and gives life, wounds and heals (32:39)."

Two short prose conclusions to the Song of Moses round off the passage in v. 44 and vv. 45-47. Verse 44 joins with 31:30 to form a pair of literary bookends around the song. Both parts of the bookends have Moses recite the poem in its entirety in the hearing of the people. Verses 45-47 of chapter 32 conclude the entirety of Moses' teaching in the book. One last time they repeat the basic themes of taking God's word to heart, teaching it to every new generation, and believing that the word constitutes the people's very life.

Moses Commanded to Die

Deuteronomy 32:48-52

Deuteronomy 32:48-52 paraphrases the contents of Numbers 27:12-14, a text near the end of Numbers, the preceding book of the Pentateuch. The section of Numbers in question comes from a source known as "HS." The writings of HS, the "Holiness School," stem from central priests akin to Ezekiel, descendants of chief priest Zadok. They prioritize God's bodily presence (God's "glory"), which radiates holiness to Israel. The thinking of HS differs markedly from Deuteronomy, which sides with Levites, not Zadokites, and which lacks any thought of an embodied God. This extract of HS, however, plays a key role here in chapter 32. It helps give the Pentateuch its present theological shape.

The ancient literary technique here is *epanalepsis*, a resumptive repetition—doubling back and repeating a bit of a preceding text in order to resume a narrative that was earlier paused. Editors used the technique as a way of sandwiching lengthy pieces of new material into a document. Here, epanalepsis acts as a literary device incorporating the whole of the book of Deuteronomy within the larger flow of the Pentateuch. This means Deuteronomy has an intentional place. It closes the Pentateuch by directing God's torah toward adaptability and continuing relevance. Throughout Deuteronomy, the reader of the Pentateuch sees Moses urging innovative reflection on, and reapplication of, torah.

The basic theme of Moses' death outside Canaan is now long familiar, but several new details within vv. 48-52 surprise, even jar, the reader. First, the Hebrew text of v. 50 presents the words "die" and "be gathered" as imperatives—direct orders. God literally commands Moses to die: "*Die* on the mountain you have climbed" (NJB).

The imperatives paint an emphatic and vivid verbal picture of God completely sovereign over life and death. As we have just read in the Song of Moses, the Lord alone freely "wounds and heals," "kills and makes alive"

(32:39). The truth is echoed in 34:5, which declares that at the end of his journey Moses dies "at the LORD's command."

Verse 50 surprises again, speaking of Moses' being "gathered" to his kin, even though he is away from all family tombs and bone depositories. Like Aaron before him, Moses appears to be gathered to his people in an experience *separate from* the burial of his body (Num 20:24; 27:13; Deut 34:6). His body is laid in an individual grave outside the promised land, but his "self" is gathered to his kin. The language points to Moses' destiny to enjoy *community* after death in the company of ancestors (Gen 25:8, 17; 35:29; 49:33; Num 20:24; 27:13; Deut 32:50; Judg 2:10; 2 Kgs 22:20). The Hebrew of 1 Samuel 28:13 gives us a feel for the idea here. In picturing the rise of Samuel from the netherworld, the text has the medium who is summoning him say, "I see preternatural beings [plural] coming up." Dead Samuel appears in the company of the kin to which he has been gathered. Notably, Sheol's touch is absent: no dust, no torn clothes, no disheveled hair. Samuel is bundled with kin, not lost in Sheol. Moses will be too!

A third surprise is the change in perspective on Moses' death in v. 51. Here, Moses is about to die because he "broke faith" with God! Up to this point, Deuteronomy has never mentioned failings of Moses in conjunction with his death outside Canaan. Rather, his death has appeared as a self-giving act in which he takes God's anger at Israel upon himself (1:37; 3:26; 4:21). With his sacrifice, Moses makes atonement for the people and allows them to enter the promised land (9:18-21, 25-29; 10:10).

A tension between different understandings of Moses' death has entered Deuteronomy. Deuteronomy 32:48-52 has repeated a non-Deuteronomic perspective from Numbers 27 (HS), according to which Moses' fate is a punishment for failing to treat God as holy at Kadesh (Num 27:14; cf. Num 20:12, also the HS source). Moses' hotheaded and presumptuous cry in Numbers 20:10 offended the Lord; he "spoke words that were rash" (Ps 106:33). The sensitive reader, however, will not dismiss Deuteronomy's composite text as "contradictory." Deuteronomy knows life is complicated; tensions and paradoxes abound this side of God's reign (e.g., see 4:19; 4:41-43; 14:21; 15:11; 23:18; 29:26). Here, the book admits that even Moses is no utopian figure. Ambiguity complicates even his sacrificial death, the noblest of offerings. Olson (150) aptly speaks of a "dialectic between Moses as *both* living and dying for the sake of others *and* living and dying as the inevitable condition of his human mortality, limitation, and sin."

The Blessing of Moses

Deuteronomy 33:1-29

Moses now takes up the role of a father figure, a responsibility about which he once bitterly complained (Num 11:12 E). A patriarch would traditionally bless his children in a deathbed scenario, just as Moses now does (see Gen 27:27-29; 48:15-16; 49:1-28; cf. 1 Kgs 2:1-4). Like a dying family head, Moses addresses the tribes gathered before him for wisdom and for oracles as his time draws to a close (cf. Gen 48:2, 11; 49:33).

The lengthy poetry of the Blessing of Moses, celebrating the election of Israel and the unique joys of the tribes, ends Deuteronomy on a high note. Whereas earlier chapters focused on covenantal curses, covenant blessings get the final word. Unlike some patriarchal testaments (cf. Gen 27:39; 49:3-4, 5-7), Moses' blessing is completely positive and encouraging. It even lacks explicit hierarchies and favoritism (contrast Gen 48:18-19). True, some tribes (Levi, Joseph) are lavishly blessed. In addition, the tribe of Simeon is missing, but this is likely due to its early historical absorption into Judah.

A poem of the divine warrior's epiphany frames Moses' testament in vv. 1-5 and vv. 26-29. The two parts of the piece interlock, with the second stanza inverting the sequence of names LORD, Jacob, Jeshurun ("upright one," a poetic term for Israel in vv. 5, 26, also 32:15). The poetic frame and other bits of shaping represent the work of exilic editors. The core blessing in vv. 6-25, however, is earlier. The northern tribes, after all, were destroyed in 722 BCE, after which one would not likely have invented these sorts of blessings for them. Extant blessings, already known, however, might continue to be preserved and treasured, inspiring hope indefinitely.

The poetry of vv. 6-25 takes the reader back in time to early monarchic circumstances. Reuben was diminished (v. 6) in eleventh-century conflicts with the Ammonites (cf. 3:16; Judg 10:7–11:33; 1 Sam 10:27–11:11). Judah was beset by Philistine "adversaries" (v. 7) up through the reign of Saul (cf. 1 Sam 31). The Levites officiated over "whole burnt offerings" (v. 10) only until Solomon's and Jeroboam's reigns, during which they were disenfranchised (see the commentary on Deut 18:6-8).

Because mentions of Davidic kingship are absent, some scholars date the Blessing of Moses prior to the Israelite monarchy. This is unnecessary. The poem merely shares Deuteronomy's antimonarchic spirit, emphasizing God as Jeshurun's true king (cf. v. 5). That is why its word about Judah in v. 7 has nothing akin to the celebration of Judah's royal preeminence in Jacob's earlier blessing of the tribe (Gen 49:10).

As the Blessing begins, the superscription (v. 1) marks Moses as a prophetic "man of God" (cf. Josh 14:6; 1 Kgs 13:1; 17:18). Such a figure delivers powerful oracles (cf. 1 Sam 9:6; 1 Kgs 17:24) and bequeaths mighty blessings (cf. 2 Kgs 4:9-10). The poetry before us is no mere parting well-wish. It is laden with force, a gift of Moses to Israel. Here, a *man of God* shares God's wisdom; Moses *prophesies* that the tribes will flourish naturally in a blessed abode (Deut 33:28), God's heavens dropping dew upon them.

The stormy appearance of the divine warrior in vv. 2-5 largely follows the standard pattern of theophanies (cf. Judg 5:4-5, 20-21; Pss 18:7-15; 68:7-8; Hab 3:3-15). The Lord marches forth from southern regions, from no-man's-land. God breaks out from realms of untrammeled ranging, from Sinai/Horeb (cf. Judg 5:5) and from Seir, the land of Edom (cf. Judg 5:4; Hab 3:3). Alongside the warrior marches an innumerable host of heaven (v. 2, cf. Judg 5:20), primed for battle. With victory won, the Lord sits enthroned as cosmic king and blesses the people as their true ruler (v. 5, cf. Ps 29:10-11).

Significantly, however, the stanza takes unexpected turns at points, giving the reader pause. The difficult Hebrew of v. 3a seems to say that God cherishes "peoples." It appears to imply that the warrior's battle will benefit *all* nations (see NAB, NRSV note). Indeed, this beginning stanza mentions no defeat of Canaanites or other individual peoples (cf. 32:42). In fact, it fails to speak even abstractly of subduing chaos (as does v. 27 below; cf. Judg 5:21; Pss 18:16; 68:12; Hab 3:8, 12-15). As in Asaphite Psalm 50:3-6, the warrior's march climaxes in the giving of the law, which evaporates all hostile threats (Deut 33:4). No substantive adversary remains, once God's word sounds forth.

The transformation of the standard form of theophany continues in v. 3b, where "holy ones," originally the heavenly host (see v. 2), now refers to God's people (cf. 7:6; 14:2, 21; 26:19; 28:9). God's people surround the Lord for instruction, gathering as disciples for catechism. "They follow in his steps and accept his teaching" (v. 3b, NLT, cf. NJPS). Verse 4 quotes Israel: "Moses charged us with the law, as a possession for the assembly of Jacob."

Understood as a quote of Israel, the verse's third-person mention of Moses is somewhat less awkward in Moses' own mouth than many commentators claim.

As in the fearful theophany on Mount Horeb, God's fiery appearance bonds Israel together as an integral "Thou." Thus, v. 5 refers to the "united tribes," the unified assembly of the Lord. The assembly welcomes God's rules, God's revealed will. God's manifestation of stormy, fiery otherness always awakens moral consciousness and longing for ethical guidance (see the commentary at 4:9-14). Now its own "heritage," Israel will vigorously instruct each new generation in divine "Teaching" (v. 4, NJPS).

In this connection, the way the Jewish scribes who transmitted the traditional Hebrew text, the Masoretes, read the end of v. 2 merits attention. They took it as referring to God's right hand giving a "fiery law" to Israel (see NET). The Masoretic text is likely corrupt, but it does convey the awesome potency of God's verbal revelation. In accord with its aura of fiery might, Israel will teach the torah aggressively, though, of course, nonviolently.

In the blessings of the tribes proper (vv. 6-25), Deuteronomy's ideal of *holism* comes to fruition. Here we find blessings associated with strong, growing community, with harmony between community and God, and with harmony in Israel's relationship with the land. This testament for the tribes is about earthy, palpable, emotive blessings. Having little to do with ethereal spirituality or lofty speculations, the text instead speaks of strength, honor, and virility. It conveys a yearning to bask in God's intimacy, the smile of the divine countenance, the safety of the divine bosom. It celebrates the earth: fresh dew, springing fountains, and beauty pouring off mountaintops.

As Mark Biddle (503) aptly states, "The Hebrew Bible stubbornly insists throughout, not just here, that relationship with the God of Israel involves ordinary, mundane, everyday life and its struggles. In fact, Israel came to know and continues to know its God not through mystical contemplation or intellectual speculation, but in encounter, often in circumstances of Israel's need and struggle for survival."

The earthiness and holism of the testament's benedictions is perhaps most apparent in the lavish blessing of Joseph (vv. 13-17), emblematic of the northern kingdom as a whole where Deuteronomy had strong roots (e.g., among the Asaphite Levites). The blessing encompasses Joseph's people, their bond with the Lord, and the bounty of their land. It speaks of an expansive populace with powerful vigor, of the "myriads of Ephraim" and the "thousands of Manasseh" (v. 17). Joseph will enjoy God's favor, the attention of the fiery God of the burning bush (v. 16, NJPS, NAB, NJB, NIV, NET, NASB, NLT). To Joseph will accrue earth's exuberant gifts and natural beauty.

The poetry of chapter 33 repeatedly celebrates strength and prowess, builds up the tribes' courage for confrontation with the Canaanites. Judah gets a strong grip on his foes (v. 7); the loins of Levi's adversaries are crushed (v. 11); Gad's population is primed for enlargement, destined to grow vast (v. 20); Naphtali too is empowered to expand its population and territory. The violent motifs and images express warrior ideals. Moses' testament in its present canonical shape, however, is *not* about physical warfare.

The language of Moses' blessing, rather, encourages wielding the "weapons" of torah and discipleship with aggressive determination. It offers an idiom of chivalry to commend fearlessness, excellence, and hardiness in spreading God's lifestyle. The task is not for the fainthearted; the world will resist the covenant aggressively.

The promise of fruitfulness in the land, so prominent in Joseph's blessing, recurs in the blessings for Zebulun and Issachar, Gad, Naphtali, and Asher. The bounty of these tribes reflects Deuteronomy's theme of Canaan's inherent fertility (see 8:7-10; 11:9-12; 32:13-14). Zebulun and Issachar, enjoying access to the Mediterranean and Lake Chinnereth, will haul in riches from the seas (v. 19b). Gad has the choicest tableland in the Transjordan area (v. 21). Spilling over with God's favor, Naphtali will be "sated" on fruitful land near the Chinnereth (v. 23). Asher will "dip his foot in oil," luxuriating in fine olive oil from the slopes of the western part of the lake (v. 24).

A patriarch's deathbed blessing often included prophetic insights into the character of his children. So too, chapter 33's blessings often point out distinctive traits of the tribes that will help direct their future. Joseph is a firstborn bull, able easily to rout enemy Canaanites; his horns are those of a wild ox (v. 17). (Note the polemical jab at Canaanite worship: neither Baal nor El, both bull gods, can offer aid against bull Joseph.)

The tribe of Gad too has the power of a beast. He lives like a lion that "tears at arm and scalp" (v. 20). This military prowess was of great service as Israel took possession of Canaan (cf. 3:18-20; Josh 1:12-14). Similarly, Dan is a "lion's whelp" (v. 22), with powerful vigor to occupy the territory it needs (cf. Judg 18:27-28).

Moses' testament is remarkable for its assumptions of divine presence. Here at the close of Deuteronomy, the delicate balance of God's absence and presence in the book tilts definitively toward divine accessibility. Verse 16, with its fertile reference to Exodus 3:1-4, anchors the theme. Speaking of the "favor of the Presence in the Bush" (NJPS), it evokes the book's several references to God speaking to Israel out of the midst of Horeb's fire (Deut 4:33,

36; 5:24, 26). God speaks to Israel directly and personally in Deuteronomy, with the divine word issuing from inside a theophanic blaze as in Exodus 3.

Joseph is far from the only tribe aglow with the otherness of the Burning-Bush Presence. Levi comes before God close enough for God to smell his offered incense. Addressing God, v. 10 in the Hebrew states that the Levites "hold sweet incense to your nose" (CEB, cf. NJPS). Benjamin too enjoys special intimacy with God. He is the Lord's beloved, resting on the Lord's shoulders. Perhaps this means he reclines at God's breast (v. 12, NAB, NET; cf. Num 11:12), or that God carries him like a lamb on a shepherd's back. Zebulun and Issachar appear particularly enthusiastic about God's presence with them. They "call peoples to the mountain," where they "offer the right sacrifices" (v. 19).

Verse 19, with its somewhat murky language, is highly suggestive. Did God once place the divine name at a sacrifice site on Mount Tabor (cf. Hos 5:1)? Does the locale of such a site, near Phoenicia, Aram, and Ammon, give v. 19 a spirit of invitation to earth's "peoples" to call on God's name there? Would this then cohere with how v. 3 seems to say that God cherishes the world's "peoples" (see NAB, NRSV note)?

The fulsome blessing of Levi and its position third in the roster right after firstborn Reuben and sovereign Judah is noteworthy. Levi's prominence here aligns with Deuteronomy's robust advocacy of the Levites (e.g., Deut 12:12, 19; 14:27; 17:18; 18:6-8; 26:12). It accords, also, with the fact that Hosea and Jeremiah, whose books are theologically akin to Deuteronomy, seem to have been Levitical priests. Similarly, it fits the Levites' status as heroes in the E strand, an important source of Deuteronomy. The E strand celebrates the tribe overtly in Exodus 32:25-29, a text to which the Blessing of Moses directly refers (v. 9). Referencing the Levites' faithfulness at the golden-calf debacle, v. 9 says the tribe's members "observed your word, and kept your covenant." When Israel dove headlong into apostasy, the Levites put loyalty to God and covenant even above family bonds.

The reference to testing and proving Levi at Massah and Meribah (v. 8) richly echoes other Scriptures, namely Exodus 17:1-7 and Numbers 20:1-13. Interestingly, Deuteronomy alters some major details of these texts. According to Exodus 17:2, 7 (E; cf. Deut 6:16), *Israel* did the testing at Massah and Meribah (also see Ps 95:8-9; Num 20:13 HS). The Blessing of Moses inverts this tradition (just as does Asaphite Ps 81:7 and Exod 15:25 E/D). It emphasizes instead Deuteronomy's theme that *God* led Israel through ordeals of "testing" in the desert wilderness with constructive intent.

The Pentateuch's texts about Massah and Meribah present *Moses*, not all of Levi, as the one under the gun, tested by harsh circumstances. Thirsting for water, the people turn on him alone: "Why did you bring us out of Egypt, to kill us and our children and livestock with thirst?" (Exod 17:3). Moses actually comes close to being stoned (Exod 17:4). Moses, however, was himself a Levite (cf. Exod 4:14; Num 26:58-59; Judg 18:30; Ps 99:6). Here, then, he becomes *the model Levite*, the paradigmatic "loyal one" (Deut 33:8). His example at Massah and Meribah epitomizes and celebrates Levi's calling to put the self at risk, to let go of all control needs, of all self-determination.

The blessing of Levi in Deuteronomy 33:8-11 singles out the tribe as a company of priests, a unique clerical guild (cf. 10:8-9; 18:1-8). Compared to the other tribal blessings, the saying imposes great obligations. The Levites bear the Thummim and Urim, devices of priestly divination (v. 8). They guard and teach the torah; they preside over incense offerings and burnt sacrifices (v. 10). The prophet Malachi holds all Levites accountable for excellence at these duties. He speaks of God's "covenant with Levi," to which *all* priests are called (Mal 2:4; see Jer 33:21-22; Ps 16:4-6). He understands the Levites to be immutably bound rightly to interpret and teach the stipulations of the torah (Mal 2:6-7; see Deut 33:10a; cf. Deut 17:10-11). They are directly responsible for cultivating reverence for God, the "awe" of God's "name" (Mal 2:5; see Deut 28:10, 58).

Some Israelites seem to have reduced priesthood to presiding at rituals and officiating over sacrifices, but not Deuteronomy. Here, Levi's special responsibility is for God's "word," God's "covenant" (Deut 33:9). What matters most is teaching and interpretation of the torah (cf. Deut 17:10-11; 2 Kgs 17:27-28; Jer 18:18; Hos 4:6; Mic 3:11; Mal 2:6-7). Deuteronomy is clear that transmitting and upholding covenantal instruction is precisely what Levites do (Deut 17:9-12, 18; 31:9, 24-26; cf. Jer 2:8; 2 Chr 31:4). Their vocation is to "guard knowledge" and propound "instruction" (Mal 2:7).

In accord with the inclusive, non-hierarchical spirit of Deuteronomy, the Blessing of Moses creates no tiers of privilege among Israel's priests. It assigns priestly authority, including altar privileges (v. 10), to all lineages descended from Levi, not merely to the Zadokites and Aaronides (see Deut 18:1-8; cf. Jer 33:18, 21, 22; contrast Num 3:32; 18:1-7; 25:10-13, HS texts). In Deuteronomy's inclusive view, even laypeople have priest-like responsibilities (Deut 7:6; 14:2; 26:19; cf. Exod 19:6).

Many through Israel's history contested the celebration of the Levites in the Blessing of Moses. Some looked at the Levites' radical claims of inclusion and exclaimed, "You Levites have gone too far!" (Num 16:7). Others took an opposite stance, finding a limitation of the priesthood to any one tribe, even

Levi, too conservative. King Jeroboam infamously "appointed priests from among all the people, who were *not* Levites" (1 Kgs 12:31-32, my emphasis; cf. 2 Chr 13:9; 1 Kgs 13:33). Levi was often fighting on two fronts. Deuteronomy 33:11 thus aptly refers to "adversaries" of Levi, to "those that hate him." Beyond reflecting Genesis 49:5's imagery, the verse reacts to a persistent challenge.

In vv. 26-29, the Blessing of Moses resumes its poetry of the divine warrior that began the chapter. True to the spirit of the combat myth, God rides through the skies like the thunderstorm (cf. Ps 18:10-15; 68:33). The Lord drives the enemy out, with the cry "Destroy!" Thanks to the Lord's victory, Israel can tread on its enemies' backs, a standard Near Eastern idiom of military triumph (cf. Josh 10:24; Ps 110:1).

The final stanza of the warrior poem employs keywords to remain connected with the blessing proper. Both the final stanza and the blessing repeat how God's people "rest in safety" (vv. 12, 28). Their land is blessed with heaven's dew (vv. 13, 28 NJPS, NJB). What is more, vv. 26 and 29 repeat the keyword "help" of v. 7. An overarching theme of chapter 33 as a whole is God's help of God's people, provoking their praise.

In this concluding stanza, the theme of military victory is more prominent than in the sister stanza in vv. 1-5. Here too, however, the poetry primarily concerns the triumph of the covenant. If the conjectural textual emendations of the NRSV are correct, God actually triumphs over the otiose gods of Canaan (v. 27). Even if not, the aim of God's "battle" is still Israel's covenantal formation. As in Asaph Psalm 78:53-55, God's aim is *sanctuary space* in which Israel can grow and mature spiritually.

The poetry of v. 28 uses idiomatic language of God's unique sanctuary zone shared across a family of Scriptures related to Deuteronomy. The texts of this family join in presenting a characteristic image of God's sacred highlands as secluded, fruitful hill-country: Deuteronomy 32:13-14; Psalm 78:54; Micah 7:14; Jeremiah 31:23 (also Exod 15:17; Num 23:8; Josh 17:18; Jer 50:19; Zeph 3:13). Micah 7:14-17 contains diction particularly close to Deuteronomy 33:26-29. In a marvelous triumph that leaves the nations reeling, God liberates God's flock and sets them "alone" in the midst of a "garden land." Just as the enemies come fawning in Deuteronomy 33:29, they "come trembling out of their fortresses" in Micah 7:17.

The Death of Moses

Deuteronomy 34:1-12

Moses now fulfills the command of God given in 32:48-52. He ascends Mount Nebo, views the land of Canaan, and dies there on the mountain. (Deut 34:1 is the only biblical text to combine the names Nebo and Pisgah in referring to the mountain of Moses' final ascent. Perhaps it understands Nebo to be a peak at the summit or on the slopes of the Pisgah mountain chain.)

In a sense, the book of Deuteronomy has been building up to the present set of events from its beginning. Moses' fate to be buried outside the promised land was announced as early as 1:37; 3:26-27; and 4:21. In fact, the preceding book of the Pentateuch, the book of Numbers, already stipulated Moses' final end outside of Canaan (Num 20:12, 24; 27:12-14; 31:2). As recently as Deuteronomy 31:2, Moses has reiterated that the Lord is not going to let him cross the Jordan.

The sensitive reader of Deuteronomy has likely thought of Moses' difficult, premature death even when reading certain key passages that do not explicitly refer to it. Texts such as 5:25-27; 9:18, 25; 31:27 highlight Moses' deprivation and self-denial, aligning with chapter 34's closing description of his final ordeal atop Mount Nebo. This final bitter cup of death outside the promised land culminates a life of other-centeredness.

The buildup to Moses' death and burial has been drawn out enough that the reader likely feels mixed reactions to the narrative at hand. It is a poignant moment, of course, to read of Moses' passing. There is also a sense of closure and release, however, at the realization of something so unavoidably inevitable and so long in coming. The narrative makes a concerted attempt here to give the reader a strong sense of an ending. The text drives home that the message of Deuteronomy has now been delivered. Its promise of a special land of covenantal formation is now on the verge of fulfillment.

As Moses surveys the tribes' lands, God reminds him, "This is the land of which I swore to Abraham, to Isaac, and to Jacob, saying, 'I will give it to

your descendants'" (v. 4). Again, the reader of Deuteronomy has come full
circle. At the start of the book, at 1:8, God had set the land sworn to the
ancestors—to Abraham, to Isaac, and to Jacob—symbolically on display
before Israel. For thirty chapters the reader has been waiting for Israel to
begin moving into this territory. More profoundly, Abraham's people have
been waiting for this moment for 400 years before Moses' speeches (see Gen
15:16 E; cf. Exod 13:5, 11 E; 32:13 E; Num 11:12 E). Deuteronomy has
often recalled this (1:35; 4:31; 6:10, 18, 23; 7:13; 8:1; 10:11; 11:9, 21; 19:8;
26:3, 15).

There it is, the promised land—and yet, *there* it is. It is still out there,
just out of reach. As the Pentateuch ends, no one has yet arrived at God's
reign. Instead, the challenge to live into the covenant goes live. God's reign
has arrived *proleptically*, "as if." Moses' prophetic vision enables him to see
the tribes firmly planted in Canaan. He sees the tribe of Dan in the north
above the Sea of Chinnereth (v. 1). He surveys Naphtali, Manasseh, and
Ephraim down west of Dan (v. 2a). He looks toward the Mediterranean and
sees the land of Judah (v. 2b). He traces the extent of Judah south toward the
Negeb and up and down the Jordan valley (v. 3). As sure as day, the tribes of
Israel are already enjoying their lands, set atop the heights, fed with produce
of the field.

Now, Moses dies at age 120 (v. 7; 31:2), an age far beyond what one
could normally expect (cf. Ps 90:10), a decade older even than Joseph's 110
years (Gen 50:26 E). Yet Moses dies with his eyesight sharp, with a spring in
his step, and with pain at being left behind as Israel moves forward. Death is
no friend of Moses, no friend at all.

Verse 5's reference to Moses as God's "servant" (cf. 3:24) strikes the
reader as particularly significant. The honorific title places Moses in the same
category as Abraham, Isaac, and Jacob, all "servants" of the Lord (9:27). It
marks him as a key instrument of God in the unfolding of God's purposes.

The special status of Moses as the Lord's servant is repeated later in
Scripture, at Joshua 1:1, 7, 13, 15; 8:31, 33; 11:12; 12:6; 13:8; 14:7; 18:7;
22:2, 4, 5; 1 Kings 8:53, 56; 2 Kings 18:12; Psalm 105:26; Malachi 4:4.
Apparently, the title "LORD's servant" was particularly fitting for him. As
Numbers 12 (E) made clear, Moses and God shared a relationship of unique
immediacy and directness. Moses, as "servant" (Num 12:7-8 E), was God's
special confidant with whom God conferred intimately, without riddle. God
declares him "entrusted with all [God's] house [Israel]" (Num 12:7).

That Moses' death is vicarious makes his sacrifice unique (1:37; 3:26;
4:21). All of God's people, however, are called as "servants," as the Lord's
confidants (cf. 26:19; 33:3). All are called to emulate Moses (32:36, 43, MT).

The entire people of God will suffer death just as Moses does and find life by passing through the ordeal. All will pass through the "death" of exile, following in the footsteps of the one who precedes them through the darkest valley (4:29-31; 30:1-3; 32:36). As Dennis Olson (165) aptly puts it, Moses dies *ahead* of the people, not *instead* of them.

Moses is last seen climbing. Not even his kinfolk know his gravesite; "no one knows his burial place to this day" (v. 6). The Hebrew text of v. 6 reads, "he buried him," the simplest meaning in context being that "the LORD buried him" (CEB, NLT). Clearly, the text takes pains to insist that readers must now get on with the trek of faith without Moses. No one is allowed so much as to venerate him at a burial shrine.

Why is Moses so definitively absented from faith's trek going forward? For one thing, Israel might be tempted to make Moses an idol, an object of worship. The risk is high indeed, given his "signs and wonders" (34:11), language used of God (4:34; 6:22; 7:19; 26:8; 29:3), his "displays of power" (34:12), again, language used of God (4:34; 26:8). Moses has to die outside the land to drive home the utter oneness of God's sovereignty over covenantal life in Canaan. As Olson (35) writes, "Moses' death shifts Israel's allegiance from a human like Moses to Yahweh, the true God."

A second reason the book absents Moses is to orient Israel definitively on Scripture. From now on, when Israel assembles at God's shrine there will be only the divine word that Moses has archived and exposited (31:9-13, 24-26). This word, not Moses, will interconnect the people with God. Through it, not through Moses, Israel of all generations will "learn to fear the LORD" (31:12, 13). Nothing will intervene between God's word, emerging as canon, and Israel, the vassal people.

Verse 10 calls Moses a *prophet*, someone focused on God's message (see Deut 18:18; cf. 1 Kgs 13:20-22). The word of a prophet, released into the world, has its own life, which must wax, while the life of the prophet must wane. Moses now falls back as the divine word pushes ahead into a future beyond the span of any one human life. He is 120; God's word must now flow through other channels (Deut 34:7; Gen 6:3).

Moses was a prophet with 20/20 vision. He died with "sight" unimpaired (34:7)—in sharp contrast with Eli, whose prophetic vision failed (1 Sam 3:1b-2), and with Balaam, who had sight worse than an ass (Num 22). Moses' acts of lawgiving at Horeb and in Moab were *foundational* for faith, but Moses' lawgiving also looks to the far future with *prophetic* potency. As long-range prophecy, Deuteronomy will perpetually be "on the move." It will push ahead toward a goal of God reigning incontestably on earth (see Mal 1:14). A fleeting foretaste of the book's final fulfillment came with Josiah. Here was a king who "fulfilled" Deuteronomy 6:5, who "turned to the LORD with all his heart, with all his soul, and with all his might, according to all the law of Moses" (2 Kgs 23:25).

Verse 10 speaks not just of a prophet with long-range vision but also of a prophet "whom the LORD knew face to face." The phrase conjures up a family of biblical texts about "Mosaic" prophets: Exodus 19:9, 19; 20:18-21; 33:11; Numbers 12; Deuteronomy 5:5, 27; 18:15-22. These texts (all E or D) are concerned with a dynamic of *Mosaic succession.* They are about a unique divine channel of prophecy, a channel active across the centuries to bring in a promised future. Moses is *sui generis* as God's prophet, but also seminal—the first in a line of authoritative "Mosaic prophets." The family of texts that resonate with Deuteronomy 34:10 all assume that future figures must arise to wear Moses' mantle. Numbers 12:6-8, for example, establishes a hierarchy of prophecy in which Mosaic prophets have ultimate authority when conflicts and doubts arise. Deuteronomy 18:15-22, for its part, is even clearer that Moses' closeness to God is a standard for Israel's use in navigating future conflicts over inspiration and authority (like the conflict in Jer 28).

Joshua, named in Deuteronomy 34:9, is the first of the successor prophets of Moses (see Josh 5:15). He eventually receives Moses' honorific title, "servant of the LORD" (Josh 24:29; Judg 2:8). Many prophets uniquely like Moses arise after Joshua, including Elijah, an archetypal prophet like Moses (see esp. 1 Kgs 19:8-9; 2 Kgs 2:8). Other notable Mosaic prophets include Samuel (see, e.g., 1 Sam 12:23), Elisha (see, e.g., 2 Kgs 2, 8, 14), and Jeremiah (e.g., note how Jer 28:16-17 echoes Deut 18:20).

Jeremiah, like Elijah before him, dynamically grabbed the baton of prophecy that Moses handed off. In accord with Deuteronomy 18:18, God puts God's words directly in Jeremiah's mouth (Jer 1:9). As the Lord "knew" Moses (Deut 34:10), the Lord *knows* Jeremiah (Jer 1:5; 12:3). Insisting on the canonical role of Deuteronomy 18:20-22, Jeremiah upholds the authority of the Mosaic prophet in cases of doubt and contradiction (Jer 28). He emulates the Mosaic role of *servant* prophet, of honored courtier who stands in the council of the Lord seeing and hearing God's word so as to proclaim it (Jer 23:18, 22).

As the Lord's unique servant akin to Moses (Deut 34:5), Jeremiah suffers profoundly. Putting personal concern and safety aside, he speaks a word direct from God that carries Israel through the arduous spiritual journey foreseen by Moses. He leads Israel through total death into the covenant's end goal (Jer 31:31-34; Deut 30:1-6).

The final shape of the Bible as a whole is bound up with the figure of Moses. The Scriptures celebrate the foundational, incomparable character of

Moses' discourse from start to finish. As we have seen, the Pentateuch concludes with the epitaph or colophon: "Never since has there arisen a prophet in Israel like Moses, whom the LORD knew face to face" (Deut 34:10). The last of the Bible's prophetic books likewise exalts Moses. The book of the prophet Malachi ends by urging as central to faith the injunction to "Remember the teaching of my servant Moses" (Mal 4:4).

Deuteronomy 34 and Malachi 4 each esteem both Moses, the "patriarch" of the covenant people, and the prophets, the carriers of the covenant into the future. Deuteronomy 34 speaks both of Moses and of prophets, figures of less stature than Moses but still God's instruments. Malachi 4 speaks of Moses, mediator of the Horeb experience, and of Elijah, Mosaic prophet of God's coming reign. Taken together, Deuteronomy 34 and Malachi 4 provide a double witness adjuring the reader to hold the Torah and the Prophets together. The two major bodies of Scripture, Torah and Prophets, offer a twin witness to God's one covenantal purpose with Israel (see Chapman 2000).

The reference to *Elijah* in Malachi 4 is significant. The covenant points to God's reign particularly strongly in Elijah's life. His prophetic career, which continued Moses' work, climaxed in a whirlwind experience of Kingdom Come. Redeemed from the power of Sheol, he ascended bodily to heaven (2 Kgs 2:11). From thence he can return alive at the day of the Lord (cf. Mark 9:4, 11). At that day, all the blessings that Deuteronomy promises for God's people, and for the world, will finally come into their own.

Works Cited

Arnold, Bill T. 2010. "Deuteronomy as the *Ipsissima Vox* of Moses." *Journal of Theological Interpretation* 4:53–74.

———. 2011. "The Love-Fear Antinomy in Deuteronomy 5-11." *VT* 61:551–69.

Barrett, Rob. 2009. *Disloyalty and Destruction: Religion and Politics in Deuteronomy and the Modern World.* New York: T&T Clark.

Berlin, Adele. 2009. "Sex and the Single Girl in Deuteronomy 22." In *Mishneh Todah: Studies in Deuteronomy and its Cultural Environment in Honor of Jeffrey H. Tigay*, ed. Nili Sacher Fox, David A. Glatt-Gilad, and Michael J. Williams, 95–112. Winona Lake IN: Eisenbrauns.

Biddle, Mark E. 2003. *Deuteronomy.* Smyth & Helwys Bible Commentary 4. Macon GA: Smyth & Helwys.

Bonhoeffer, Dietrich. 1995. *The Cost of Discipleship.* New York: Touchstone.

Calvin, Jean. 1950. *Commentaries on the Four Last Books of Moses: Arranged in the Form of a Harmony.* Translated and annotated by Charles William Bingham. Grand Rapids MI: Eerdmans.

Cayley, David. 1992. *Northrop Frye in Conversation.* Concord OT: Anansi.

Chapman, Stephen B. 2000. *The Law and the Prophets: A Study in Old Testament Canon Formation.* FAT 27. Tübingen: Mohr Siebeck.

———. 2013a. "Martial Memory, Peaceable Vision: Divine War in the Old Testament." In *Holy War in the Bible: Christian Morality and an Old Testament Problem*, ed. Heath A. Thomas, Jeremy Evans, and Paul Copan, 47–67. Downers Grove IL: InterVarsity.

———. 2013b. "Perpetual War: The Case of Amalek." In *The Bible and Spirituality: Exploratory Essays in Reading the Bible Spiritually*, ed. Andrew T. Lincoln, Gordon McConville, and Lloyd K. Pietersen, 1–19. Eugene OR: Cascade.

Childs, Brevard S. 1974. *The Book of Exodus: A Critical, Theological Commentary*. Philadelphia: Westminster.

Cook, Stephen L. 2004. *The Social Roots of Biblical Yahwism*. SBL Studies in Biblical Literature 8. Leiden: Brill.

———. 2010. "Deuteronomy." In Oxford Bibliographies Online, accessible at http://goo.gl/Hrj08X.

———. 2011. "Those Stubborn Levites: Overcoming Levitical Disenfranchisement." In *Levites and Priests in History and Tradition*, ed. M. A. Leuchter and J. M. Hutton, 155–70. SBL Ancient Israel and its Literature 9. Atlanta: SBL.

———. 2013. "God's Real Absence and Real Presence in Deuteronomy and Deuteronomism." In *Divine Presence and Absence in Exilic and Post-Exilic Judaism*, ed. Izaak J. de Hulster and Nathan MacDonald, 122–50. FAT II. Tübingen: Mohr Siebeck.

Coote, Robert B. 1991. *In Defense of Revolution: The Elohist History*. Minneapolis: Fortress.

Fretheim, Terence E. 1991. *Exodus*. Interpretation. Louisville: John Knox.

Frost, Robert. 1995. *Collected Poems, Prose and Plays*. New York: Library of America.

Geller, Stephen A. 1996. *Sacred Enigmas: Literary Religion in the Hebrew Bible*. London: Routledge.

Girard, René. 1977. *Violence and the Sacred*. Translated by Patrick Gregory. Baltimore: Johns Hopkins University Press.

Graupner, Axel. 2002. *Der Elohist: Gegenwart und Wirksamkeit des Transzendenten Gottes in der Geschichte*. WMANT 97. Neukirchen-Vluyn: Neukirchener.

Hagedorn, Anselm C. 2007. "Taking the Pentateuch to the Twenty-First Century." *ExpTim* 119:53–58.

Halpern, Baruch. 1991. "Jerusalem and the Lineages in the Seventh Century BCE: Kinship and the Rise of Individual Moral Liability." In *Law and Ideology in Monarchic Israel*, ed. B. Halpern and D. Hobson, 11–107. JSOTSup 124. Sheffield: Sheffield Academic Press.

Heschel, Abraham Joshua. 1955. *God in Search of Man: A Philosophy of Judaism*. New York: Farrar, Straus and Giroux.

Janzen, J. Gerald. 1997. *Exodus*. Westminster Bible Companion. Louisville KY: Westminster John Knox.

Jenks, Alan W. 1977. *The Elohist and North Israelite Traditions*. Missoula MT: Scholars Press.

Knafl, Anne K. 2010. "Deuteronomy, Name Theology, and Divine Location." Paper presented at the annual meeting of the Society of Biblical Literature. Atlanta, 22 November.

Launderville, Dale. 2003. *Piety and Politics: The Dynamics of Royal Authority in Homeric Greece, Biblical Israel, and Old Babylonian Mesopotamia*. Grand Rapids MI: Eerdmans.

Leuchter, Mark A. 2009. "The Priesthood in Ancient Israel." *BTB* 40/2:1–11.

Levinson, Bernard M. 1997. *Deuteronomy and the Hermeneutics of Legal Innovation*. New York: Oxford University Press.

Lindquist, Maria. 2010. "King Og's Iron Bed." Paper presented at the annual meeting of the Society of Biblical Literature. Atlanta, 21 November.

Lohfink, Norbert. 1992. "Opfer und Säkularisierung im Deuteronomium." In *Studien zu Opfer und Kult im Alten Testament mit einer Bibliographie 1969-1991 zum Opfer in der Bibel*, ed. A. Schenker, 15–43. FAT 3. Tübingen: Mohr.

Luther, Martin. 1955. *Works*, vol. 9, *Lectures on Deuteronomy*. Edited by Jaroslav Pelikan and Helmut T. Lehmann. Saint Louis: Concordia.

MacDonald, Nathan. 2003. *Deuteronomy and the Meaning of "Monotheism."* FAT 2, 1. Tübingen: Mohr Siebeck.

Maul, Stefan M. 1992. "*Kurgarrû* und *assinnu* und ihr Stand in der baby-lonischen Gesellschaft." In *Außenseiter und Randgruppen: Beiträge zu einer Sozialgeschichte des alten Orients*, ed. Volkhert Haas, 159–71. Konstanzer Althistorische Vorträge und Forschungen 32. Konstanz, Germany: Universitätsverlag.

Mays, James Luther. 1969. *Hosea: A Commentary*. OTL. Philadelphia: Westminster.

McBride, S. Dean. 1969. "The Deuteronomic Name Theology." Ph.D. dissertation, Harvard University.

————. 1973. "Yoke of the Kingdom: An Exposition of Deuteronomy 6:4-5." *Interpretation* 27:273–306.

————. 2007. "Deuteronomy, Book of," in *The New Interpreter's Dictionary of the Bible*, ed. Katharine Doob Sakenield, 2:108–17. Nashville: Abingdon.

McConville, J. Gordon. 2002. *Deuteronomy*. Apollos Old Testament Commentary 5. Downers Grove IL: IVP Academic.

Miller, Patrick D. 2007. *The Way of the Lord: Essays in Old Testament Theology*. Grand Rapids MI: Eerdmans.

————. 2009. *The Ten Commandments*. Interpretation. Louisville KY: Westminster John Knox.

Moberly, R. W. L. 1999. "Toward an Interpretation of the Shema." In *Theological Exegesis: Essays in Honor of Brevard S. Childs*, ed. Christopher Seitz and Kathryn Greene-McCreight, 124–44. Grand Rapids MI: Eerdmans.

Nelson, Richard D. 2002. *Deuteronomy: A Commentary*. OTL. Louisville KY: Westminster John Knox.

Olson, Dennis T. 1994. *Deuteronomy and the Death of Moses: A Theological Reading*. OBT. Minneapolis: Fortress.

Olyan, Saul M. 1996. "Why an Altar of Unfinished Stones? Some Thoughts on Ex 20,25 and Dtn 27,5-6." *ZAW* 108:161–71.

————. 2004. *Biblical Mourning: Ritual and Social Dimensions*. Oxford: Oxford University Press.

Otto, Rudolf. 1970. *The Idea of the Holy: An Inquiry into the Non-Rational Factor in the Idea of the Divine and its Relation to the Rational.* Translated by John W. Harvey. New York: Oxford University Press.

Overberg, Kenneth. 2006. *Ethics and AIDS: Compassion and Justice in Global Crisis.* A Sheed & Ward book. Oxford: Rowman & Littlefield.

Pedersen, Johannes. 1973. *Israel: Its Life and Culture, Volumes 1–2.* London: Oxford University Press.

Rad, Gerhard von. 1966. *Deuteronomy: A Commentary.* Translated by Dorothea Barton. OTL. Philadelphia: Westminster.

Rattner, Abraham, and Allen Leepa. 1970. *Abraham Rattner.* New York: H. N. Abrams.

Rofé, Alexander. 1985. "The Laws of Warfare in the Book of Deuteronomy: Their Origins, Intent and Positivity." *JSOT* 32:23–44.

Rouillard, Hedwige. 1999. "Rephaim." In *Dictionary of Demons and Deities in the Bible (DDD)*, ed. K. v.d. Toorn, B. Becking, and P. W. v.d. Horst, 692–95.Leiden: Brill.

Sommer, Benjamin D. 2009. *The Bodies of God and the World of Ancient Israel.* Cambridge: Cambridge University Press.

Spronk, Klaas. 1986. *Beatific Afterlife in Ancient Israel and in the Ancient Near East.* AOAT 219. Kevelaer: Butzon & Bercker.

Steiner, George. 1989. *Real Presences.* Chicago: University of Chicago Press.

Stern, David. 2008. "Recent Trends in Biblical Source Criticism." *JBQ* 36:182–86.

Sweeney, Marvin A. 2001. *King Josiah of Judah: The Lost Messiah of Israel.* Oxford: Oxford University Press.

Terrien, Samuel L. 1978. *The Elusive Presence: The Heart of Biblical Theology.* San Francisco: Harper & Row.

Tigay, Jeffrey H. 1996. *Deuteronomy [Devarim]: The Traditional Hebrew Text with the New JPS Translation.* Philadelphia: Jewish Publication Society.

Vedeler, Harold Torger. 2008. "Reconstructing Meaning in Deuteronomy 22:5: Gender, Society and Transvestitism in Israel and the Ancient Near East." *JBL* 127:459–76.

Vogt, Peter T. 2006. *Deuteronomic Theology and the Significance of Torah: A Reappraisal*. Winona Lake IN: Eisenbrauns.

Weinfeld, Moshe. 1972. *Deuteronomy and the Deuteronomic School*. Oxford: Clarendon.

Welch, Adam Cleghorn. 1928. *Jeremiah, His Time and his Work*. London: Oxford University Press, H. Milford.

Wright, Christopher J. H. 1996. *Deuteronomy*. NIBCOT 4. Peabody MA: Hendrickson.

Other available titles from

#Connect
Reaching Youth Across the Digital Divide
Brian Foreman

Reaching our youth across the digital divide is a struggle for parents, ministers, and other adults who work with Generation Z—today's teenagers. *#Connect* leads readers into the technological landscape, encourages conversations with teenagers, and reminds us all to be the presence of Christ in every facet of our lives. *978-1-57312-693-9 120 pages/pb* **$13.00**

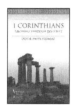

1 Corinthians (Smyth & Helwys Annual Bible Study series)
Growing through Diversity
Don & Anita Flowers

Don and Anita Flowers present this comprehensive study of 1 Corinthians, filled with scholarly insight and dealing with such varied topics as marriage and sexuality, spiritual gifts and love, and diversity and unity. The authors examine Paul's relationship with the church in Corinth as well as the culture of that city to give context to topics that can seem far removed from Christian life today. *Teaching Guide 978-1-57312-701-1 122 pages/pb* **$14.00**
Study Guide 978-1-57312-705-9 52 pages/pb **$6.00**

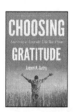

Choosing Gratitude
Learning to Love the Life You Have
James A. Autry

Autry reminds us that gratitude is a choice, a spiritual—not social—process. He suggests that if we cultivate gratitude as a way of being, we may not change the world and its ills, but we can change our response to the world. If we fill our lives with moments of gratitude, we will indeed love the life we have. *978-1-57312-614-4 144 pages/pb* **$15.00**

Choosing Gratitude 365 Days a Year
Your Daily Guide to Grateful Living
James A. Autry and Sally J. Pederson

Filled with quotes, poems, and the inspired voices of both Pederson and Autry, in a society consumed by fears of not having "enough"—money, possessions, security, and so on—this book suggests that if we cultivate gratitude as a way of being, we may not change the world and its ills, but we can change our response to the world. *978-1-57312-689-2 210 pages/pb* **$18.00**

To order call **1-800-747-3016** or visit **www.helwys.com**

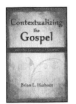

Contextualizing the Gospel
A Homiletic Commentary on 1 Corinthians

Brian L. Harbour

Harbour examines every part of Paul's letter, providing a rich resource for those who want to struggle with the difficult texts as well as the simple texts, who want to know how God's word—all of it—intersects with their lives today.   *978-1-57312-589-5 240 pages/pb* **$19.00**

Dance Lessons
Moving to the Beat of God's Heart

Jeanie Miley

Miley shares her joys and struggles a she learns to "dance" with the Spirit of the Living God.   *978-1-57312-622-9 240 pages/pb* **$19.00**

A Divine Duet
Ministry and Motherhood

Alicia Davis Porterfield, ed.

Each essay in this inspiring collection is as different as the mother-minister who wrote it, from theologians to chaplains, inner-city ministers to rural-poverty ministers, youth pastors to preachers, mothers who have adopted, birthed, and done both.

978-1-57312-676-2 146 pages/pb **$16.00**

The Enoch Factor
The Sacred Art of Knowing God

Steve McSwain

The Enoch Factor is a persuasive argument for a more enlightened religious dialogue in America, one that affirms the goals of all religions—guiding followers in self-awareness, finding serenity and happiness, and discovering what the author describes as "the sacred art of knowing God."   *978-1-57312-556-7 256 pages/pb* **$21.00**

Ethics as if Jesus Mattered
Essays in Honor of Glen H. Stassen

Rick Axtell, Michelle Tooley, Michael L. Westmoreland-White, eds.

Ethics as if Jesus Mattered will introduce Stassen's work to a new generation, advance dialogue and debate in Christian ethics, and inspire more faithful discipleship just as it honors one whom the contributors consider a mentor.   *978-1-57312-695-3 234 pages/pb* **$18.00**

Healing Our Hurts
Coping with Difficult Emotions
Daniel Bagby

In *Healing Our Hurts*, Daniel Bagby identifies and explains all the dynamics at play in these complex emotions. Offering practical biblical insights to these feelings, he interprets faith-based responses to separate overly religious piety from true, natural human emotion. This book helps us learn how to deal with life's difficult emotions in a redemptive and responsible way. *978-1-57312-613-7 144 pages/pb* **$15.00**

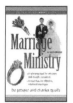

Marriage Ministry: A Guidebook
Bo Prosser and Charles Qualls

This book is equally helpful for ministers, for nearly/newlywed couples, and for thousands of couples across our land looking for fresh air in their marriages. *1-57312-432-X 160 pages/pb* **$16.00**

Hope for the Thinking Christian
Seeking a Path of Faith through Everyday Life
Stephen Reese

Readers who want to confront their faith more directly, to think it through and be open to God in an individual, authentic, spiritual encounter will find a resonant voice in Stephen Reese.

978-1-57312-553-6 160 pages/pb **$16.00**

A Hungry Soul Desperate to Taste God's Grace
Honest Prayers for Life
Charles Qualls

Part of how we *see* God is determined by how we *listen* to God. There is so much noise and movement in the world that competes with images of God. This noise would drown out God's beckoning voice and distract us. Charles Qualls's newest book offers readers prayers for that journey toward the meaning and mystery of God. *978-1-57312-648-9 152 pages/pb* **$14.00**

I'm Trying to Lead... Is Anybody Following?
The Challenge of Congregational Leadership in the Postmodern World
Charles B. Bugg

Bugg provides us with a view of leadership that has theological integrity, honors the diversity of church members, and reinforces the brave hearts of church leaders who offer vision and take risks in the service of Christ and the church. *978-1-57312-731-8 136 pages/pb* **$13.00**

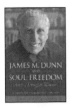

James M. Dunn and Soul Freedom

Aaron Douglas Weaver

James Milton Dunn, over the last fifty years, has been the most aggressive Baptist proponent for religious liberty in the United States. Soul freedom—voluntary, uncoerced faith and an unfettered individual conscience before God—is the basis of his understanding of church-state separation and the historic Baptist basis of religious liberty.   *978-1-57312-590-1 224 pages/pb* **$18.00**

The Jesus Tribe
Following Christ in the Land of the Empire

Ronnie McBrayer

The Jesus Tribe fleshes out the implications, possibilities, contradictions, and complexities of what it means to live within the Jesus Tribe and in the shadow of the American Empire.

978-1-57312-592-5 208 pages/pb **$17.00**

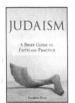

Judaism
A Brief Guide to Faith and Practice

Sharon Pace

Sharon Pace's newest book is a sensitive and comprehensive introduction to Judaism. What is it like to be born into the Jewish community? How does belief in the One God and a universal morality shape the way in which Jews see the world? How does one find meaning in life and the courage to endure suffering? How does one mark joy and forge community ties?   *978-1-57312-644-1 144 pages/pb* **$16.00**

Let Me More of Their Beauty See
Reading Familiar Verses in Context

Diane G. Chen

Let Me More of Their Beauty See offers eight examples of how attention to the historical and literary settings can safeguard against taking a text out of context, bring out its transforming power in greater dimension, and help us apply Scripture appropriately in our daily lives.

978-1-57312-564-2 160 pages/pb **$17.00**

Living Call
An Old Church and a Young Minister Find Life Together

Tony Lankford

This light look at church and ministry highlights the dire need for fidelity to the vocation of church leadership. It also illustrates Lankford's conviction that the historic, local congregation has a beautiful, vibrant, and hopeful future.   *978-1-57312-702-8 112 pages/pb* **$12.00**

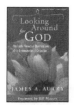

Looking Around for God
The Strangely Reverent Observations of an Unconventional Christian
James A. Autry

Looking Around for God, Autry's tenth book, is in many ways his most personal. In it he considers his unique life of faith and belief in God. Autry is a former Fortune 500 executive, author, poet, and consultant whose work has had a significant influence on leadership thinking.

978-157312-484-3 144 pages/pb **$16.00**

Making the Timeless Word Timely
A Primer for Preachers
Michael B. Brown

Michael Brown writes, "There is a simple formula for sermon preparation that creates messages that apply and engage whether your parish is rural or urban, young or old, rich or poor, five thousand members or fifty." The other part of the task, of course, involves being creative and insightful enough to know how to take the general formula for sermon preparation and make it particular in its impact on a specific congregation. Brown guides the reader through the formula and the skills to employ it with excellence and integrity.

978-1-57312-578-9 160 pages/pb **$16.00**

Meeting Jesus Today
For the Cautious, the Curious, and the Committed
Jeanie Miley

Meeting Jesus Today, ideal for both individual study and small groups, is intended to be used as a workbook. It is designed to move readers from studying the Scriptures and ideas within the chapters to recording their journey with the Living Christ.

978-1-57312-677-9 320 pages/pb **$19.00**

The Ministry Life
101 Tips for New Ministers
John Killinger

Sharing years of wisdom from more than fifty years in ministry and teaching, *The Ministry Life: 101 Tips for New Ministers* by John Killinger is filled with practical advice and wisdom for a minister's day-to-day tasks as well as advice on intellectual and spiritual habits to keep ministers of any age healthy and fulfilled.

978-1-57312-662-5 244 pages/pb **$19.00**

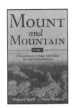

Mount and Mountain
Vol. 1: A Reverend and a Rabbi Talk About the Ten Commandments
Rami Shapiro and Michael Smith

Mount and Mountain represents the first half of an interfaith dialogue—a dialogue that neither preaches nor placates but challenges its participants to work both singly and together in the task of reinterpreting sacred texts. Mike and Rami discuss the nature of divinity, the power of faith, the beauty of myth and story, the necessity of doubt, the achievements, failings, and future of religion, and, above all, the struggle to live ethically and in harmony with the way of God.   *978-1-57312-612-0 144 pages/pb* **$15.00**

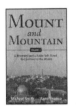

Mount and Mountain
Vol. 2: A Reverend and a Rabbi Talk About the Sermon on the Mount
Rami Shapiro and Michael Smith

This book, focused on the Sermon on the Mount, represents the second half of Mike and Rami's dialogue. In it, Mike and Rami explore the text of Jesus' sermon cooperatively, contributing perspectives drawn from their lives and religious traditions and seeking moments of illumination.   *978-1-57312-654-0 254 pages/pb* **$19.00**

Of Mice and Ministers
Musings and Conversations About Life, Death, Grace, and Everything
Bert Montgomery

With stories about pains, joys, and everyday life, *Of Mice and Ministers* finds Jesus in some unlikely places and challenges us to do the same. From tattooed women ministers to saying the "N"-word to the brotherly kiss, Bert Montgomery takes seriously the lesson from Psalm 139—where can one go that God is not already there?   *978-1-57312-733-2 154 pages/pb* **$14.00**

Overcoming Adolescence
Growing Beyond Childhood into Maturity
Marion D. Aldridge

In *Overcoming Adolescence*, Marion D. Aldridge poses questions for adults of all ages to consider. His challenge to readers is one he has personally worked to confront: to grow up *all the way*—mentally, physically, academically, socially, emotionally, and spiritually. The key involves not only knowing how to work through the process but also how to recognize what may be contributing to our perpetual adolescence.

978-1-57312-577-2 156 pages/pb **$17.00**

Quiet Faith
An Introvert's Guide to Spiritual Survival
Judson Edwards

In eight finely crafted chapters, Edwards looks at key issues like evangelism, interpreting the Bible, dealing with doubt, and surviving the church from the perspective of a confirmed, but sometimes reluctant, introvert. In the process, he offers some provocative insights that introverts will find helpful and reassuring. *978-1-57312-681-6 144 pages/pb* **$15.00**

Reading Ezekiel (Reading the Old Testament series)
A Literary and Theological Commentary
Marvin A. Sweeney

The book of Ezekiel points to the return of YHWH to the holy temple at the center of a reconstituted Israel and creation at large. As such, the book of Ezekiel portrays the purging of Jerusalem, the Temple, and the people, to reconstitute them as part of a new creation at the conclusion of the book. With Jerusalem, the Temple, and the people so purged, YHWH stands once again in the holy center of the created world.

978-1-57312-658-8 264 pages/pb **$22.00**

Reading Hosea–Micah
(Reading the Old Testament series)
A Literary and Theological Commentary
Terence E. Fretheim

Terence E. Fretheim explores themes of indictment, judgment, and salvation in Hosea–Micah. The indictment against the people of God especially involves issues of idolatry, as well as abuse of the poor and needy. The effects of such behaviors are often horrendous in their severity. While God is often the subject of such judgments, the consequences, like fruit, grow out of the deed itself. *978-1-57312-687-8 224 pages/pb* **$22.00**

Sessions with Genesis (Session Bible Studies series)
The Story Begins
Tony W. Cartledge

Immersing us in the book of Genesis, Tony W. Cartledge examines both its major stories and the smaller cycles of hope and failure, of promise and judgment. Genesis introduces these themes of divine faithfulness and human failure in unmistakable terms, tracing Israel's beginning to the creation of the world and professing a belief that Israel's particular history had universal significance. *978-1-57312-636-6 144 pages/pb* **$14.00**

Sessions with Revelation (Session Bible Studies series)
The Final Days of Evil
David Sapp

David Sapp's careful guide through Revelation demonstrates that it is a letter of hope for believers; it is less about the last days of history than it is about the last days of evil. Without eliminating its mystery, Sapp unlocks Revelation's central truths so that its relevance becomes clear. *978-1-57312-706-6 166 pages/pb* **$14.00**

Silver Linings
My Life Before and After *Challenger 7*
June Scobee Rodgers

We know the public story of *Challenger 7*'s tragic destruction. That day, June's life took a new direction that ultimately led to the creation of the Challenger Center and to new life and new love. Her story of Christian faith and triumph over adversity will inspire readers of every age. *978-1-57312-570-3 352 pages/hc* **$28.00**
978-1-57312-694-6 352 pages/pb **$18.00**

Spacious
Exploring Faith and Place
Holly Sprink

Exploring where we are and why that matters to God is an ongoing process. If we are present and attentive, God creatively and continuously widens our view of the world. *978-1-57312-649-6 156 pages/pb* **$16.00**

The Teaching Church
Congregation as Mentor
Christopher M. Hamlin / Sarah Jackson Shelton

Collected in *The Teaching Church: Congregation as Mentor* are the stories of the pastors who shared how congregations have shaped, nurtured, and, sometimes, broken their resolve to be faithful servants of God. *978-1-57312-682-3 112 pages/pb* **$13.00**

Time for Supper
Invitations to Christ's Table
Brett Younger

Some scholars suggest that every meal in literature is a communion scene. Could every meal in the Bible be a communion text? Could every passage be an invitation to God's grace? At the Lord's Table we experience sorrow, hope, friendship, and forgiveness. These meditations on the Lord's Supper help us listen to the myriad of ways God invites us to gratefully, reverently, and joyfully share the cup of Christ. *978-1-57312-720-2 246 pages/pb* **$18.00**

To order call **1-800-747-3016** or visit **www.helwys.com**

A Time to Laugh
Humor in the Bible
Mark E. Biddle

An extension of his well-loved seminary course on humor in the Bible, *A Time to Laugh* draws on Mark E. Biddle's command of Hebrew language and cultural subtleties to explore the ways humor was intentionally incorporated into Scripture. With characteristic liveliness, Biddle guides the reader through the stories of six biblical characters who did rather unexpected things. 978-1-57312-683-0 164 pages/pb **$14.00**

The World Is Waiting for You
Celebrating the 50th Ordination Anniversary of Addie Davis
Pamela R. Durso & LeAnn Gunter Johns, eds.

Hope for the church and the world is alive and well in the words of these gifted women. Keen insight, delightful observations, profound courage, and a gift for communicating the good news are woven throughout these sermons. The Spirit so evident in Addie's calling clearly continues in her legacy. 978-1-57312-732-5 224 pages/pb **$18.00**

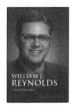

William J. Reynolds
Church Musician
David W. Music

William J. Reynolds is renowned among Baptist musicians, music ministers, song leaders, and hymnody students. In eminently readable style, David W. Music's comprehensive biography describes Reynolds's family and educational background, his career as a minister of music, denominational leader, and seminary professor. 978-1-57312-690-8 358 pages/pb **$23.00**

With Us in the Wilderness
Finding God's Story in Our Lives
Laura A. Barclay

What stories compose your spiritual biography? In *With Us in the Wilderness*, Laura Barclay shares her own stories of the intersection of the divine and the everyday, guiding readers toward identifying and embracing God's presence in their own narratives.

978-1-57312-721-9 120 pages/pb **$13.00**

Made in the USA
San Bernardino, CA
24 March 2017